CAMBODIAN REFUGEES IN ONTARIO:
RESETTLEMENT, RELIGION, AND IDENTITY

JANET McLELLAN

Cambodian Refugees in Ontario

Resettlement, Religion, and Identity

UNIVERSITY OF TORONTO PRESS
Toronto Buffalo London

ISBN 978-0-8020-9962-4

Printed on acid-free, 100% post-consumer recycled paper with vegetable based inks

---

Library and Archives Canada Cataloguing in Publication

McLellan, Janet, 1952–
  Cambodian refugees in Ontario : resettlement, religion, and
  identity / Janet McLellan.

  Includes bibliographical references and index.
  ISBN 978-0-8020-9962-4

  1. Cambodians – Ontario – History.   2. Cambodians – Ontario –
  Social conditions.   3. Refugees – Cambodia.   4. Refugees – Ontario.
  5. Cambodian Canadians – Ontario – History.   6. Cambodian
  Canadians – Ontario – Social conditions.   I. Title.

  FC3100.C27M35 2009   305.895′930713   C2009-902852-2

This book has been published with the help of a grant from the Canadian Federation for the Humanities and Social Sciences, through the Aid to Scholarly Publications Programme, using funds provided by the Social Sciences and Humanities Research Council of Canada.

University of Toronto Press acknowledges the financial assistance to its publishing program of the Canada Council for the Arts and the Ontario Arts Council.

University of Toronto Press acknowledges the financial support for its publishing activities of the Government of Canada through the Book Publishing Industry Development Program (BPIDP).

Dedicated to all Cambodians in resettlement

A KHMER MONK'S POEM TO CAMBODIANS IN CANADA

For thousands of years our ancestors have passed on our culture to
   guide us through the hardships in life.
Generation after generation, our culture is passed on from soul to
   soul – and we invite everyone to join us, whether you are young or
   old.
Our rituals are sacred and real, pure and true. But it is up to all of us
   to treasure them and make sure that they are not forgotten.
Never forget who you are and where you come from, for it is your
   culture and religion that makes up the moral fibre of your soul.
Be proud of what you have. Cherish every moment. Accept today for
   what it is, treasure tomorrow for what it may bring.
Happiness is deep within you. You will find it when you look past
   your despair; for life is a journey that never ends.

Written in Khmer by the Venerable Srey Kinthan, Wat Khmer
Santivararam, Windsor, Ontario. Translated by Sarorn Sim from the
video *Memories: Celebrations of Remembrance*, 2006.

Contents

Acknowledgments

Meeting and interacting with Cambodians is a humbling experience. In recognizing their horrific past, one realizes the enormous courage of those who came to Canada and faced overwhelming obstacles and barriers in their resettlement. To laugh with them, share good meals and conversations, observe their joy in celebrating traditional festivals, see the love within families and between friends, and participate in shared hugs and smiles upon greeting is to witness their triumph over the ever-present inner pain. The willingness of Cambodians to struggle with resettlement issues, to preserve what they can of Khmer culture and community ties, and to steadily rebuild their lives are all testament to the strength and tenacity of the Khmer spirit. The aspiration of this book is to honour Cambodians in Canada and to celebrate their spirit, despite their ongoing suffering, difficulties, and disappointments. Cambodians are 'survivors who can teach us a great deal about the strength that human beings can call forth in the face of the most extreme deprivations and cruelties' (Chan 2003: x). Cambodians have relied on this strength both in their shattered homeland, and in their initial resettlement, adaptation, and integration into Western countries.

Sincere gratitude and appreciation is given to the many Cambodian refugees and second-generation youth who have generously contributed to this book. Their personal experiences, thoughts, insights, and concerns have made this book possible. Heartfelt thanks are given to the Khmer service workers and Khmer religious, cultural, and community leaders whose contributions to their communities verge on the heroic. Special recognition goes to Sarorn Sim, who produced the documentary videos *Memories: Celebrations of Remembrance* and *I Am Khmer*. The research benefited greatly from the support and contribution of several

Cambodian assistants: Ratha In, Shanda Soukchamroeung, Vireak Ly, and especially Kosal Ky, who accompanied me to Cambodia in 2002.

Michael Lanphier, at the Centre for Refugee Studies, York University, was consistently supportive of the research, facilitating financial assistance through the Social Cohesion Project funded by the Social Sciences and Humanities Research Council of Canada and providing unfailing encouragement. I thank him and Anthony Richmond for reading an earlier draft and making helpful suggestions for revision. The support of my colleagues at the Department of Religion and Culture at Wilfrid Laurier University is appreciated, as is the Short-Term Research Grant provided by Wilfrid Laurier University that enabled travel to Cambodia. Thank you to Melodee Martinuk and Marion Robinson for their editorial assistance on the mansucript, as well as to reviewers who provided valuable comments and critiques. The University of Toronto Press is acknowledged for permission to include material from previous publications, notably *Many Petals of the Lotus* and *Encyclopedia of Canada's Peoples*. Clyde McLellan is given special appreciation for editing the drafts from a layman's perspective, for technical assistance, and for his companionship and skill in driving throughout Ontario in all kinds of weather.

This book has been published with the help of a grant from the Canadian Federation for the Humanities and Social Sciences, through the Aid to Scholarly Publications Program, using funds provided by the Social Sciences and Humanities Research Council of Canada.

Preface

Civil and regional war during the late 1960s and early 1970s, followed by genocidal persecution and starvation, forced more than half a million Cambodians to flee their country. The Khmer Rouge regime from 1975 to 1979 systematically destroyed and destabilized families and communities in order to provide obedient workers for the new communist state. Almost two million Cambodians died during this time, over one-quarter of the country's population. Cambodians faced further disjunction when they fled to Thai refugee camps, and when sponsored for resettlement in Western countries. Throughout the 1980s, resettlement was considered the most 'durable solution' to the Cambodian displacement (Van Hear 2006: 9). In resettlement, Cambodians have had to shift from a Khmer Buddhist ethics-regulated society of hierarchy and extended family dependency to the predominant emphasis on individualism, secularism, materialism, self-reliance, and competition. This transition has affected all facets of their lives, impacting religious identities, family and generational dynamics, community social cohesion, and coming to terms with the past and its lingering effects.

Cambodian refugees who resettled in Ontario now consist of three generations: adult survivors of the Khmer Rouge; the children and older youth who accompanied them; and the children born and raised in Canada. Although identified as people born in the country known as Cambodia (also referred to as Kampuchea), most Cambodians refer to themselves as 'Khmer,' a term designating the ethnic and linguistic identity of 90 per cent of the population. This book details their multiple, overlapping, and sometimes contradictory images of cultural, religious, and ethnic identities in flux. Identity construction is a reflection of the different experiences of the three generations in being Khmer and in being Canadian, particularly in regards to the influence of transnational and homeland allegiances.

Although there have been several books on Cambodian resettlement in the United States, including the studies by Ebihara et al. (1994), Hopkins (1996), Smith-Hefner (1999), Chan (2003), and Ong (2003), there is scarce literature on Cambodian refugees in Canada. Data on Cambodians are generally not included in the extensive body of material on Indochinese refugees (which tends to focus on the large influx of people from Vietnam), or in general studies on ethnic and minority groups in Canada. In Ontario, approximately five thousand Cambodians live in the city of Toronto and the nearby regions of Maple, Newmarket, and Vaughan, with a similar number living in communities in Ottawa, Hamilton, London, Kitchener-Waterloo, and Windsor. This book begins to redress the absence of 'Cambodians' in Canadian academic studies.

The specific characteristics of Cambodian resettlement in Ontario, however, represent only one facet of the nuanced and complex picture of Cambodians in diaspora. As Ebihara et al. (1994: 22) note, Cambodians in resettlement entail endless themes of transformation and persistence, loss and continuity. Three interrelated frameworks of analysis are implicit throughout this book. The first is of particular significance to first-generation Cambodian refugees and involves the long-term consequences of their pre-migration experiences. The second, common to other studies in global migration and diaspora, reflects the complex dynamics of resettlement, adaptation, and integration into new social contexts that arise alongside new forms of transnational linkages. The third framework is the shifting and contested nature of ethnic and religious identity within three generations, most notably its inherent capacity for compromise, situational flexibility, instability, and transformation. It is no coincidence that the discussion of ethnoreligious identities of Asian immigrants and refugees involves such words as 'reconfiguration,' 're-creation,' 'redefinitions,' 'reconstructing,' 're-envisioning,' 'reappropriation,' or 'revitalization' in describing how historical, religious, and cultural heritages are retained and modified to remain a viable part of new identities. As Lowe notes, hetereogeneity, hybridity and multiplicity mark Asian Americans, particularly as their multifaceted negotiations of ethnicity, religion, and ancestry entail a complex process of 'becoming' and 'being' (1991: 24).

The transliteration of Khmer terms and words is problematic since most books or articles tend to have their own rendering. Khmer terms in this book reflect those utilized by different authors in their publications and unless otherwise noted, are derived from interviews with Cambodians in Ontario. Although these transliterations may be viewed as inadequate by some scholars, their inclusion is a way of honouring those who gave their time and commitment to making this book possible.

In documenting Cambodian resettlement struggles in Ontario and their strategies for renewal and success, material is taken from the author's 1995 study on Cambodian adaptation and integration, fieldwork in Cambodia during the summer of 2002, and interviews with Cambodians throughout Ontario from 2002 to 2005. The initial study was the first in-depth investigation of Cambodian resettlement in Canada. It identified difficulties and assessed the outcomes of their resettlement in the Ontario cities of Ottawa, Kingston, Toronto, Hamilton, London, St Thomas, and Windsor (McLellan 1995). The research, from December 1992 to March 1994, was funded by Canada Employment and Immigration, Ontario Resettlement Division (through the Centre for Refugee Studies, York University), and included a two-day workshop in which more than a hundred Cambodians from Ontario participated. The Cambodian fieldwork in 2002, to explore transnational connections and linkages of Canadian-Khmer who return to Cambodia for personal, political, or economic reasons, was funded by a short-term research grant from Wilfrid Laurier University. More extensive research on Cambodians in Ontario was funded by the 2002–05 SSHRC Social Cohesion and Transnationalism Project, under the direction of Michael Lanphier, at the Centre for Refugee Studies, York University. This research identified activities that enhance social cohesion and overcome divisions within Cambodian communities, including generational dichotomies and differences in religious belief and practice. In association with the Canadian Cambodian Association of Ontario, a two-day youth leadership workshop entitled 'Retaining and Expressing Khmer Identities in Ontario' was held in July 2005, attended by over fifty Khmer youth from different Ontario cities and towns. The SSHRC funding was also used to make the 2005 documentary film *Memories: Celebrations of Remembrance* by Sarorn Sim, a second-generation Khmer Canadian.

CAMBODIAN REFUGEES IN ONTARIO:
RESETTLEMENT, RELIGION, AND IDENTITY

Introduction

A common theme throughout Canadian immigration history has been the setting of the priorities and principles of selection as to who is admissible and under what conditions. Total numbers, specified categories, availability of candidates, or criteria for rejection arise through the issuing of various Orders-in-Council, government regulations, and amendments (Kubat 1979: 23). The roles and status of immigrant populations are influenced by policies of admissibility and category identification, particularly as they encourage or discourage permanent settlement, facilitate or impede citizenship participation, and either offer or withhold social benefits (Richmond 1988: 47). Bureaucratic behaviour, interpretation in the implementation of legislated regulations, the media, and public opinion also exert powerful influences on policy, selection, admission, and administration. Prior to 1975, Canada did not have an official policy for refugees, but a series of ad hoc measures that classified or accepted refugees according to group characteristics (Lanphier 1981). The Canadian response to refugees was stimulated more by prevailing governmental perceptions of them, the advantages that they could provide for Canada, and their subsequent 'absorptive capacity,' rather than a realistic sense of their situational immediacy and urgency (Andras 1980; Dirks 1977).

In 1976, a new Immigration Act included a plan to govern Canada's annual refugee intake; to expedite resettlement assistance; and to work in close cooperation with the United Nations High Commission for Refugees (UNHCR), Canadian foreign aid agencies, the provinces, and voluntary agencies. It provided a procedure for persons whose collective situation placed them in a de facto refugee situation when UNHCR status could not be met, such as humanitarian movements of people fleeing war zones. This allowed the Canadian government to classify an entire group of refugees under a 'designated class' specification and enabled them to enter Canada as 'landed immigrants' (Lanphier 1981). Through this legislation, groups of refugees began to arrive: Kurds from Iraq; Portugese Angola/Mozambique returnees; Lebanese; and Indochinese from Vietnam, Laos, and Cambodia. Between 1975 and 1978, almost ten thousand Indochinese refugees (primarily Vietnamese) were resettled in Canada. Refugees who were middle class, anti-communist, and persecuted for political and economic reasons were considered especially worthy of Canadian humanitarian assistance. Those without skills and personal qualities deemed useful to Canada, who had health difficulties, or who held ideological beliefs at variance with traditional Canadian norms encountered greater difficulty in gaining entry (Dirks 1979/80).

In 1979, a new policy identified refugees as individuals towards whom the Canadian government had specific obligations, and an annual intake quota was set of ten thousand, with a further two thousand contingency spots (Adelman et al. 1980). This was influenced by the late 1978 drama of the *Hai Hong*, a freighter full of Indochinese stranded off the coast of Malaysia. Malaysian guards threatened to shoot anyone who attempted to land and join the already tens of thousands of unwanted Indochinese on the shores and frontiers of Thailand and Malaysia. By May 1979, the flow of Indochinese refugees into Malaysia and Thailand (as well as Indonesia, Hong Kong, and Singapore) rose to over fifty thousand per month, severely straining the social, economic, and political stability of these countries (Stubbs 1980). The mass exodus of Indochinese refugees received much international media attention, facilitating humanitarian gestures from the Canadian government and the general public. Canada regarded Indochinese refugees as freedom seekers fleeing communist states to avoid oppression, and drew parallels between the ethnic Chinese in Vietnam and the Jews under Nazi Germany (Adelman 1983). Toronto newspapers gave extensive coverage to the horrendous plight of Indochinese refugees, particularly to the Vietnamese, whom they referred to as 'boat people.' Although Vietnamese boat people comprised the majority of refugees admitted to Canada, this reference did not acknowledge the smaller numbers of refugees from Laos and Cambodia who had fled to Thailand on foot.

To supplement the 1979 refugee quota, the Canadian government appealed to the private sector to sponsor an additional four thousand Indochinese refugees (Annual Report to Parliament on Immigration

Levels, 1980). Non-governmental sponsorship enabled groups of five or more adult Canadian citizens or permanent residents (privately or corporately) to sponsor refugee groups and individuals, and to support them and their subsequent dependents for one year. A 'master agreement' between national organizations (religious or humanitarian) and the federal government enabled local chapters, parishes, and congregations to participate in sponsorship activities with few formalities other than material assistance and orientation. The government provided emergency hospital, medical, and dental care before arrival; supplemented transportation loans; organized employment services; and funded language training (in French or English), occupational training, and skills upgrading (Lanphier 1981).

On 24 June 1979, Operation Lifeline, an Ontario-based private sector sponsorship plan, began advocating for more refugee sponsorship, and within two weeks, sixty chapters were established (Adelman et al. 1980). By October 1979, thirty-six hundred groups had applied to sponsor more than nineteen thousand Indochinese refugees (Adelman et al. 1980; McCrasson 1980). To further encourage private initiative, the Canadian government proposed a matching formula that would admit one refugee for each one brought in through private sponsorship (Annual Report to Parliament on Immigration Levels, 1983). By year's end, 13,400 privately sponsored and 11,200 government sponsored refugees had arrived in Canada. In 1980, the total of privately sponsored refugees rose to thirty-five thousand (Lanphier 1981). Due to a growing public backlash against further influxes of Indochinese refugees, the matching formula was halted (Adelman et al. 1980). Canadian media coverage shifted from an emphasis on sympathy for refugee flight and camp conditions, to the theme of refugee resettlement and the problems of racism, unemployment, and cultural compatibility (Adelman 1983).

As emphasis on the boat people declined, Canada gave greater attention to the sponsorship of Cambodian refugees, particularly as a humanitarian response to their escalating conditions of starvation and the subsequent squalor, violence, and deprivations in the Thai border camps. From late 1979 through the 1980s, hundreds of thousands of Cambodians had fled into Thailand, and some into Vietnam. Although initiated by the disruption of the Khmer Rouge regime, the mass exodus was fuelled by fear of Vietnamese communist rule and by Cambodia's social and economic devastation that had resulted in the collapse of its food production. The sudden and disorderly movement of Cambodians comprised a 'migration crisis' (Van Hear 1998: 23). As a 'reactive migration,' these movements are dictated by catastrophic events and chaotic dispersal that severely constrain choices in seeking refuge (Richmond 1994: 60). Chapter 1 provides an overview of the conditions (nationalist movements, Vietnam War, Communist Khmer Rouge regime, and Vietnamese occupation of Cambodia) that forced Cambodians from their homeland. Also included are facets of their flight, conditions in Thai refugee camps, and the Cambodian health concerns that initially deterred their resettlement in Western countries.

Although Thailand was willing to grant temporary asylum, Cambodians were expected to return to their homeland or seek resettlement elsewhere. Approximately three hundred thousand of them eventually found resettlement in Western countries, with nearly half going to the United States (Douglas 2003). More than fifty thousand went to France, while Canada and Australia received the third- and fourth-largest Cambodian refugee populations (UNHCR 2000: 99). During the 1980s, Canada received almost twenty thousand Cambodian refugees as part of its 'designated class' category. Most resettled either in southern Ontario (approximately five thousand in Toronto and another five thousand in smaller cities and towns) or in Quebec (primarily Montreal). Chapter 2 describes the process of sponsorship into Canada, the pre-migration characteristics of Cambodian refugees, and their geographical dispersal across Canada (with particular detail about communities in Ontario). It assesses past resettlement programs in Ontario, and current community development programs. Specific resettlement challenges that faced Cambodian men, women, and children in Ontario are noted, but extensive details on the legacy of genocide, trauma, and social devastation (particularly its effect on Khmer women) are not included from McLellan's 1995 report.

Diaspora and Transnationalism

Cambodians who resettled in Ontario remain part of the larger diaspora of Cambodian refugees. Their social fields are linked through the transnational domain of the homeland, countries of first asylum (Thailand and Vietnam), and various resettlement locations in the wider diaspora (Van Hear 2006: 11). Cambodians in diaspora have a shared sense of a common cultural identity that involves issues of loss and idealization of pre-war Cambodia. They also share, in varying degrees, a commitment to the maintenance and restoration of the homeland through multiple economic, demographic, social, political, and cultural links.

Yet, there are several class, ethnic, and status differences among Cambodian refugees. Chapter 3 introduces these distinctions and divisions within Ontario Cambodian communities, including Kampuchea Krom, ethnic Khmer born in Vietnam. These sometimes divisive identities are connected with specific kinds of cultural retention, youth aspiration for higher education, employment patterns, participation in homeland aid programs, and various transnational linkages and networks. Ontario Cambodian identities and cultural practices in diaspora are influenced and expressed as a result of their displacement and transnationality. They also embody various elements of hybridity that arise through adaptation and integration in specific locales, including troubled relationships with and partial alienation from the host society (Cohen 1997: 180; Van Hear 1998; Haller 2004).

In Canada, the ethnic, political, and religious identities of most recent immigrants and refugees are constructed in response to global transformations and the emergence of transnational communities across multiple borders and boundaries (Satzewich and Liodakis 2007: 206). As Cheran (2006: 3) notes, there are numerous ways to belong and to incorporate both 'home' and 'host' experiences. Local expressions of identity involve negotiations to re-create and redefine social relations that may require new responses to the prevailing social norms and patterns of integration. Traditional hierarchies, ideologies, lines of power, religious and political authority, however, often remain embedded in connections to the homeland or other communities of resettlement.

To sustain transnational relations and networks, new forms of community, communication, cultural production, travel, flows of capital, and types and sites of political and social engagement emerge (Vertovec 1999). Social connections involve multinational kinship ties; global institutions that support cultural, religious, and political circuits; and groups or individuals who share everyday activities or practices across national borders (Ebaugh and Chafetz 2002). They engage in reciprocal patterns of change that can be identified and analysed both symbolically and in a systematic and grounded fashion (ibid.: 8). Models of political and cultural immigrant adaptation are best understood through both vertical networks and relationships within local contexts of specific nation-states, and lateral networks with the homeland and other communities in diaspora (Levitt 2001; Faist 2000; Tambiah 2000; Vertovec 1999). Tibetan and Southeast Asian refugee communities that resettled in Canada maintain various connections with their respective homelands that reflect historical and current political and economic conditions there (McLellan 1999; McLellan and White 2005). Global conferences; annual workshops; and the transnational circuitry of monks, religious teachers, cultural performers, and political advocates provide local communities with doctrinal authority and legitimacy that help reaffirm and revitalize ethnic and religious identities. Asian refugees in resettlement maintain day-to-day family, community, ceremonial, and ritual facets of life through both local and transnational leadership, linkages, and networks (McLellan 1999; Ebaugh and Chafetz 2002; Guest 2003).

In Canada, the political, ideological, ethnic, and religious identities of refugees are shaped by their status as racial, religious, and cultural minorities. Many of the resettled non-Christian Asian refugees have faced exclusion, social marginalization, and racial and religious discrimination, often without recourse to friends and family who had settled elsewhere or remain in the homeland (McLellan 1999; McLellan and White 2005). Ong (1995: 808) identifies 'minoritization' as the social process of 'cultural citizenship' wherein dominant institutions and everyday encounters teach lessons about how refugees can belong, yet continue to be differentiated from others. The social status of Cambodian refugees is even more ambivalent since their extensively disadvantaged economic, political, and social circumstances render them a 'flawed element' in the Asian American model minority continuum (Ong 1995: 809).

The global agendas of the nation-states in which refugees resettle and the degree of political recognition given to their original homeland, or of those who occupy it, further affect their representation and recognition. This can be seen in the Canadian government's attitude towards resettled Tibetans after trade relations were assumed with China (McLellan 1999: 97). Disadvantaged Asian refugees are in sharp contrast to the cosmopolitan and affluent Asian immigrants who 'have the material and symbolic resources to express a complex agency in manipulating global schemes of cultural difference, racial hierarchy, and citizenship' (Ong 1993: 746). Asians with high social and economic capital can use it 'to make strategic choices of citizenship that do not inhibit their business activities worldwide or threaten the economic and political security of their families' (ibid.). The public discourse and counter-narratives about transnational communities and diasporic networks express various power struggles concerning their spacial, ideological, and social control (Haller 2004). Local and global contexts of power (or lack thereof) simultaneously re-create, redefine, and negotiate the social relations and identities that reaffirm and revitalize traditional and modified forms of authority and social legitimacy. Chapters 4 and 5 demonstrate these contexts within Cambodian religious identities and institutions in Ontario.

Within the process of religious restructuring, Cambodian individuals and groups in Ontario resettlement communities seek confidence in traditional systems of identity and Buddhist rituals that sustain collegial trustworthiness, and create opportunities to break free from the restraints of local religious habits to transform past practices and identities (Giddens 1990: 20). The struggle to generate new grounds of identity and legitimacy not only results in readjusted power relations and privileges, but also alterations in ideas, behaviours, and attitudes towards authority or social innovations. Chapter 4 details Cambodian attempts to re-create traditional Khmer Buddhism in Ontario, examining how Buddhist beliefs, practices, and institutions enhance their social and cultural identity, moral and ethical authority, and community cohesion. For many older Khmer, Buddhism, especially the role of the Buddhist monk, is the most culturally appropriate mechanism for psychological and community healing. The different types of transnational and homeland connections that sustain Khmer Buddhism in resettlement entail both continuities and transformations, as well as discord, particularly among the youth, Kampuchea Krom, and Khmer Christians. New identities among Khmer Christians are presented in Chapter 5. Cambodians converted to Christianity in the refugee camps and through the resettlement sponsorship process. Christian Khmer employ innovative adaptive strategies through non-traditional religious beliefs and practices, and they struggle to generate their own grounds of Khmer identity and legitimacy. They represent a small but significant minority in Ontario Cambodian communities.

Social Capital

Social capital is a key interpretive category and a constant theme in examining the circumstances involved in negotiating identity and adaptive success among resettled Cambodians. Social capital consists of those social structures that make it possible for groups and individuals to achieve particular goals, and to replicate familiar structural relations between people by generating networks of obligations, expectations, and trustworthiness (Coleman 1988, 1990). It is contained in ethno-specific community ties and leadership, intra-religious affiliations and networks (beyond the specific ethnic community), and individuals who act on behalf of an identifiable group within the larger ethnic community. Pre-migration experiences and backgrounds especially influence a community's or group's social capital, and its capacity or need to seek social capital from others (Makio 1997; McLellan and White 2005; Taylor 1994; Zhou and Bankston 1998: 11–12). Refugee communities, particularly, require a high degree of social capital to facilitate culturally familiar resettlement needs, to enhance educational and employment opportunities, to encourage the retention or rejection of traditional religious and cultural identity, and to actively contribute to different types of transnational networks and linkages (McLellan 2004; Guest 2003; Zhou and Bankston 1994; Wuthnow 2002). With greater social capital, broad transnational networks can extend beyond basic family linkages and remittance patterns to more complex political, economic, or social involvements in the homeland.

Three categories of social capital are bonding, bridging, and linking (Woolcock 1998; Putnam 2000; Voyer 2003). Each is associated with specific adaptive strategies useful in resettlement and the development or maintenance of transnational linkages. Bonding capital is a cohesive mechanism within families, groups, communities, and religious institutions. It especially helps newcomers to maintain and support ethnic and cultural identity, traditional family and homeland values, and global connections with others (Zhou and Bankston 1994; Warner and Wittner 1998; McLellan 1999; Ebaugh and Chafetz 2000; Eck 2001; Wuthnow 2002). Religious institutions are highly effective in providing bonding social and spiritual capital necessary for transnational networks and homeland linkages (Guest 2003). Bonding social capital contained within local families and communities limits the venues for programs and services in resettlement or in the homelands. It is most effective in sustaining surviving family members or religious institutions in the homeland through remittances or special donations, and in keeping abreast of social issues and political allegiances in the homeland and/or other resettlement countries. Bridging social capital extends beyond the particular group or community to connect with others in order to enhance cooperative activities. An example is the role of Christian churches in the sponsorship, resettlement, and conversion of Southeast Asian refugees (McLellan 1999; Winland 1992). Patron-client relationships between the private sponsor and refugees reflect the kind of social capital that Bezanson (2006: 429) identifies as ties between relatively powerful and relatively weak people. Linking capital expands on bridging capital by facilitating relations between different groups to enhance social recognition, wealth, or influence. Woolcock (2001: 13) recognizes the capacity of linking capital to leverage resources, ideas, and information beyond a particular community. Thich Nhat Hanh's Tiep Hien Order, for example, expanded its original Vietnamese membership to include non-Vietnamese in North America and Europe (McLellan 1999: 116–18). The transnational membership dramatically enhanced the group's ability to provide social assistance to individuals and groups in Vietnam, and to advocate for political and economic reform there.

The degree of social capital necessary to mobilize a community to provide homeland aid programs or participate in political activism depends on high levels of trust, solidarity, and social cohesion. These are especially absent among those who have experienced extensive mistrust, fear, and broken relationships, inhibiting their confidence to develop a sense of place and identity in new social contexts. Without high levels of social capital, it is difficult to develop and maintain the kinds of transnational networks that facilitate monetary flows; technological exportation of cultural traditions; satellite transmissions; the circulation of religious, cultural, and ethnic images, artefacts, and personnel; and innovative identity changes that serve a range of emotional, personal, social, and economic interests in resettlement.

Numerous studies identify a lack of trust, solidarity, and social cohesion within Cambodian resettlement communities, and excessive experiences of isolation, lack of leadership, and fear of authority (Beiser et al. 1989; Boehnlein 1987; Mollica et al. 1997; DePaul 1997; Kinzie 1988; Stevens 1995; Chan 2003). The 1975–79 Marxist-based Khmer Rouge regime completely devastated Cambodia, destroying its economic infrastructure and most of its social, cultural, religious, and political leadership. During those years of repression and terror, millions of Cambodians were evacuated from their homes; separated from their families; subjected to physical and verbal assaults; imprisoned in concentration and 're-education' camps; forced to undergo or witness cruel punishment, abduction, and/or execution; and deprived of food and shelter. Those who fled to refugee camps in Thailand survived in what Ebihara et al. (1994: 20) describe as a state of liminality, living a life of limbo (often violent) and further powerlessness. The legacy of traumatized survivors, broken families, and shattered communities has exacerbated Cambodian efforts to rebuild social capital in countries of resettlement.

Depleted levels of social capital were notable among the Cambodians who resettled in Ontario. Low educational levels and high illiteracy rates further hindered the extent to which traditional social, cultural, political, and religious bonds could be reaffirmed and re-established in a Western social context. Compared with Cambodians who resettled in Quebec, France, and the United States, Ontario Cambodians have had limited influence and impact on other transnational communities or the homeland. The kinds and degrees of transnational networks and linkages that they have developed and maintain, primarily reflect bonding capital. Homeland connections among first-generation Cambodians are with extended family and opportunities to enhance their retention of traditional religious, cultural, and ethnic identity. They do not extend to political or wider-scale economic involvements. Bridging and linking forms of social capital are, however, found in the transnational networks and activities of Christian Khmer and Kampuchea Krom.

As Cambodia slowly recovers its infrastructure and strives to maintain social, political, and economic stability, Cambodian refugees in Ontario have been rebuilding their lives, families, and community institutions, with the two processes being dependent upon each other. For Cambodians in Ontario, the ability to re-create or redefine traditional ethnic and religious identities, and to reach beyond them, has been restricted by material resources and levels of social capital. Both impact the ability of Cambodian refugees to cultivate public recognition and representation; to develop adaptive and integrative strategies; to overcome community and individual mistrust; to negotiate the values, organizations, and mechanisms of global communication; and to maintain the continuity of relationships with their homeland and among themselves.

To understand the Cambodian people who resettled in Ontario, one must appreciate the extent and gravity of their suffering in Cambodia. First-generation Cambodians in Ontario cannot be separated from their identity as survivors of genocide: that is why they are here, and that is who they are. As Langer notes, fifty years after the Jewish Holocaust, testimonies of the survivors recount that they still remain 'hostages to a humiliating and painful past that their happier future does little to curtail' (1991: xi). Tensions remain between self-imposed isolation and the need for community. Their deep memories remain unresolved, particularly when they strive to communicate the memories of annihilation and survival to others (ibid.: 23). Like Jewish Holocaust survivors, first-generation Cambodians experienced extensive social disruption, unimaginable horror, inhumane deprivations, absence, and irreversible losses that they find difficult to understand, let alone speak about. Similar to the children of Jewish Holocaust survivors, second-generation Cambodian children often grasp a different kind of truth that denotes pride in the strength of their parents' survival, ability to build new lives, retain rich cultural and religious heritages, and express hope (ibid.: x). Enormous difficulties remain in attempts to bridge these two kinds of truth.

The intergenerational perspective on the effects of trauma and the experiences of war have been given little attention, particularly the role of the family in an individual's perceptions and reactions (Bek-Pedersen and Montgomery 2006: 108). How families communicate about traumatic experiences not only influences the transmission of trauma, but can lead refugee youth and children of survivors to regard the world as basically unpredictable, insecure and dangerous (ibid.: 96). In Long Beach, California, the largest Cambodian resettlement community has only recently held one of the first American events to discuss the effects of the Khmer Rouge regime on survivors and their American-born children (*The Desert Sun*, 31 March 2008, B8). Cambodian children of survivors are only now beginning to understand the emotional silence of their parents and its psychological and social consequences. Chapter 6 details the concerns and experiences of Cambodian youth in Ontario. It highlights their struggle to identify and position themselves as Canadian children of Cambodian refugee parents. Older Khmer youth and those born and raised in Canada must negotiate identities amid the lure of secular materialism and non-Khmer avenues for status or power, and the expectations of older Cambodians who reify traditional Cambodian cultural heritage and religious identities as the essence of being Khmer.

Second Generation

The negative contextual factors that many immigrant and refugee youth face in resettlement create vulnerability to 'adversarial subcultures' and an inability to cope with difficult situations (Portes and Zhou 1993: 83). Racial discrimination, inner-city concentrations, various levels of social capital, and the absence of a strong receiving co-ethnic community lead to complex patterns of adaptation specific to the second generation (Zhou and Bankston 1998: 3–7). Rumbaut refers to this as 'segmented assimilation' (1996: 124), a situation that negatively affects ethnic identity formation and the reaffirmation of ethnic solidarity. As refugees, and as Canadian-born children of refugees, Cambodian youth in Ontario have had to cope with hostile social environments, language challenges, school performance issues, parent-child generational conflicts, and contentious peer relationships. The low educational goals of many Cambodian parents account for the particularly low educational achievements among Cambodian youth (Portes and Rumbaut 2001: 103).

In their broad operational definition of the second generation, Portes and Rumbaut (2001: 23) include both native-born children of foreign-born parents and foreign-born children who migrated before adolescence. Within Ontario Cambodian communities, the distinctions between the youth who arrived as refugees, and those born and raised in Canada are acknowledged through referring to them as older Khmer youth and younger Khmer youth. Kwon and Kim identify foreign-born youth as the '1.5 generation' (1993: 75), situated between the first and second generations, and who experience structural marginality within new social contexts and within their own communities. Among older Khmer youth in resettlement, this structural marginality can be seen in their struggle for identity while being an adaptive bridge for their parents and a role model to the younger generation. As survivors of the Khmer Rouge, their resettlement experiences are not only associated with high levels of emotional and psychological distress, but also with positive aspirations for social functioning that were often found lacking among the first generation (Mollica et al. 1997; DePaul 1997). The combined strain of post-traumatic stress disorder (PTSD) symptoms and resettlement expectations, however, left them particularly vulnerable to social isolation (Clarke et al. 1993: 65; Stevens 1995; Bek-Pedersen and Montgomery 2006). Younger Cambodian youth born and/or raised in Canada also reflect what Portes and Rumbaut refer to as consonant, dissonant, and selective patterns of acculturation (2001: 52). Both foreign- and Canadian-born Cambodian youth in Ontario traverse multiple sites of belonging and express complex allegiances that are continually being constructed in response to local and global influences, and that are quite distinct from the first generation.

Among second-generation immigrants and refugees in Canada, transnationalism has become a type of consciousness that particularly invokes multiple and overlapping identities (Satzewich and Liodakis 2007: 215). Cultural productions created by these youth emphasize the continuity of ancestral traditions and their family experiences of resettlement. Maira (2002: 23) refers to the ways in which second-generation youth negotiate the politics of ethnicity, race, gender, and cultural beliefs and practices as a process of 'reflexive hybridity.' The vitality and complexity of music particularly offers a way through the oppositions of essentialism versus pluralism and tradition versus modernism, as do new understandings or 'countermemories' of dance (Bottomley 1991: 312–13; Maira 2002). Cambodian youth in Ontario also reflect their hybrid identities through an engagement with homeland-based art, music, and cultural forms and in their ability to maintain multiple ways of interaction and communication. Simmons and Plaza (2006: 143–6) refer to this social fluidity as 'code-switching,' that is, to oscillate between speech patterns and references meaningful only to other Khmer youth or community members and those common to mainstream institutions, employment sites, and non-Khmer friend networks.

Cambodian youth are innovative in their modes of cultural reproduction. Their styles of clothing, music, different types of social interactions and groupings reflect attempts to balance Cambodian-based heritage with local community identities and broader Canadian social inclusion. Strong disparities, however, exist among the second generation in understanding or accepting traditional religious practices and institutions, particularly the role of Buddhism, Buddhist monks, and the meaning of traditional rituals. Although second-generation youth have become a central focus of recent studies on North American immigrants, little is known about their shifts in religious affiliation, or the kinds of hybridity and multiplicity entailed in their ethnic and religious identities (Stepick 2005: 19–20). While some youth are deeply engaged in their ethnic religious communities (Bankston and Zhou 1995), many second-generation adolescents and young adults do not participate in substantial numbers, even when congregational-style formats and organized Sunday schools are available (Ebaugh and Chafetz 2000: 431; Suh 2004: 65). In Ontario, Cambodian youth do not have weekly English-language religious services, and there are few specialized programs of religious education available, a lack that contributes to their difficulties in Buddhist participation and conflicted Buddhist identities.

Many Cambodian youth no longer identify Buddhism as an integral part of their personal, cultural, or ethnic identity. New cultural symbols of belonging are increasingly utilized to validate innovative ways of being Khmer that are not defined by Buddhist practices, ethics, and values. Many of them arise through transnational networks, but especially through visits to Cambodia. Chapter 7 recapitulates essential facets of the Cambodian resettlement in Ontario highlighting the impact that developing and maintaining linkages and connections to the homeland has had on generational continuity. Disparate concepts of identity are increasingly accepted as being authentic ways of building ties with the homeland, and with Cambodians in other countries of resettlement. Strong transnational linkages and connections help older Cambodians maintain a variety of Khmer ethnic and cultural identities in Canada, and affirm the second generation's shifting and adaptable notions of what it is to be Khmer in Canada.

Research Methods and Data Collection

Data collection in Ontario has involved interviews (formal and informal) and participant-observation at a variety of Cambodian community ceremonies, cultural and religious festivities, and social events. Over a twelve-year period, at least two hundred Cambodians in Ontario and twenty-one in Cambodia were interviewed by the author, with some sessions involving small groups consisting of family and friends. Interviews were in people's homes, at community health organizations, government offices, resettlement agencies, Cambodian associations, Buddhist temples, and Christian churches. Khmer research assistants helped to contact and arrange interviews, providing translation when necessary. Unless specific individuals spoke during a public forum, or requested that their names be used, identification of participants is anonymous and their location in smaller communities is usually excluded from specific quotes.

Formal interviews were conducted with non-Khmer and Cambodian individuals affiliated with government-funded institutions, while semi-structured interviews were held with community leaders, and representatives of cultural and religious associations. Interviews with Cambodians not involved in leadership positions tended to be informal and unstructured. Cambodian interviewees included community leaders; health and social service assistants; resettlement workers; Buddhist monks, nuns, and elders; Christian pastors and individuals associated with different Christian institutions; teachers of heritage language programs; students from high schools, colleges, and universities; business owners; cultural leaders and performers; factory workers and well-educated professionals; parents; independent women with home-based employment; abandoned and isolated women; elderly Khmer; Chinese-Cambodians; and Kampuchea Krom. Individuals provided insights relating to their personal experiences in Cambodia, to being Khmer, to facing challenges of resettlement and adaptation, and to how the Cambodian identity in Ontario is being re-created and redefined.

During interviews in the early 1990s, many Cambodians spoke about their horrendous experiences of suffering, even though it was not asked of them. These experiences were disturbing to hear and distressing to those who related them. Although reassured that they did not have to talk about their painful memories, many wanted to recount their stories of survival, insisting that I hear what had happened to them so I could understand. In several instances, it was the first time these experiences were shared with anyone. At times people wept openly when speaking or listening to one another. During some interviews, after the Khmer translator from a health or service agency finished translating and the interviewee had left, the translator would then want to share his or her own particular experiences as well. One non-Khmer health care worker who sat in on this kind of secondary interview had no idea that the Khmer translator with whom she had worked so closely for six months had endured such horrors, or that the traumatic experiences of a shared client of theirs were not unusual among Cambodian refugees.

Ten years later, Cambodians did not express the same need to share their survival stories, and the research was more focused on their successful strategies for social cohesion rather than the difficulties of resettlement. During small social gatherings, some Khmer engaged in joking behaviour, laughing as they retold stories of outwitting the Khmer Rouge or catching rodents for food, delighting in the expressions of horror on the faces of the younger children as they gave cooking details. In individual interviews, however, it was still evident that when people did relate experiences under the Khmer Rouge or fleeing to Thailand, their pain and suffering had not lessened over time, and the retelling was profoundly disturbing to them.

Interviews in Ontario with first-generation Cambodians were only handwritten. During the early 1990s, interviewees were especially concerned with being taped and the possibility that others would hear their words. To help overcome their mistrust of a stranger asking questions, a long period of time would be spent going over the interview consent form, the nature of the research, and answering personal or general questions. The notepad that was being used to record information was often given to the Cambodians being interviewed to provide them with the opportunity to write down names, phone numbers, or addresses themselves, to read what had been recorded already, and in subsequent interviews, to refer back to information for further qualification or comment. During the 2002–05 interviews, being tape-recorded was no longer a concern. The second generation not only encouraged the use of a tape recorder, but laughed at the 'old-fashioned' equipment and suggested more sophisticated technologies. Taped interviews were transcribed and returned to interviewees with an invitation to correct any mistakes or to provide further comments.

During the 1993 Cambodian workshop at York University, the larger gatherings were bilingual in Khmer and English. In the smaller group sessions, participants were encouraged to speak in Khmer to further their involvement and understanding. During the smaller sessions participants were requested to complete a ten-page survey on Cambodian settlement and adaptation in Ontario, written in both Khmer and English. Two hundred were handed out during the workshop, and another hundred were mailed to Khmer throughout Ontario. Over one hundred completed questionnaires were translated into English.

In the early 1990s, formal and semi-structured interviews with non-Khmer were conducted with Canadian government representatives at the federal, provincial, and municipal levels; service providers from a variety of agencies and organizations (past and present); principals at public schools and ESL teachers; journalists; private sponsors active in resettling Cambodians; and individuals associated with Cambodian communities. Several types of immigration statistics and census data were also consulted. Immigration statistics from Employment and Immigration Canada provided an accurate account of total numbers of Cambodians who arrived in Canada, detailed the primary years of resettlement from 1980 to 1992, and highlighted characteristics of the community upon arrival (age, gender, education, previous employment, family composition, mode of sponsorship). Census data included Cambodian population characteristics as well as customized cross-tabulations (ethnic origin with language, place of residence, religion, employment, education).

Distinct from Cambodian communities in Quebec, the United States, and other Western countries, Cambodians who resettled in Ontario suffered an initial lack of support from government and other agencies in providing culturally appropriate services. A second distinction was the near total absence of Khmer educational, medical, religious, economic, and professional leaders in Ontario. The lack of external support as well as community capital created extensive resettlement challenges that in some cases led to successful adaptive and integrative strategies.

Utilizing data from the 1995 report on Cambodian refugees, this book gives attention to the modes of sponsorship; the Cambodian presence and numbers in various cities; the availability of resettlement services; the types of difficulties; the extent of community distinctions, divisions, and cohesive activities; the re-creation and redefining of religious identities, practices, and traditions; cultural and ideological continuities and transformations in the second generation; and the importance of transnational linkages and connections for individuals and families.

Much of the material on second-generation Cambodian youth is from the Khmer Youth Workshop for second-generation Cambodians, held 16–17 July 2005, at the University of Toronto Hart House Farm. Most of the sessions were videotaped by youth members of the Canadian Cambodian Association of Ontario (CCAO) and audio-taped by the author. Both were transcribed. The executive director of the CCAO suggested that the workshop focus on youth initiatives and leadership:

> Bring in twenty to thirty strong core individuals from around Ontario to do a weekend leadership retreat. We build these leaders by teaching them the concepts of social justice, community development, empowerment, and Cambodian Canadian social and political, economic, and religious issues, proposal-writing skills, management skills, organizational skills, and the list can go on ... Having worked with youth for a while now, I see that they want to build their community but don't know how to ... build the Cambodian community leadership capacity. (personal interview, 2004)

Ultimately, the workshop reflected a range of interests including social cohesion, transnational influences on ethnic and religious identities, leadership training, and skills development. Most of the fifty or so participants were second-generation youth in their late teens and early twenties who expressed a strong interest in becoming leaders and in strengthening their Ontario communities. These individuals embody the increase in community social capital and the recognition and representation of Khmer Canadians.

1 A Brief History of Cambodians

Ninety per cent of the population of Cambodia is Khmer, a people whose history in Indochina dates back to 1500 BCE (Garry 1980). The Khmer lifestyle of rice cultivation and animal husbandry developed in symmetry with the annual monsoons and two main seasons (a dry, cool winter and a hot, wet summer). The serpent Naga was venerated as the primary guardian spirit of the land, and later, as a protector of Buddha. Following the marriage between an Indian prince and a Khmer princess in the first century CE, Khmer people became known as Kampucheans. The influences of India and, to a lesser degree, China helped to create a rich and varied cultural and religious heritage (Mabbett and Chandler 1995; Majumdar 1980). The Buddhist religion, Sanskrit language, Indian alphabet, judicial laws, and Hindu conceptions of the monarchy were incorporated into Khmer culture and society. The Khmer language, however, retained a structure and basic vocabulary quite distinct from these historical influences (Mabbett and Chandler 1995: 3). Traditional Cambodian art, classical dance, music, and dramatic presentations are rooted in ancient Hindu and Buddhist legends and myths. In the latter half of the first millennium, the Khmer became a significant polity (Ebihara et al. 1994: 9).

By the mid-twelfth century Kampuchea was a strong centralized state encompassing territories that are now Laos, central Thailand (Siam), South Vietnam, parts of Burma, and the Malay Peninsula. Cambodians refer to this period of Khmer history as the 'golden age.' Sophisticated hydraulic networks sustained a vast and dependable agricultural production. It was a time of political stability, military power, religious learning, performance arts, and the building of the great temple city of Angkor Wat. Featured predominately in the Cambodian national anthem and flag, Angkor Wat remains a powerful symbol of Khmer achievement and cultural identity, representing a glorious past and the potential for a modern nation-state. Themes that were carved into the Angkor Wat walls continue to inspire classical dance and other art forms now practised in Cambodia and in Khmer communities around the world. Angkor Wat images appear everywhere: on T-shirts, beer bottles, and uniforms; and on logos for Cambodian banks, airlines, and businesses. One Cambodian businessman in Toronto depicts the Angkor Wat on his delivery vans, several Ontario restaurants use the image or name to identify themselves as Cambodian, and most Ontario Khmer families have at least one picture of it on a wall in their home.

Beginning in 1432, Kampuchea faced increased territorial encroachments from Siam and Vietnam. Losing huge areas of land and political autonomy, Khmer control dwindled to a region that approximates present-day Cambodia (Ebihara 1985). By 1834, a large area of Kampuchea had been annexed to Vietnam and smaller areas to Siam. Numerous Khmer-speaking people located in Eastern Siam became referred to as Khmer Sarin, and those in Vietnam as Kampuchea Krom. The Vietnamese initiated a systematic Vietnamization of the more than one million Kampuchea Krom, who lived in the annexed territory, attempting to destroy their language, traditions, and religion (Garry 1980). Despite Vietnamese efforts, the Kampuchea Krom retained a strong Khmer identity by continuing to speak the Khmer language, practising Theravada Buddhism, and keeping their concept of nationhood firmly embodied in Cambodia. Following the Vietnamese annexation, Kampuchea requested and received French protection, becoming the French colony of Cambodge in 1863 (Chandler 1991). The French influence pervaded government, language, and education. Cambodge was eventually anglicized to Cambodia, although many Cambodians still refer to themselves as Khmer and their country as Kampuchea. Despite foreign occupation and some minorities, the population in Cambodia has remained relatively homogeneous, the majority being ethnic Khmer (Chandler 1991).

Ethnic and Class Distinctions in Cambodia

Cambodian ethnic minority groups include the Vietnamese, Chinese, Burmese, Lao, Cham Muslims (Sunni Muslims known as Khmer Islam), and several hill tribes (such as Khmer Loeu). In 1973, the population of Cambodia had been estimated at 7.3 million, with the following ethnic divisions (Garry 1980: 35): Khmer (6,200,000), Chinese (450,000), Vietnamese (450,000), Khmer Islam (150,000), and Khmer Loeu (50,000).

Ethnic Khmer in Ontario say that they are racially distinct from Vietnamese and Chinese, citing their darker skin, taller bodies, upturned and slightly larger noses, curlier hair, fuller mouths, and straighter eyes (McLellan 1995). Further, the Vietnamese and Chinese practise Mahayana Buddhism, while Khmer identify with Theravada Buddhism.

Teochiu-speaking Chinese, known as Chen, first settled in Cambodia seven hundred years ago (Whitmore 1985). Clustering in small towns and urban areas, they frequently intermarried with local Khmer giving their offspring a mixed-race appearance. Many Chen assimilated into Khmer society, while others attempted to balance competing ethnic and religious identities. Cantonese-speaking Chinese migrants tended to dwell in large urban areas (Phnom Penh, Battembang, and Kampong Cham) and retained a distinct identity that separated them from Khmer (ibid.). In the early 1970s, approximately 7 per cent, of Cambodia's population maintained some form of Chinese identity (Chandler 1991).

Traditional Khmer society had developed into three distinct class and status groups: royalty and government officials who lived in small towns and urban areas, rural-based peasants, and Buddhist monks (Bit 1991). Each group was shaped by patron-client networks that extended from the king, down through bureaucratic officials and the Buddhist monastic order, to village officials and powerful kinsmen (Chandler 2000: 105). These vertical relations of patronage and personal deference were tempered in the villages by bilateral kinship ties and the Khmer-Buddhist ethos of compassion that shaped male and female roles in family and community affairs (Ong 2003: 32).

The French colonial influence increased the dichotomy between rural and urban life and the differences between Khmer royalty and Khmer peasants. Two value systems were created. One emphasized Western ideals and education, classical Khmer culture, and a modern approach to Buddhism referred to as Thommayut (Dhammayut) that privileged Pali scripture and textual study over customary practices (Hansen 2007: 99). The other remained entrenched in traditional, conservative lifestyles of rural agricultural production that did not encourage educational or business aspirations, and a village-based Buddhism called Mahanikay (Mysliwiec 1988). Whereas elite expressions of classical dance were traditionally performed for and under the patronage of the royal family, rural people embraced the more popular performances of shadow plays, folk dramas, and folk dances that reflected regional differences, political and social parodies, and improvisational techniques. The urban-based Thommayut (Dhammayut), a reformed monastic fraternity from Thailand known as *thor thmei* (the modernizers), initially developed in opposition to *thor cah*, the predominately rural Mahanikay traditionalists, and influenced Mahanikay's eventual inclusion of more rationalized and demythologized facets (Harris 2005: xii; Hansen 2007: 110).[1] The critical discourse of Buddhist modernism became a significant part of anti-colonial nationalism. These new forms of knowledge within a variety of literary and narrative genres also influenced new ideas about ethical and ritual purity, emphasizing moral development and self-cultivation for both monastics and laypeople (Hansen 2007: 181).

French rule widened class divisions among the minority ethnic groups and Khmer. Vietnamese were encouraged to assume administrative functions and vocational occupations, Chinese to pursue financial and commercial activities, and Khmer to remain in agricultural and intensive labour roles (fishing, construction, carpentry, weaving). The development of a Khmer middle class began after the country became independent in 1953 when urban Khmer moved into government administrative and white-collar positions. Older Cambodians now residing in Ontario still classify themselves and evaluate one another according to these ancestral class and ethnic differences, past livelihoods, and urban or rural locale. During the early years of resettlement, these distinctions thwarted attempts to integrate and unite the various Khmer communities, even though more than 80 per cent of the Cambodians arriving in Canada had been rural-based, with many younger adults having little memory of rural village life before the war.

Repercussions of the Vietnam War

In 1953, Cambodia gained independence under the political leadership of Prince Norodam Sihanouk, aided by several political factions, among them the rural-based Cambodian communist resistance forces (Khmer Isarak) and the Vietnamese communists (Vietminh). During the next fifteen years, Cambodia became caught up in the escalating Vietnam War, oscillating between Western and communist pressures. By the late 1960s, North Vietnamese communists were moving arms and troops into the rural eastern provinces of Cambodia, and Prince Sihanouk, in defiance of U.S. pressure, openly affiliated with the Chinese communist government (Chandler 2000). In 1969, a massive

American bombing of Cambodia began in conjunction with a South Vietnamese invasion, both supposedly directed towards Vietcong soldiers in Cambodia (Shawcross 1979). The royalist government of Prince Sihanouk was replaced in 1970 by the U.S.-backed regime of Lon Nol, a former general and defence minister under Prince Sihanouk. With Sihanouk forced into exile, Cambodia was renamed the Khmer Republic and used increasingly as a military strike zone to prevent North Vietnamese troop movements into South Vietnam. The Lon Nol government encouraged hatred towards Vietnamese living in Cambodia, and allowed American bombing raids to intensify inside Cambodia. During the five-year bombing campaign, well over a million Khmer were forced from their rural homes into the capital Phnom Penh, which grew from a city of two hundred thousand to over two million people (Chandler 1983). Thousands of other displaced rural Khmer joined the growing Khmer Communist Party.

In the 1960s, Prince Sihanouk began calling the Cambodian communists 'Khmer Rouge.' After his overthrow, he sanctioned and supported Khmer Rouge efforts from his exile in China. Sihanouk's call for Khmer resistance against the Lon Nol government escalated Cambodia into civil war. Through the early 1970s, for every story Khmer people heard about Khmer Rouge atrocities, there were counter-stories about the Lon Nol regime's massacres of ethnic Vietnamese citizens, generalized corruption, and lawlessness (Ngor 1987: 71). When the Americans abandoned Cambodia two weeks before the fall of Saigon in April 1975, Khmer Rouge forces under the leadership of Pol Pot took over the country, renaming it Democratic Kampuchea. Lasting until early 1979, the extremist rule of the Khmer Rouge enforced an administration based on open force, intimidation, and inhumane treatment. Their brutal approach to power consolidation and implementation utilized idealistic and nostalgic notions of Khmer nationalism and past glory.

Khmer Rouge Regime, 1975–1979

Khmer Rouge forces entered Phnom Penh on 17 April 1975. Many of the soldiers were twelve- to sixteen-year-old uneducated rural orphans (Ngor 1987). Few had ever been to a city and all were indoctrinated into communist ideology. Within three days of their occupation, the Khmer Rouge evacuated all the inhabitants of Phnom Penh. Resistors and hesitators were shot. For weeks, roads leading to rural areas were clogged by the over two million evacuees. No food, shelter, or water was provided, only orders to keep moving away from the city. Simultaneous evacuations occurred from every major city and town in Cambodia. Khmer now resettled in Ontario speak of men, women, children, and even hospital patients being forced, at gunpoint, to leave, and tell that during this time, family members were separated or died of exhaustion, thirst, exposure, and illness by the roadside. Throughout the country, schools, hospitals, banks, post offices, libraries, and Buddhist temples were systematically plundered and destroyed by Khmer Rouge cadres. Individuals associated with these institutions were either immediately shot (often in front of family members), or imprisoned and eventually executed. The Khmer Rouge hastily established rural work communes across Cambodia to accommodate the millions of displaced people from cities and small towns. This began what the Khmer Rouge referred to as 'Year Zero' of their radical communist state. During the initial chaos, thousands of Khmer were able to escape to Vietnam (150,000) or Thailand (35,000–40,000) (Ebihara 1985). For most Khmer, however, the next four years consisted of continual transfers of masses of people from one rural labour camp to another. Vickery (1983) details the sectoral and temporal differentiation within Democratic Kampuchea, with particular zones and regions (*damban*) characterized by extreme hardship and brutality and others more conducive to survival through diversity of food sources or relatively benign attitudes of the cadres.

In many areas, Khmer Rouge cadres encouraged people to tell their life stories, thus enabling them to identify former government officials, educated individuals, merchants, and landlords as 'class' enemies. Purges of class enemies, based on Maoist methods learned by Khmer Rouge leaders during China's Cultural Revolution, became common. Of the almost two million Cambodians who died during the Pol Pot regime, more than a hundred thousand died as direct targets of torture and executions, the rest from starvation, forced labour, lack of medical care, and as victims of war (Kiljunen 1983; Welaratna 1993). Ontario Cambodians who survived this ordeal easily recall the hard labour in fields, working days and nights without rest, the lack of food, being under constant surveillance, and being witness to innumerable acts of brutality and killing. They speak of watching their children and parents die of starvation and family members being shot and beaten, of the numerous acts of petty cruelty, suffering, and personal indignities, and the unceasing feelings of despair, fear, and terror. An older Cambodian woman now living in Ottawa recalled:

Fourteen days after 17 April, my husband committed suicide because if he didn't turn himself in, the whole family would be killed. My seven children, an eight-month-old baby to twelve years, and I were moved to a different area and forced to work. We were forced to live with three other families. One can of rice was given for the whole family to eat for three days, no salt. Lots of bodies became swollen with the flesh hanging down because of the lack of salt and excessive water retention. Many people ate ash because there may be salt [in it].

In the first five months, five of my children died from illness. Me and the three families were picked on because our husbands were all associated with the government. In 1977, they found out I used to be a teacher and they took me to kill me. One of my daughters had been taken to the soldiers' troop but my smaller son stayed with me and he was to be killed with me. He was three years old then. We were included with thirty or forty people, and they killed my son first and other people. I was shot in the side and smashed with a rifle over my back and left for dead. Later that night I woke up and crawled far away and stayed in a banana tree for three days ... This is how I survived ...

My memories are with me all the time. I am always feeling that sadness. All I want is [Khmer service worker] to be my friend to listen to my nightmares, which don't go away. Many are like me. They don't go to the temple because when they have so much pain they want to be isolated. (personal interview, 1994)

The violence inflicted on Cambodian people was carried out in the name of 'Angka,' a nameless, faceless organization whose leaders were not known. One Toronto Khmer woman felt that the pervasive terror of Angka was worse than hunger, because nothing could be done about it:

I remember when we were in the work group and we had to hold hands coming back to camp because we were starving and had no energy to walk. We had no clothes, only black. We had to keep our hair short. For four years we had no soap or shampoo. We could only wash our hair with water. All of us had head lice. We had to work in the rice fields, in deep water, and as soon as we went into the water, the leeches came and attached on.

We always cried. It was so horrible. We had to do everything. Plant rice, digging, irrigation. Little bowls of watery rice everyday. Only two cups of rice cooked with water for twenty people ...

Friends would slowly die in front of us and we thought that's what would happen to us. Nighttime was the most fearful because Angka would come then and call people out and they would disappear. They were always there to listen, to watch, to try and catch you up. You had to be always careful. One word could kill you. Every morning when we saw the sun we thought we have survived one more day. We kept thinking this every day. In my group there were three women who used to be university students. They spoke French with one another one evening and Angka heard this and the next day they were taken away and killed. We know this because their clothes were brought back. Everybody knew but nobody could talk about it. We just worked and kept quiet. Our life was in danger all the time, we were scared to talk, scared to do anything. (personal interview, 1994)

Social/Class Distinctions under the Khmer Rouge

The Khmer Rouge regime divided Cambodian people into three social groups: Khmer Rouge cadres and soldiers were leaders and authority figures; 'new people' (*moulatan thmai*) were slave labour; and 'old people' (*moulatan chass*) were overseers of new people, acting as administrators of labour, housing, and food distribution. Only Khmer Rouge cadres had full rights and privileges, with 'new people' having none (Chan 2003: 11). 'Old people' were rural based and had consented to Khmer Rouge rule during 1970–75. Although skilled in agriculture and rural living, they were generally illiterate and uninformed about urban life and global events. Also referred to as 'base people,' they were allowed to speak in Khmer Rouge meetings and make some independent decisions. Traders and farmers from areas not previously under Khmer Rouge control were identified as 'candidates' and given fewer rights (ibid.). 'New people' were displaced rural people who had fled to Phnom Penh as a result of American bombing, farmers who had large plots of land, and anyone living in towns and cities at the time of the Khmer Rouge occupation. Urban-raised evacuees were given especially harsh treatment, being identified as enemies of the state with no rights whatsoever. Those immediately targeted for execution, imprisonment, and torture included government officials, soldiers, merchants, educated and professional people, classical dancers, musicians, members of the royal family, artists, Buddhist monks, and those perceived as being Western influenced (wearing glasses, speaking French). A Cambodian woman from Ottawa noted that this targeting often extended to families:

I was born 1965. I left Cambodia in 1979 at age fourteen. My father was the minister of justice before 1975. From 1975 to 1979, most of my family was killed by the Khmer Rouge. There were only five of us left when we left Cambodia – myself, my brother, sister, mother (she died three years ago), and nephew. We left Cambodia because of the communists and all the killing. I saw with my own eyes how they killed and how they put me in what they called re-education schools. I was there one week because they considered me of the bourgeois class, me and my family. But they didn't know my father was minister of justice; if they knew it, they were going to kill my whole family. (personal interview, 2002)

One young Cambodian woman now living in London recalled the continual targeting:

In 1975, I was in Grade 13. During Pol Pot I had to pretend I was only in primary school and had to change my name because father was a teacher. We pretended we were a poor family with no education. They kept asking questions about the past trying to trick us. When father was sick, he couldn't work, and then they sent father away to die because he couldn't work. If we cried in public we would all be killed. He was forty-seven. One of my uncles worked in the office and one day was taken away with another group of men, supposedly to plan something, but we knew the group was taken to be killed. My mother had two older sisters and all of them are widowed. (personal interview, 1994)

Social ideals of morality and aspiration changed from that of the Buddhist monk or the Western-educated professional to the 'revolutionary' figure whose raw labour power and absolute control of others would create a new utopian communism (Ong 2003: 18). This horrific experiment in social engineering sought to completely eradicate traditional Cambodian society by engaging everyone in state-controlled rural production and by forcibly erasing cultural and social identity. Classical Khmer dance and music were denounced as corrupt and replaced with Chinese communist propaganda plays. Chinese songs glorifying the great success of the Chinese Cultural Revolution were broadcast throughout the camps when people returned from the fields at night. Buddhist practices and traditional ceremonies, including merit-making (the offering of food), and funeral and memorial rites were forbidden. Children over five years old were taken from parents and placed in children's work camps to be interrogated and tricked into disclosing their parents' class identity. Wives were separated from husbands, each to live in cramped, dormitory-like conditions wherever their labour was required. Communal food was provided only for workers; the elderly, sick, weak, and disabled were expected to die. Forced marriages were common; those who resisted were punished, as revealed by one Khmer woman in Ottawa, who said:

> In mid-1977 I was put in jail with my feet in the stocks [because] the Khmer Rouge tried to force me to marry someone against my will. There, I suffered from lice, mosquito bites, starvation, and threats upon my life. These threats were in the form of electric shocks, plastic bags placed over my face until I fainted, and bayonets held to my temple. Lastly, they beat me all over my body, accusing me of being an agent for the CIA. During this period I despaired of life. Few survived this jail. Two years later I emerged alive, even though I had been reported dead. (personal interview, 1994)

In a drastic departure from traditional social and gender hierarchy, young women, referred to as *mit neary*, were given power and authority to command people and to identify 'enemies' of the Khmer Rouge state. Children as young as ten years old were purposely exposed to widespread violence and intensive indoctrination. They were given food or reduced labour as incentives to turn them into cadre to carry out aggressive and violent actions against the perceived 'enemies' of the Khmer Rouge. The constant threat of being identified as enemies created extensive mistrust among families, friends, relatives, and co-workers. One Khmer man now living in Ottawa recalled:

> There were always spies in the camps listening in at night to try and catch you ... Even families turned each other in. This mistrust cannot be mended. During Pol Pot no one could say anything for fear of punishment, even to best friends. All this changed Cambodians. Now they are trying to change back, but some of them can't after what happened to them. Mistrust and fear are still in the communities here. (personal interview, 1994)

During the last two years of Khmer Rouge control, several internal purges occurred among Khmer Rouge cadre and leaders (Vickery 1983). The *moulatan chass* ('old people') were increasingly subjected to the forced relocations, slave labour, violence, and inhumane living conditions (Kiernan 1983). By the end of 1978, many of the perpetrators of Khmer Rouge control were themselves victims. One Khmer Canadian woman described those who survived, including herself, as 'leftovers from the dead.'

The Exodus into Thailand

In early 1979, Vietnam invaded Cambodia to quell intensifying Khmer Rouge incursions into Vietnamese territory. A Vietnamese-backed Khmer government was installed, controlled by Heng Samrin, Hun Sen, and other defectors from different factions of the Khmer Rouge. Cambodia was renamed the People's Republic of Kampuchea. Khmer Rouge collective farms and forced systems of labour collapsed throughout the country, and people were free to begin searching for family. Fearing oppression by the Vietnamese communist invaders and the possible return of the Khmer Rouge, thousands of Cambodians sought asylum in Thailand. Thai soldiers, renegade resistance soldiers, and bandits all preyed upon Cambodian refugees fleeing into Thailand. Even though the majority of Cambodian refugees were ill, wounded, exhausted, and starving, women and young girls were frequently raped, and any goods, extra clothes, or hidden gold was confiscated (Kong 2003: 76). Thousands of land mines planted by retreating Khmer Rouge caused jungle paths into Thailand to become littered with Cambodian corpses and body parts. One young Khmer woman in Toronto remembered:

> We walked through waters, bushes, and minefields on our way to Thailand. Wherever I turned, I could see corpses, some stacked in piles. I saw men crowded around a wounded person ... I can still see the wounded man covered with blood and without a right arm and with one leg blown off. (personal interview, 1994)

By April 1979, over forty thousand Cambodians had sought asylum in Thailand. Many were surviving members of the Khmer urban middle class, shopkeepers, teachers, and civil servants (Kiljunen 1983). Thailand quickly closed its borders to the mass influx, forcing several thousand back into Cambodia. Many attempted to flee again, while others were caught in border camps established by the Khmer Rouge, or by smugglers, criminals, and right-wing guerrilla movements. Between April and August, the most catastrophic famine in Cambodia's history forced hundreds of thousands more Cambodians from every class and ethnic group to leave Cambodia. In September 1979, the numbers of Cambodian refugees seeking asylum reached nearly five hundred thousand. International pressure forced Thailand to open its border again and allow the creation of large holding centres to be managed by the United Nations High Commission for Refugees (UNHCR 2000).

Garry described their plight at this time, 'The situation in Cambodia is dramatic: generalized starvation; abominable public health, which cannot be improved for lack of doctors and medicine; sterility among women; high infant mortality; and, everywhere, hordes of runaways trying to reach Thailand and deserting the young, the old, and the sick who are unable to continue. Over a million refugees are now in camps in Thailand or near the border of Cambodia' (1980: 42).

By 1980, Thailand had closed its border once more. The Thai military directed Khmer refugees escaping Cambodia into non-UNHCR border camps. More than two hundred thousand Cambodian refugees were in these border camps, with at least twenty camps controlled and supervised by various Cambodian political and military organizations. Eleven border camps, with over 122,000 thousand people, were controlled by Khmer Rouge (Garry 1980: ibid.). The re-emergence and reinforcement of the Khmer Rouge system of control and military capacity was abetted through American, Chinese, and Thai military aid, and several international relief organizations (Reynell 1989: 39–41). American foreign policy makers expected the Khmer Rouge to serve as an indirect U.S. proxy to continue the fight against the Vietnamese; Thailand wanted the Khmer Rouge border camps to act as military buffer zones; and China continued to sell arms (Chan 2003: 17). For the next eight years, refugees in these border camps were used as human shields between Khmer Rouge fighters and the Vietnamese-backed government of Cambodia. Reynell (1989: 152–60) details the massive psychological consequences among the thousands of Cambodian refugees who spent years moving from one border camp to another before making it to Thai-based UNHCR camps, such as Khao I Dang and Sakeo, and their consequent resettlement opportunities. Khmer in Ontario who had experienced several of these border camps described being constantly on the move, always afraid of being forced back into Cambodia, or of being caught by Khmer Rouge leaders who would hold families as ransom to force the men to fight. One man who had fled to Thailand in the early 1980s recalled this pattern:

The first time we escaped the government caught us and demanded money. We went back to Phnom Penh but one week later we tried again with a different strategy. I left my children (age three years and one year) and wife, and went first. Then my wife joined me later, then our children were brought out with the guides (traders). I went to a border camp and waited for the rest of the family. This camp was under the control of [Prince

Sihanouk's Royalist Party known as] FUNCINPEC [Front Uni National pour un Cambodge Indépendant Neutre Pacifique et Coopératif]. By the end of 1981, we moved to Khao I Dang and stayed there about six to eight months and applied to Japan, Canada, and France. In August 1983, we left Khao I Dang for Shimbourea Camp, which is the transit to resettlement. We stayed there for six months then applied again and were accepted for Canada in the Kitchener area. (personal interview, 2005)

In UNHCR camps, Cambodian refugees received a regular supply of food, chlorinated water, and medical treatment. International aid groups provided education for children, retraining programs for men, and most importantly, hope for resettlement. There was, however, a high incidence of rape in the camps by Thai soldiers. Women refugees were especially targeted at night, after the camp administrators had left (Ngor 1987: 419; Chan 2003: 18; Kong 2003: 77). UNHCR camp administrators also found it difficult to distinguish between refugees. In Sakeo Camp, for example, over two-thirds of the population were identified as Khmer Rouge soldiers who continued to control other Cambodians there (Ngor 1987: 412). Later, thirty thousand Khmer Rouge were transferred from Sakeo to Khao I Dang for resettlement purposes (Kiljunen 1983).

The Cambodian exodus demonstrates the complex politics of asylum in Thailand, the enormous range of quality and opportunities in the different camps, and the ambiguities of labelling those who flee their homeland as 'displaced persons,' 'illegal entrants,' 'evacuees,' or 'refugee-seekers' (Chan 2003: 25–8).

Difficulties in Obtaining Canadian Resettlement Opportunities

A big obstacle facing Cambodians seeking resettlement in Canada was the perception that they were not good candidates. Thomson (1980: 126) wrote that Cambodian refugees were of a different background and motivation from other Indochinese refugees, and only Cambodian-Chinese with formal education and professional or trade skills were suitable for Canadian resettlement. Because most Khmer refugees came from rural cultural settings, it was assumed that Western foods, technology, values, and styles of interpersonal interaction would be too overwhelming for them. In 1979, the majority of the more than fifty thousand Indochinese refugees accepted for resettlement in Canada were from Vietnam (Adelman et al. 1980). Rather than consider Cambodians for government sponsorship, Canadian funds were diverted to Cambodian relief in the Thai refugee camps (ibid.). Canada's selection policy reflected considerable self-interest. Refugees accepted for resettlement were assessed according to their skills and motivation, with well-educated professionals being favoured (ibid.). Educated and skilled Cambodians who could fit the selection criteria represented a very small minority of all applicants, and most of those resettled in Quebec.

Church spokespeople and leaders of private sponsorship organizations criticized the selection policy as too inhumane and pushed for higher admission rates of Cambodians to be based on humanitarian criteria. Even when Cambodians were accepted, processing delays were common. One private sponsor related an important interview that detailed these issues:

> There was numerous [sic] red tape with Canadian immigration. They identified Cambodians as being uneducated, having nothing to offer Canada ... Catholic Immigration were never officially told not to sponsor Cambodians, but their applications were always slower to accept. In 1979–80, the American ambassador in Canada and his wife were very interested in Cambodians ... She arranged a meeting with the minister of immigration at her residence, with myself, a member of the Catholic Immigration Board, the head of the Refugee Section for Immigration, and the head of the Canadian Immigration Section in Thailand, who was doing the interviews which decided who got resettlement. The head of Canadian immigration in Thailand called Cambodians 'betel-nut chewing women and uneducated people. If I put them all on a plane you would not want them when you see them.' This made the minister of immigration realize the bias against Cambodians, and there were no longer any delays in the processing. (personal interview, 1994)

Another reason for delay was the uncertainty government officials felt concerning Khmer Rouge infiltrating Cambodian applicants. One government sponsor who made selection decisions in the Thai refugee camps commented:

> A lot of Khmer Rouge were in the camps, mixed in with regular people. Canadian immigration officers were very sensitive to past activities but had a hard time to figure out who was who. After a couple of years it became easier for them to weed regular people out from the Khmer Rouge, and this speeded up the process of applications. (personal interview, 1994)

Distinct from other Indochinese, Cambodian refugees had high numbers of 'free cases,' individuals who did not have close relatives or extended family members (Ebihara 1985). The large numbers of unaccompanied minors (orphans) and female-headed households reflected the extremely high mortality rates of Khmer adults, especially men. Another distinction of Cambodian refugees was their very poor physical health, showing more symptoms of malnourishment, more tuberculin reactors, higher hepatitis B indicators, more parasites, and much lower mean haemoglobin and red blood count volumes than other Southeast Asian refugee groups tested (Cantanzaro and Moser 1982). Cambodians also suffered extraordinarily high rates of social and emotional impairment, and more serious psychological disorders than other Southeast Asian groups, particularly Cambodian women without spouses (Beiser 1990; Mollica et al. 1987; Kinzie 1988; Kinzie et al. 1986). More than 90 per cent of all Cambodian refugees experienced sustained trauma and inhumane living conditions, regardless of age, gender, religion, ethnicity, or class status. Among most refugee groups in Canada, primary cases of trauma and torture are usually identified in adult political prisoners or with an individual's particular ethnoreligious identity. Surveys on Cambodian refugee children in the United States document that they endured multiple catastrophic events: family separation, starvation, slave labour, near death experiences, participating in or witnessing killings and torture, and the loss/death of at least one family member, with an average of three members per nuclear family (Kinzie et al. 1986, 1989; Carole 1991; Bit 1991; Clarke et al. 1993; DePaul 1997). In Cambodian communities today, nearly all adults over age thirty-five share and remember these experiences.

Survivors of torture and trauma have had their trust, self-esteem, and values so devastated that most of them carry reactions of depressive withdrawal, anxiety, and fear long after the situation of helplessness and hopelessness is over (Payne 1990; Reid and Strong 1988; Eisenbruch 1991; Kral et al. 1967; Beiser 1990; Mollica et al. 1987; Kinzie 1988). The acute and chronic symptoms of this carryover are recognized as posttraumatic stress disorder (PTSD) and 'torture syndrome' (ibid.). PTSD has been applied to survivors of the Jewish Holocaust, abused children, and prisoners of war. Some of the symptoms, which may not emerge until later in an individual's life, include interpersonal, social, and employment difficulties; acute loneliness; insomnia and nightmares; recurrent, intrusive, and disturbing thoughts; reduced involvement with ordinary activities; memory impairment; reduced concentration;

emotional liability; dissociation; and survivor guilt (Reid and Strong 1988).

The distress of fleeing their homeland, living in refugee camps, vying for resettlement opportunities, adapting and integrating into a foreign country, and losing familiar social and cultural networks has compounded the suffering of Cambodian refugees. Beiser (1989: 183) notes the additional stress for Indochinese refugees in Canada when their private sponsorship and support was carried out by individuals or groups whose religion differed from their own. Eisenbruch (1991) identifies the anguish among resettled Cambodian refugees as 'cultural bereavement,' finding it especially evident in North America, where there is great pressure to leave their old culture behind. In his study on the relevance of grief and mourning among Cambodian refugees, Boehnlein comments on the extent of their losses: 'Many individuals have lost their spouses, children and parents, along with lifetime savings and possessions. Others lost their means of livelihood, previous social status or social role. In addition, all Cambodian refugees have literally lost their homeland and many aspects of their rich and centuries-old cultural traditions' (1987: 765).

Payne (1990: 3) suggests that people who have undergone extreme trauma and loss tend to cope through defences of repression and suppression (underreporting or denying the distress), social withdrawal (to avoid confronting painful memories), and depression (lack of interest, mental confusion, brooding). When these tendencies are magnified by the Cambodian cultural propensity to keep silent about one's suffering, especially with strangers, community and individual needs remain unstated and go unnoticed. Switzerland, the United States, Australia, and New Zealand each coordinated teams of medical and mental health staff to develop effective systems of mental health treatment for Cambodian refugees based on the study of Khmer concepts of well-being (Boehnlein 1987; Kinzie 1988; Eisenbruch 1991; Wicker and Schoch 1988; Carole 1991; Reid and Strong 1988; Abbot 1989). These early interventions provided clear models to facilitate Cambodian resettlement and reduce long-term family and community difficulties. In Ontario, similar systems of treatment by coordinated health professionals were not developed (McLellan 1995; Chan et al. 1999).

2 Cambodian Resettlement in Canada

Upon resettlement, Cambodians faced a radical disjunction from their pre-migration experiences under the Khmer Rouge, the Vietnamese communist occupation, and within the Thai refugee camps. Ong describes their experience, noting that 'Cambodian refugees moved from a regime of power over death to a regime of power over life, from a state that governed by eliminating knowledge to one that promotes the self-knowing subject, from a system based on absolute control to one that governs through freedom, from a society that enforced initiative for collective survival to one that celebrates individualistic self-cultivation ... and pressures to perform as knowing subjects who are "free" to refuse or accept rules, "free" to govern themselves' (2003: 18).

Western social ethics of individualism, secularism, materialism, self-reliance, and autonomy are distinct from a Khmer Buddhist ethics-regulated society of hierarchy and extended-family dependency. Making this transition has had an impact on all facets of Cambodian lives in resettlement: their religious identities, family and generational dynamics, community social cohesion, transnational networks and linkages, and coming to terms with the past and its lingering effects.

Arrival in Canada

In contrast to the United States, which experienced three major waves of Cambodian resettlement (Ebihara 1985), most of the Cambodians in Canada came in one refugee flow during the 1980s. The few Cambodians living in Canada before 1980 were Khmer diplomats, businesspeople, and students who resided mainly in Quebec. These individuals were granted permanent resident status when Cambodia became internationally isolated after 1975. Several Khmer from outside Cambodia also came to Canada before the 1980s as UNHCR Convention refugees. Subsequently, both groups were able to sponsor surviving family members, former friends, colleagues, and classmates from Thai refugee camps. One Cambodian sponsored in this way related:

> I left Cambodia in 1961 to go to high school in Montreal. I stayed there to study civil engineering and got my B.Sc. in 1965. I continued in school 'til September 1967, when I received a master's in Civil Engineering at the École du Polytechnic in Montreal. I went back in 1967 to Cambodia to work in dam construction and hydro power plants for the State Company of Dams until 1975 when the Khmer Rouge came. I was pulled to the country with my wife, four children, and two mothers, and I stayed there until the Vietnamese came in. In 1979, two mothers and two sons were dead, so we were only four out of eight. I left for Thailand with my wife and two sons.
>
> We stayed in the refugee camps until friends in Montreal sponsored us. I wrote to my friends from my university class and they sponsored us. Through the United Nations and United Nations authorities, I was able to write to my classmates to let them know that I was alive. We arrived around 1980 in Montreal and started to work. (personal interview, 2002)

The majority of Cambodians arrived in Canada after 1979 as 'designated class' refugees through federal government and private sponsorship programs. Immigration data indicate that 18,602 Cambodians entered Canada between 1980 and 1992, with 8,342 through private sponsorship (Employment and Immigration Canada 1980–92). The majority were under thirty-four years of age, with approximately equal numbers of males and females. Those over the age of forty-five were more likely to have had private sponsorship.

Arrival rates over the twelve-year span vary considerably. In 1980, 3,269 Cambodians entered Canada, but only 1,302 in 1981. Higher numbers resumed in 1983, fluctuating slightly until 1989. In 1984, the Canadian government sponsored 1,236 Cambodians, with only 283 arriving in Canada through private sponsorship. By 1988 and 1989, these numbers were reversed, with private sponsorship at 1,190 and 1,487, compared with 315 and 527 through the government (ibid.). In 1990, the numbers dropped dramatically to a total of 720 persons, dwindling further to only 214 persons in 1992 (ibid.). These low numbers reflect a new UNHCR emphasis on repatriation rather than resettlement.

The UNHCR did not take into account the difficulties Cambodians in Canada would have in sponsoring family members from Cambodia. The numbers of Cambodians arriving in Canada since 1992 indicate a steady but small rate of approximately two hundred people per year. These low sponsorship rates are a reflection of the difficulties Cambodians in Canada have with bureaucratic procedures, as well as an inability to meet the minimum financial requirements for immigration.

Private Sponsorship

Most private sponsorship of Cambodian refugees was through Christian congregations under the 'Master Agreement,' made with the government of Canada, of three main groups: the Christian Reformed Church, Catholic Immigrant Aid, and the Mennonite Church. The extent of private sponsorship varied considerably throughout Ontario. In London and St Thomas almost all Cambodians were privately sponsored; in Ottawa more than half; in Windsor and Kingston, less than one-third; and in Toronto and Hamilton, less than a tenth. Private sponsorship was initially higher than government sponsorship (in 1980), but declined drastically until 1987 when government sponsorship waned. This resurgence of private sponsorship reflected the strong advocacy of Cambodian groups to encourage private sponsors to resettle their friends and relatives. Church sponsors worked with one another to help reunite Cambodians. St Peter's Catholic Church in Goderich sponsored two brothers and their families in December 1980. They invited a third brother and sister with her accompanying family, who had been sponsored by the town's Knox Presbyterian Church in March 1980, to live together in a former convent that had been renovated by members of the St Peter's congregation. In Kingston, one church sponsored over twenty-three individuals from one fractured extended family (an elderly mother, her widowed daughters, and their children and orphaned cousins). The Christian Reformed Church reunited hundreds of Cambodian families in Ontario.

In addition to reuniting Cambodian families, private sponsorship provided other advantages. In Ottawa, St Thomas, Hamilton, and London, church and individual sponsors were often the front-line service providers for Cambodian refugees. They provided housing (sometimes in their own homes or nearby apartments); took people shopping for clothing, food, and kitchen utensils; enrolled the children in school and adults in ESL classes; advised on vocational training and other educational opportunities; and arranged for medical appointments. Through personal contacts, private sponsors were more successful than the government in finding employment for Cambodians and in mediating between employers and workers if difficulties or misunderstandings arose. Some sponsors became 'fictive kin' to the Cambodian families, helping them to bridge the cultural gap between Cambodians and Canadians, especially by sharing each other's food, music, dances, and games. In Ottawa, Catholic Immigrant Services organized monthly meetings for refugees, sponsors, and church workers to discuss issues and organize summer picnics. In the opinion of a Khmer man in Ottawa:

Cambodians are too shy to make the attempt to reach out to Canadians. Those who have connections with Canadian families through sponsorship have encountered friendship with Canadians but those who were government sponsored or those who came through family have no relationships with Canadians. (personal interview, 1994)

One former federal government worker commented:

I felt that people got a better start if they were privately sponsored, despite all the problems. Good sponsors provided a safe environment for the first year. One can question if this can be a factor in the differences between Laotian (who are very successful) and Khmer. (personal interview, 1994)

Difficulties did arise, as one sponsor remembered:

Cambodians were overwhelmed by the material prosperity of Canada. Sponsors felt that the Cambodians had an inadequate response to the living accommodations offered to them. For example, too many would end up living in one small room, they would be doing all sorts of washing in the bathroom, and not using laundry facilities.
    The cultural differences were the most difficult to deal with, especially language differences. There was more sign language between sponsors and Cambodians than translation. One major lack was that sponsors 'told' the Cambodians what to do, but not how to do. There was a lack of education about Khmer people, and sponsors were not aware of what to expect. Many sponsors didn't take time to review the available literature in booklets, and just went at it ad hoc. (personal interview, 1994)

For some Cambodian refugees, close contact with private Christian sponsors enabled them to learn what were regarded to be Christian attitudes and values. Pressures to convert and their subsequent distancing from the larger Buddhist community, however, became contentious issues (see chapter 6). The overall effectiveness and influence of private sponsors greatly decreased after 1985, when there were family members or friends already in Ontario to greet newly arrived refugees. In 1986–87, large numbers of Cambodians were sponsored to St Thomas, London, and Toronto by the Christian Reformed Church, through the influence of the church's previously sponsored Cambodians. By this time, it was not uncommon that local sponsoring churches were situated in different towns and cities from where the Cambodians would resettle, and thus members of their congregations would never actually meet them.

Demographics of Cambodians in Canada

The number of Cambodians living in Canada is difficult to estimate. Immigration data do not include Cambodians who arrived prior to 1980, nor the few thousand Khmer Kampuchea Krom listed as Vietnamese refugees and/or nationals, nor those Khmer from Thai refugee camps who claimed they were Vietnamese in order to gain a better opportunity for resettlement in Canada. The 2001 Census reports almost the identical number of Cambodians (18,745) that Immigration Canada data show for the twelve-year period 1980 to 1992. Census numbers reveal the absence of adult Cambodians sponsored by family members and spouses during the 1990s. The 2001 Census reported only 20,430 Canadian residents of Cambodian ethnic origin, including 5,595 who indicated more than one ethnic origin. The underrepresentation of Cambodians in census data stems from a variety of factors. Language difficulties have been a major barrier in understanding or completing census forms, and experiences in Cambodia and the refugee camps left many Cambodians suspicious about divulging personal information. During the 1980s and 1990s a significant number of Cambodians lived in government-assisted housing with strict occupancy regulations. There may have been hesitancy to reveal the number of Khmer families and individuals living in one household.

Residential Distribution

Resettlement was not evenly distributed across Canada. Cambodians resettled in small towns and cities as single individuals or in small groups ranging from two to fifty families. The greatest concentrations of Cambodians are in the large urban centres of Montreal and Toronto, with smaller numbers in Ottawa, Hamilton, London, and Vancouver. Cambodian community sources in the 1990s indicated that there were approximately 10,000 Cambodians in Ontario, with almost half of them in the Toronto area.[1] Government workers, service providers, and Cambodian community leaders favoured resettlement in smaller urban areas. One government worker commented:

> In small communities people resettle faster and children can catch up faster. The more they mix with Canadian families, the better the way of thinking, way of life. (personal interview, 1994)

A Cambodian social worker in Toronto during the 1990s also supported this view:

> Cambodians who live in smaller towns fare much better. They are forced to learn English, but in Toronto, no necessity. They can get by with no language. (personal interview, 1994)

A community leader in Hamilton felt that smaller communities were better for Cambodians to know each other, and to get help. In 1994, he said that he knew 90 per cent of the community there. This sentiment was shared by a Cambodian leader in Kingston:

> I have many friends in Ottawa and Toronto but like to live in Kingston because of the quality of schools and the small-town nature ... In large areas like Toronto, Ottawa, and Montreal 50 per cent of Cambodians have problems with loneliness and isolation. Kingston has good support for newcomers. More help is available for people to apply for assistance. Larger communities such as Toronto and Ottawa are so big it is hard to understand how to get to places, to use transportation; people need to rely more on friends. (personal interview, 1994)

Most Cambodians preferred to live in large urban areas. Waves of secondary migration from within Canada followed initial resettlement, resulting in concentrations of Cambodians in larger cities. These movements reflected the desire to be reunited with family members, friends, and relatives, and to access better employment opportunities, support services, shopping, and Khmer cultural activities. One Cambodian man explained:

> I came to Canada in 1983. I lived in Winnipeg for six years. I moved to St Thomas in 1989 because Cambodians who lived in Winnipeg had no jobs and just moved to Toronto. I have my older family who lives in St Thomas. (personal interview, 1994)

A fifty-year-old woman detailed her preference for Toronto:

> When I first came to Canada, about seventeen years ago, it was fairly difficult to get items from Cambodia. Even getting cooking ingredients was difficult; there were not many grocery stores that sold Asian products. I remember that we had to go all the way to [a] Chinatown to do our grocery shopping. Now, there are plenty of Asian grocery stores, you can practically get almost any ingredient you need, although you are paying a lot more for them, especially when it comes to fruit. It is also very easy to get music and videos, especially here in Toronto, you can get them at grocery stores, little shops that cater to this sort of information, and some people even sell them from home. (personal interview, 2004)

The Ontario Cambodian population significantly increased during the late 1980s (Statistics Canada 1981, 1986, 1991: Catalogue 93). London (+4%), Hamilton (+3.8%), and Toronto (+8.8%) experienced influxes due to perceived employment opportunities, while Montreal (–4%), Ottawa/Hull (–7%), and Quebec City (–6%) experienced declines, suggesting a trend to move from French- to English-speaking centres. In addition to the core resettlement area of Toronto, several Cambodian concentrations emerged in the nearby newly developed areas of Newmarket, Brampton, Vaughan, and Maple. Newmarket has attracted more than five hundred families since the mid-1990s. In the smaller cities of Kingston and St Thomas, Cambodians were dispersed throughout several residential areas, living in private homes and government-assisted housing. In larger urban centres such as Windsor, Ottawa, Hamilton, London, and Toronto, they initially clustered in low-cost and subsidized housing areas, usually large apartment blocks. In Ottawa and Hamilton, these apartments are located in different parts of the city, but in Toronto and London they are concentrated more in one area.

The initial placement of Cambodians into subsidized housing has had several consequences, particularly regarding experiences of racism and discrimination.[2] In London, Cambodians frequently commented on racist experiences involving white Canadians.[3] Across Ontario, Cambodians spoke of being the subject of racist and discriminatory remarks, made even by members of sponsoring church groups. One young man, born in Cambodia but raised in Windsor, recalled:

> My earliest memory is one of the most traumatizing for us. My father was trying to get an education and was going to ESL classes and he didn't have a car so he would drive his bike to and from classes, even in the winter. As he would ride by, these white guys would be yelling and swearing at him, and he would come home so frustrated. He didn't understand what was going on in this society and what it was he was being exposed to. These were just local people. I remember seeing him when he was driving home. I was so young at the time. I would wait for my father to come home; I was so eager to see him and I would see that these people throwing snowballs at him, yelling at him. My sisters and brother, they also have these memories. I'm sure they also encountered it at work. (personal interview, 2005)

During the late 1980s and the early 1990s, at least thirty Cambodian families in the North York area of Toronto moved from one subsidized apartment block to another due to what was described as 'intolerable racial difficulties,' citing fear and intimidation from established Caribbean-Canadians and a new influx of African refugees.[4] By the mid-1990s, Cambodians who had moved to new apartments faced the same difficulties.[5] A young man raised in this area commented:

> It's a matter of understanding the turf, that's the problem. But also you get picked on too, especially by the Black people. They are aggressive. Our people are more passive, you know don't rock the boat, just live peacefully. Jane-Finch had a lot of violence, a lot of drugs and gangs. (personal interview, 2005)

During the mid-1990s, an elementary school vice-principal said that the majority of students at her school would be classified as visible minorities, with Cambodian children 'at the bottom of the totem pole.' At another elementary school in the same area, where the majority of the student population was primarily Indochinese, the principal stated that a racial hierarchy was not evident. A Khmer community leader from Jane-Finch said:

In race relations, Cambodians are very submissive. They don't want any more trouble, so they are shy and withdrawn. In public housing large numbers of people are Black, and Cambodian parents complain that the Cambodian children are being beaten up in the school playground and in the streets. What can be done? During a meeting that the Cambodian Association held on this issue, only one Black member (the guest speaker) came from the community. Also there is the problem of drug trafficking, noise all night, and parties which disturb sleep patterns. (personal interview, 1994)

The structural and racial conditions of subsidized public housing in rundown neighbourhoods in Toronto were similar to the Khmer images of urban violence that Frank Smith (1994: 156) depicts and what Ong describes for American Cambodians in Oakwood and San Francisco: 'The everyday chores of earning, buying, spending, and distributing resources among family members required a great deal of work on the part of people who mostly couldn't drive, or didn't own cars, or didn't even understand the morphology of the cityscape. Older women told me they were afraid of venturing out because they might get disoriented, lost, or mugged. Fathers walked to the bus stops to meet their children coming home from school, to protect them from being jumped on and pummelled by other kids. Initially, there were tensions with long-resident blacks in the neighborhoods, and some resentment over what was seen as competition for welfare support' (2003: 123).

Starting in the late 1990s, Cambodians throughout Ontario began to move from concentrated city neighbourhoods into the suburbs, many of them purchasing homes in new housing developments. Although these residential moves are indicative of upward mobility and successful adaptation, the need to pay large mortgages negatively affected the post-secondary educational opportunities for Cambodian youth.

Cambodian Resettlement Services

Cross-cultural adaptation is an ongoing complex process requiring personal, social, and economic adjustments that individuals undergo at differential rates. For many Indochinese newcomers, the initial turmoil associated with relocation tended to subside after the first five years as language skills improved, psychological well-being increased, and the financial situation stabilized (Haines 1985; Dorais 1991; Zhou, Bankston, and Kim 2002; Hein 1995). With government funding, service agencies provided front-line aid to help integrate new Indochinese arrivals under the assumption that dependence on front-line aid would diminish as adaptation increased. To this end, Cambodian refugees in Ontario sponsored by the government received federal government funding through the Adjustment Assistance Program. Assistance was provided for approximately one year to cover living costs, medical treatment, and transportation. Privately sponsored refugees received similar support through their sponsors.

Service agencies that provided programs for newcomers (those who have lived in Canada less than three years) received federal support through Immigration Settlement, Department of Citizenship and Immigration Canada (formerly Employment and Immigration Canada). Each province had its own Immigrant Settlement and Adaptation Program (ISAP) to fund Language Instruction for Newcomers to Canada (LINC) and various ad hoc 'seed' grants. Monies provided by the Secretary of State (which became Multiculturalism and Citizenship Canada) were primarily core funding (to sustain service agencies) or project oriented, accessible through yearly applications for grants. ISAP funding was normally renewed annually, although appeals could be made for three-year funding blocks to give greater security for settlement service workers to develop more effective programs. In 1980, ISAP and LINC were the two primary programs available to Cambodian refugees, both geared to providing essential settlement services and to facilitate integration. Throughout the 1980s, ISAP provided salaries and benefits for Khmer settlement/service workers, with specific projects supplemented by small 'seed' grants.

The majority of Cambodian refugees accepted for resettlement in Canada were among the least educated of all Indochinese refugees, being rural people with little knowledge of urban life. Immigration statistics note that of the 18,602 Cambodians who resettled in Canada between 1980 and 1992, only about 8 per cent reported some fluency in French or English; 5,678 had no education; 9,980 had some primary school in Cambodia, with 624 having completed the equivalent of Grade 9; 1,513 had some and 393 had completed secondary school; while 488 had some post-secondary school education (Employment and Immigration Canada 1980–92). Over half of the Khmer men and the majority of Khmer women were functionally illiterate in Khmer. Their low educational and literacy statistics clearly demonstrated the Cambodians' need for extensive language and job skills training to facilitate secure employment and adaptation. The horrific pre-arrival experiences of most Cambodian refugees also indicated that the entire Cambodian community would require prolonged and increased specialized settlement services. Despite these unique needs, English-language training classes (ESL) in Ontario were offered to Cambodian refugees primarily during the first six months after their arrival, a period of enormous culture shock. Initially, language classes were restricted to 'heads of households,' who were assumed to be men, and discontinued when they found employment.[6]

Accessing Resettlement Services

Immediately upon arrival in Ottawa and Toronto, the small numbers of Chinese-Cambodians who culturally and linguistically identified themselves as Chinese were able to receive community and resettlement services from providers within the Chinese community. Organizations such as the South East Asian Services or the Vietnamese, Laos and Cambodian Association provided broad-based community networks, services, and advocacy for Sino-Cambodians. For Cambodian refugees who resettled in Quebec, the existing Khmer community of well-educated professionals was quickly mobilized to provide extensive and highly effective resettlement services.

French-speaking Khmer who lived in Quebec were not asked to provide interpretive services or arrange orientation and support activities for Cambodian refugees in English-speaking Ontario. Consequently, for those who resettled in Ontario during the early 1980s, there were few Khmer translators available to help the thousands of new arrivals to Hamilton, Kingston, London, Ottawa, Toronto, and Windsor. Most Cambodian refugees needed translation assistance to register for the Ontario Health Insurance Plan (OHIP); visit doctors, dentists, and hospitals, or in crisis situations; look for suitable housing and employment; apply for welfare; register children in school; sponsor relatives; and access education (especially ESL training). Without Khmer translators, their culture shock was exacerbated, and the concept of resettlement services frequently misunderstood. A Khmer man from Ontario described his first weeks in Canada:

When I arrived in Canada I was twenty-two years old. I had problems when I first came. I was very afraid of Canada. Canada is a clean country, even the toilet is very clean. This place is a place like heaven, that is, different from our Cambodia, especially the camps that we lived in was like hell.

And I was frightened here at first because I had never seen the lights that brightened, glittered. In the apartment was also very difficult. Even though they let me stay in a very old place, they said it was good enough for me.

And I was very scared of people other than Cambodians from the beginning. I was afraid when I was met at the airport. I thought maybe they were not nice to meet. You know, how can anyone help a person who does not know me at all? They maybe will take me into the forest and give me the land and start to farm, you know farming. And instead of doing that, they put me in the hotel, isolate me from the first comer [other Khmer]. They don't know [about us] until seven days later, and my wife cannot eat the food because she eats rice, and she almost starved. The immigration worker was a Vietnamese. So I was isolated and scared because a lot of people were drinking and sleeping, you know, they sleep around the hotel. I was scared to walk out for four or five weeks. (personal interview, 1994)

One Khmer service worker commented on the fearfulness that Cambodians had:

Ethnic Khmer do not access services and remain isolated … People are very conservative. In this country, 'social service' is a new concept. Services provided by the government have not been experienced before. People think the government officer has power to control them. Therefore, people are distrustful of public service and service providers. People avoid services to protect themselves. (personal interview, 1994)

In Cambodia, all forms of Khmer social relationships, cultural attitudes, political power, and economic interactions were essentially shaped by the pervasive nature and extent of the hierarchical system of patronage (Mortland and Ledgerwood 1987: 294). Relationships between a patron and client are symmetrical. Patronage expresses disparities in wealth, power, status, and influence, reflecting the patron's ability to provide assistance and resources to a client. When Cambodians first resettled in Western countries, they believed patronage was the only mechanism through which they could acquire assistance or resettlement services (ibid.). Initially, Cambodians did not understand the idea of 'volunteering' (providing services or 'doing good' by giving freely of one's time) or the motives of those who would help strangers. This is illustrated in the comments of one St Thomas man:

Although I spoke some English that I learned in the refugee camp, I did not understand the system of sponsorship and was concerned what the Christian Reformed Church was going to do with me and my family. I was afraid that my family would be taken, and I was worried that I didn't know how to get them back. When the sponsor visited, I thought he was sizing up the family to sell them into labour. I quickly realized my mistaken ideas, and now remember how the sponsors were really good and patient, and that they gave good advice to me. (personal interview, 1994)

Toronto was the only city in Ontario where a Cambodian community association, the Canadian Cambodian Association of Ontario (CCAO), was able to offer government-funded settlement services to Khmer newcomers.[7] Dr Vanroeung Chek, the only Khmer-speaking physician in Ontario (now retired), and president of the CCAO in the early 1990s, identified some of the difficulties facing Cambodians:

War of any kind or size can influence one's mental health. The brutality of war has an impact on survivors. The scenes of horror may return in the form of nightmares ... During the first three years, we were happy because we received support from the government. Then we had to face a new culture and language. Many of us suffer from mental health problems as a result of war. This is PTSD ... We need to expand the Cambodian Association. We need a Cambodian psychologist who understands our psychology and culture. Most Cambodians with problems hide them, and they need someone to visit them at home. Serious cases need to be referred to organizations such as Hong Fook in Toronto. (personal interview, 1994)

In the early 1990s, the Hong Fook Mental Health Centre in downtown Toronto employed a full-time Khmer worker to do outreach work with Cambodians. Through Canada Employment and Immigration funding, Hong Fook produced a twenty-minute documentary, *A Land of Hope?* (in Khmer with English subtitles), to demonstrate Cambodian difficulties in resettlement and the availability of their organization to help. The emphasis of the documentary was on stories of success.[8]

In smaller Ontario cities, such as Ottawa, Hamilton, Kingston, London, Windsor, and Kitchener/Waterloo, resettlement services and integration programs were provided through larger multicultural and multilinguistic agencies. Only a few employed the full-time services of a Khmer translator (e.g., London and Ottawa). Although a variety of community development or education programs were available, without a Khmer service worker, most Cambodians were not able to access

LINC opportunities or receive translation, documentation, and escort services. In the absence of a Khmer worker, many Cambodians had to rely on family and friendship networks (if available) to assist with resettlement needs.

Until the mid-1990s, Cambodians in St Thomas were the only ethnic or newcomer group living there, and they were immediately recognized as having unique needs. All were privately sponsored and supported by local Christian Reformed churches. The first Khmer man to arrive in 1983 had converted to Christianity in the refugee camps and was asked to volunteer as a counsellor to other refugees. He worked closely with the churches and provided valuable assistance in documentation, interpretation, orientation, health issues, and general needs. A Cambodian heritage class was held for many years at the St Thomas YMCA. In the early 1990s, the Elgin-St Thomas Health Unit employed a full-time non-Khmer community development worker, and a Ministry of Citizenship grant funded a Khmer-speaking Cambodian community worker. Through the joint efforts of these two workers, Cambodians in St Thomas were able to access the effective community development programs developed by the London Cross Cultural Learner Centre (CCLC).[9]

Ottawa's, initial resettlement services were provided through the Catholic Immigrant Aid Centre. ISAP funding kept two full-time Cambodian service workers for eight years. Through aid from Ottawa Carleton Immigration Services Organization (OCISO), the local board of education was able to develop a pilot project that employed a Khmer translator to liaise between local schools and Cambodian parents. This was successful for several years, until funding ceased. By 1994, Cambodians in Ottawa were seeking settlement services from Community Health Centres (CHCs).[10] The executive director at the Somerset CHC in Ottawa explained:

> CHCs receive money from the provincial Ministry of Health. This is quite separate from the squeeze happening in ISAP immigrant settlement agencies. Therefore, ISAP-funded agencies are looking to CHCs as new growth areas. Also, CHCs have already been doing a lot of resettlement work with family-sponsored relatives who cannot access settlement agencies, as well as with refugee claimants, some of whom have been here for years. Also, many refugees don't want to go to a 'settlement agency,' but want to go to a mainstream organization or institution. At the CHC, anyone can access our services and we hope we can provide them in a culturally sensitive

manner, but no one is identified as being eligible or ineligible. (personal communication, 1994)

The staff at the Carlington and Somerset West CHCs were acutely aware that Cambodians in resettlement were extremely vulnerable.[11] They recognized that special approaches were needed to connect with a community that had a high proportion of women as heads of families, and of people who had had multiple exposures to war trauma, who had witnessed the deaths of family members through violence or starvation, and who had lost years of education and employment. The non-Khmer social worker with the Carlington CHC explained:

> The idea is to catch people before they fall into accepting a lack of service. When I started in 1986, I met newcomers who had not seen a service worker for years and the problems were huge in terms of family isolation, and not knowing anything about the system, for example, living with broken stoves and fridges, and not knowing how to deal with housing authorities. Many of these refugees had no phone or no connection with ESL or had school problems with their children ... By the time we began to connect with people, they had been in Canada up to seven years. Many had not been in any contact with a service worker during all this time. Since they were no longer eligible for ISAP-funded services, they fell through the cracks because they knew of no alternatives. Refugees are often poorly equipped to understand the complexities of our highly bureaucratic systems both in health and social services ...
>
> If some time and effort is invested in educating people to the appropriate ways to use Canadian systems, problems can be averted, to everyone's benefit. This must be viewed as part of the 'acculturation process.' Refugees have frequently been the victims of or have been witness to war, famine, torture, etc. This is not usually the case with immigrants. In providing health and social services to refugees, there is a tremendous need for service providers to be sensitive to their need and be willing at times to make accommodation ...
>
> Our needs assessment comes from community-based individual outreach workers, who attend ESL classes, talk to sponsoring church groups and boards of education, visit Ottawa Housing and public health, and generally hang out in lobbies of apartments as well as going door to door ... The word of mouth on services available at Carlington CHC is also important. When I go door to door, I am accompanied by a member of whatever ethno-specific community we are targeting, and when we meet

someone we tell them about Carlington CHC services, give ESL a push, and we ask where more people live, for example, are there any more on the floor, in the block and so on who might not know of our services. I then visit ESL classes to help with 'problems.' Through this one-on-one work, I started to hear about Cambodian needs. For example, in one week, eight women told of their isolation and depression. This resulted in the creation of a women's program. (personal communication, 1994)

The CHC mandate for providing culturally appropriate services has enabled some programs to be available for Cambodians as long as needed. Twenty-five years after the initial resettlement of Cambodians, the Somerset Community Health Centre in Ottawa still retained a full-time Cambodian social service worker. Ottawa CHCs have been especially effective in addressing and meeting the special needs of Cambodians.

Unfortunately, in other Ontario cities government and social service programs have tended to be oriented towards the considerably larger Sino- and ethnic Vietnamese groups (Nguyen 1983). The general lack of understanding for the special needs of Khmer refugees was evident in a 1983 report on the health needs of the Southeast Asian community, in which one Toronto physician wrote: 'I strongly recommend that the City of Toronto allow space and opportunity for Vietnamese professionals, such as doctors, dentists, lawyers, teachers, to be trained and employed as mental health workers and paraprofessionals in the department. Many Cambodians and Laotians know how to speak Vietnamese ... so that these are also effectively serviced by a Vietnamese-speaking worker' (Dang 1983: 7).

In fact, very few Cambodians knew how to speak Vietnamese (except for the Kampuchea Krom), and the historical animosity between Cambodia and Vietnam would have inhibited Khmer people from trusting or associating with Vietnamese. As a very small portion of Indochinese refugees, Cambodians were frequently assumed by government personnel and private sponsors to be 'Vietnamese boat people.' One major newspaper even used a picture of a Cambodian mother with her baby to symbolize 'boat people' in Canada (*Ottawa Citizen*, 11 October 1980, 43). A former Khmer service worker in Toronto commented:

By 1985, the label Southeast Asian meant Sino-Vietnamese or Vietnamese. So most projects on Southeast Asians were started by and focused on non-Lao and non-Khmer peoples. Southeast Asian got co-opted by Vietnamese Indochinese. All these studies and projects floating around didn't address

the Khmer situation. No one heard the 'silent scream' of Cambodian people. (personal interview, 1994)

As Asians, Cambodians in Ontario were expected to adhere to the
'model minority' stereotype given to the Japanese, Chinese, and Vietnamese in Canada, that is, to be excellent students, industrious workers,
and resourceful business owners. One scholarly paper characterized all
Indochinese as 'over-achievers' (Adelman 1988). It detailed the contributions they could make to Canada, but ignored the ethnocultural distinctions and the barriers to success that characterized Cambodians. A
non-Khmer resettlement worker in Windsor, who did not recognize the
distinct needs of Cambodian refugees, gave this statement:

> Cambodians didn't need introductory services. Friends, relatives, the pop-
> ulation base operative in the community allowed for those introductory
> settlement needs; for example, the first meeting with doctors, first enrol-
> ment in school, first home search, all these were met by the Cambodian
> community ... In Windsor, at the beginning, their services and needs were
> the same as everyone else's – in language and economics. Cambodians
> advanced in the economic field. People gained a level of affluence that is
> enviable. (personal interview, 1994)

This attitude contrasts sharply with that of a former Khmer service
worker in Windsor, who said:

> My boss was very negative towards the problems of Cambodians. She had
> no sympathy for them, looked at escorting services as treating them like a
> babysitter. She laid me off because she said there was nothing for me to do.
> She came from [Europe] as a refugee and said if she could learn English,
> everyone should. She didn't understand the difficulties Cambodians had,
> and the way she treated them made them feel ashamed and frightened.
> She reprimanded them for not being more self-sufficient ... She didn't
> encourage me to go with Cambodians and would provide no transporta-
> tion support, not even to pay for my gas or parking when I would use my
> own car to take people. (personal interview, 1994)

The lack of recognition and sensitivity to the distinct needs and his-
tories of Cambodians was evident elsewhere in Ontario.[12] Low levels
of advocacy and cultural brokering for specialized resettlement services reflect Cambodian refugees' scarcity of social capital. Many gov-

ernment-funded resettlement workers and private sponsors lacked the experience and/or resources to effectively recognize and deal with the traumatized background and psychological requirements of Cambodian refugees, especially of widows and unaccompanied minors.[13]

In all of the Ontario Cambodian communities, the few Khmer-speaking settlement/service workers were under tremendous pressure to provide an enormous range of services. Most Cambodian service workers were recently arrived refugees themselves, as much in need and as stressed as those for whom they provided services. The majority of Cambodians (service workers as well as clients) had little understanding of social services, the rationale, and approach behind aid or how services were allocated. Cambodian resettlement workers were expected to meet new arrivals at the airport, arrange accommodation, and provide cultural and social orientation for each family as it arrived (clothing, transportation, technology, shopping). These same service workers were also expected to facilitate counselling; offer translation, interpretation, and documentation services; escort individuals to schools, health care facilities, and government departments, and law offices; give instructions on accessing employment, housing, ESL, social services, banking, telephones, etc.; advise on dealing with child or wife abuse; and engage in advocacy, community outreach, and mediation between sponsors and refugees. One former Khmer settlement worker recalled:

During the first year people needed to be led slowly, to get shelter, to get ESL. Unlike other counsellors with high caseloads and tight schedules, the Khmer settlement services were labour-intensive, and Khmer were not strict on showing up on time. Khmer people would need to personalize relations with the settlement worker, for example, calling her sister (*srei*) or some other term of respect indicating age, wisdom, or knowledge, rather than name. I knew the ice was broken between me and the clients when terms of respect were replaced by familial terms ...

In 1985, outside of the Cambodian Association, there was no one who could speak Khmer. Cambodian Association people were asked to deliver the impossible. They couldn't do referral, there was no one to refer to. In 1984–85, there was a steady input of new families. One family equaled two solid days of work with helping to sign immigration papers, orientation, shopping, etc. ISAP gives a list of specific things to buy, but the Cambodian Association had to translate and interpret. Staff phone numbers were available for calls during the middle of the night – but, of course, no pay for this. People called for all sorts of emergencies. Women's concerns were always a problem. (personal interview, 1994)

In the early 1980s, there were few female resettlement workers to accompany Khmer women to doctors, to the hospital for childbirth, to explain Canadian procedures on the feeding and care of babies, or to mediate between health care practices.[14] Traditional medical practices among Khmer include herbal medicines, cupping (*Choup*), coining (*Kos Kjol* or *Choup Kchall*), moxibustion (placing a herbal compound on the skin then igniting it, known as *Oyt pleung*), post-partum steaming and 'roasting' (*ang pleung*), humeral (hot and cold) theories of illness, acupressure, and massage, as well as wearing amulets around the neck or protective threads on the wrist. Several of these practices were misinterpreted and misunderstood by non-Khmer.[15] A Khmer worker explained:

A mother in Ottawa did *Kos Kjol* for her kid. *Kos Kjol* is given first before anything else will be given. When someone is sick you scratch the body with a coin (or like) and oil which makes red bruises. When the kid went to gym and took off his clothes, his teacher saw the bruises. The teacher asked him but he could not explain. He said, 'I don't know my mom did it.' So the teacher called the police and caught her. They asked me to translate. I said this is a cultural thing that we do when someone is sick. Somebody might translate that word as 'scratch the wind' because *Kos* means to scratch, and *Kjol* means wind. I had to bring several doctors to explain the situation before they released her. (personal interview, 1994)

Many of the Khmer service workers in the early 1980s were unsuitable, either due to their lack of understanding of the job or their inability to gain the trust of the community. Toronto especially had a high turnover of service workers. A former Khmer service worker in Toronto said:

The concept of 'grants' are very difficult to understand and very difficult to explain to Khmer who are not familiar with them. It is not charity, but there are expectations such as financial accountability. These are new concepts. In 1985, people at the Cambodian Association were still struggling with these concepts. The two staff people doing escort and interpretation services were young men in their early twenties and not familiar. Also, what had these people gone through? They endured Pol Pot, very little education, and lacked English capacity. Yet these jobs, as settlement workers, were so demanding and extensive. Even the coordinator was not skilled in administration. Every time a job ad was put out, there was a terrible time getting people to apply. There was no one with minimal skills that could be 'qualified,' according to funders and mainstream service providers ... The problem with funding applications and writing proposals for grants is not lack of awareness of the issues but the ability to write reports with the proper buzz words. Khmer people didn't know proper English and had a difficult time writing. (personal interview, 1994)

In contrast to the early years of resettlement, when few Cambodians would apply for resettlement worker jobs, by the 1990s there was increasing competition for a declining number of available positions. A common perception among Cambodians at that time was that resettlement positions required no training, involved little work, paid well, and could be obtained through patronage. By the mid-1990s, some of the younger Khmer with community college diplomas in social work and community development expressed anger that they could not find work as qualified service providers.[16] Most service workers by that time, however, were highly motivated Cambodian women, effective and experienced in dealing with contentious issues.

Despite the efforts of Khmer service workers on behalf of the Cambodian community, cultural and linguistic difficulties continued. One non-Khmer agency worker stated:

Communication with Cambodians is constantly difficult, and there is always misunderstanding on both sides. You misunderstand them and they misunderstand you. (personal interview, 1994)

One Khmer service worker noted the kinds of misunderstandings towards service workers that can arise from within the community:

Just last week, a woman needed to go to welfare and [the Khmer service provider] made the appointment, but the welfare worker cancelled the appointment and the woman didn't understand. The woman blamed [the Khmer service provider] for making it difficult. It took [the Khmer service provider] over an hour to explain to the woman but there is no guarantee the woman understood. When things are misunderstood, people blame the Association and the worker. They feel other people don't have a hard time and therefore the fault must be with the worker. (personal interview, 1995)

In other cases, people would phone Khmer service workers and request immediate help, which, if not forthcoming, was then used as an excuse to criticize the agency and the worker. The need for assistance did not decline, as one service worker at the Cambodian Association in Toronto illustrated:

> Every day we get a lot of phone calls from other agencies, for example, welfare, doctors, dentists, schools, teachers, social workers, unemployment counsellors. We also have to call unemployment counsellors, child tax benefits, metro housing, etc., on behalf of the client. We do both referrals in and networking out. This increases at the half-month (15th) when the income report statement doesn't come and at the end of the month when mailed-out cheques don't come (e.g., welfare, child tax credit). On the 16th, everyone has to send an income statement. When people don't get this, they ask the Cambodian Association to call the social worker or someone. Some people don't know their worker, but even those who do still feel insecure to call the worker and depend on the Cambodian Association to call for them.
>
> People don't know how to complete their forms. Month after month, we serve the same people, even though copies are made. They are explained very slowly and clearly, but they don't trust themselves. Every month, new people also request help. They are totally dependent on the Association, especially the single parents who have lost their network of friends. Most of the time now is taken up with translation needed in social services, family separation, children in school, divorce, family violence ... Many people who are so dependent on us have had no education background in Cambodia. Also, many of these are single mothers with children. These people have no understanding of forms or how to manage within the system on their own. (personal interview, 1994)

By the late 1990s, funding for Cambodian resettlement services ended. Only a few organizations, such as the Cambodian Community Association of Ontario, Jane-Finch Family and Community Centre, and Hong Fook in Toronto; two community health centres in Ottawa; and the London Cross Cultural Learner Centre were able to support small programs for Cambodian youth and women, or provide advocacy.

Learning English as a Second Language

Ninety-two per cent of all Cambodians who resettled in Canada from 1980 to 1991 could not speak either of Canada's official languages

(Employment and Immigration Canada 1980–92). Among older adults, English-language acquisition remains a critical resettlement difficulty. In 1995, the majority of Cambodian women and older Khmer in Ontario faced enormous communication barriers, still requiring translators for interviews with government and social service workers, teachers, and medical personnel. Most were unable to access ESL classes and programs (McLellan 1995).[17] Difficulties in speaking and writing English among Cambodian youth contributed to their high dropout rate from school (ibid.). The Toronto-based Cambodian Association recognized that the lack of English among Cambodians generated the continued need for providing front-line services in the mid-1990s, especially when dealing with schools and social agencies. A Khmer service worker noted:

A lot of our time is spent on the telephone dealing with emergency calls for the Children's Aid Society and with school problems. Elementary schools call concerning no attendance, coming to school too early, behaviourial problems, coming home late, violence to children, cleanliness, nutrition not adequate, no proper clothing. Sometimes the telephone is not enough and they need a translator in person. This happens with the Children's Aid and school board, who need immediate assistance with parent interviews. Problems increase when the kids reach teenage years, and there are more problems now than a few years earlier. This is due to increasing family separation. It is not only the children's problem, but the problem of mother, she is isolated and depressed. (personal interview, 1994)

The necessity of using whatever translators were available increased issues of mistrust among the Cambodians. Since translators are not generally trusted (people fear gossip or embarrassment to have their problems known), few completely disclose difficulties, resulting in misunderstanding of the situation at hand. Until the late 1990s, public schools throughout Ontario required Cambodian translators to mediate between school officials and Khmer parents. Without a translator, parents had little contact with the schools and inadequate participation in their child's education. A Khmer translator who worked for one of the public schools in Toronto identified several difficulties:

The common experience is for parents not to show up in school, for example, to see the teacher on parents' night. They want to go, but can't speak English and don't understand the context of school. Also parents can't read notes to them in English. Parents don't understand report cards. To arrange with parents to meet the teacher, I have to make a phone call and be there when they meet. They come if they are called in Khmer, but if the note arrives or if kids tell them, they don't come. Parents are too shy and too fearful to come on their own. They feel they don't belong to the school. But the schools can't afford this kind of outreach.

Funding is being reduced for translators. Therefore, more and more parents won't come. More and more phone consultations will be the norm, having the Khmer assistant speaking with parents about the child's report. But this leaves the teacher out of the interaction. Also those people who could do translation are very rare. Most people don't feel their English is good enough or, in young people, they don't feel their Khmer is good enough. With the few translators available and teacher interviews held at the same time, sometimes there are three or four jobs at different schools within one night ... Middle schools also use translators but by the time the child is in Grade 7 and 8 many teachers just use the child. But, the child won't translate problems to parents and many children don't have good grasp of English to act as translator. (personal interview, 1994)

Many of the older Cambodian youth who arrived in the 1980s dropped out of school because of language difficulties. They tended to marry young and their children also had difficulty in learning English. In the mid-1990s, teachers in elementary schools throughout Ontario recognized that these second-generation Cambodian children needed ESL instruction but were not eligible for assistance.[18] Cambodian youth who did not finish high school faced additional challenges with their limited ability to find meaningful work or access educational opportunities later in life. One Khmer service worker commented:

Before 1989, there were few incidents of people so dependent as people tended to find work without needing English skills. There were lots of high school dropouts with lots of energy who needed jobs to support families here and back home. It was more important to work and send money back than to go to school. Now with the recession, they have high unemployment. Most teenagers when they first arrived in Canada were placed in high school and middle schools and never received extra help. They had no schooling in Cambodia and no consistent education in the camps. Therefore, ten years were lost. Also, with the massive trauma experienced, they couldn't concentrate so well. They tended to drop out early. It was more meaningful to go out to work and support family and relatives.

These people are now in their twenties and they have no future except for welfare. They have lost hope and direction. (personal interview, 1994)

It is not surprising that the children of these Cambodians who had arrived as older youth also face serious issues in school and in society. In the mid-1990s, alienation among Cambodian youth manifested itself in depression and dropping out of school. By 2003, gang and drug issues among Cambodian youth in the larger Ontario cities characterized their alienation, although more youth were completing high school.

Current Trends in Ontario Cambodian Communities

By the late 1990s, with the majority of resettlement and other program funding coming to a halt in Ontario, Cambodians involved in religious groups and small networks of family and friends increasingly provided counselling, translation, and documentation services for one another. In 2003, Cambodian individuals in Toronto, Hamilton, St Thomas, and Ottawa noted that the levels of family stress and violence seen in the early years had significantly declined and marriages were more stable. The leader of one Cambodian association in Ontario pointed out:

> There were lots of divorces in the beginning ... This was because people came from such poor living conditions in the camps where they had no clothes, no makeup, no fun. Then, when they come to Canada they would go overboard with wanting to go to parties, with buying nice clothes. Many went to parties twice a month, even more. But, there is still struggle in the homeland, and they don't think of that, both men and women. Over here they are just buying, buying, new cars, new house. There is no one here to control them. Their family is away, in other places. Because the family was not here, the problems really started. People don't want to get education, good jobs, skills to support their family, but they do gambling, drinking, and get a bad image. Then the problems start as the families start to break apart. Now things are more settled and this [divorce] is no longer such a problem, except when older men get a very young wife [from Cambodia], and this creates different issues. (personal interview, 2003)

Given the excessive challenges and the lack of social capital within Cambodian communities, their resiliency in facing cultural and language setbacks, and their overall adjustment to Canadian society has been impressive. Cambodians have slowly recognized their own inner capacities and are building upon them. It is only recently that Cambodians in Ontario are beginning to achieve avenues of upward mobility. Cambodian employment in Ontario has been steady since the late 1990s, with greater instances of Cambodian adults accessing employment and retraining opportunities. Expressions of financial stability through home ownership have become more common. Other forms of social capital are characterized by the development of Buddhist temples, small businesses, and an increasing number of Cambodian youth who enter the professions after college and university, thus gaining community status.

Long-term effects of isolation and marginalization remain, however, particularly among inner-city youth and those families headed by single parents or widows who fall outside of family, friendship, and community networks. These two groups are highly vulnerable, and often lack either institutional or informal support. The lack of culturally sensitive services and recognition of their needs affect Cambodians at both the personal and community levels and continue to be resettlement challenges. A Khmer man from Hamilton commented on the lingering frustration that remains among alienated Cambodians:

> Still no one in the government or society knows who we are. Government workers always think we are Chinese or Vietnamese. Cambodian people get so tired of this fight to let people know they are Cambodian and now, Cambodians don't know who to go to or where to get recognition. (personal interview, 2001)

3 Community Distinctions and Divisions

Class, Education, and Employment

Khmer elites and professionals who survived the Khmer Rouge tended to choose France for resettlement. Having been educated in French, their qualifications were readily accepted. Merchants and business-people, former government officials, and soldiers from several political factions (Lon Nol, Khmer Rouge, Khmer Serei) chose the United States. A military record or previous business dealings with Americans made their acceptance for resettlement easier. Canada, Australia, and New Zealand became resettlement options for those without professional, business, or military backgrounds. According to Employment and Immigration Canada immigration statistics, almost 85 per cent of Cambodians who resettled in Canada from 1980 to 1992 were rural people with very little education or urban experience.[1]

The minimal educational background of Cambodians in Ontario seriously inhibited their resettlement endeavours. One Cambodian service worker in the mid-1990s noted the affect of this on children born or raised in Canada:

If the family has a background of education, the children are encouraged to stay in school. If the family has no education, it becomes more important for the youth to help support the family financially, for example, to get extra cash. This makes education a low priority for both parents and youth. Among rural people there is no environment for studying, no support or encouragement to go to school, no parents to ask about school life, or activities, or how the child is doing. Parents only see the social aspect of school and that makes them want to take the girls out before they date.

They don't see the worth of school. Children of parents who had some education or know the value of education are pushed and encouraged. This leads to further class divisions in the community. Also the majority are uneducated and only a minority of parents are interested in the children, go to a school play, etc. (personal interview, 1994)

In the early 1990s, perceptions of class differences contributed to the difficulties that Cambodian service workers faced. Ontario's social policies and practices during the 1980s and early 1990s favoured ethnic leaders who were well educated, spoke English, and had an appreciation of the power dynamics in regard to government funding. Few Cambodians in Ontario met these criteria, and those who did were especially supported by government and social service workers. Many Cambodians from rural backgrounds felt that the Cambodian service workers only acted with respect towards the educated urban class of Khmer. One Cambodian woman said:

Cambodian Association people act arrogant and pompous. They talk insulting to Khmer; they use loud voices and very short speech. The people at the Association talk differently to the classes of Khmer. They talk loud and rude to the uneducated but when they find they are speaking to an educated Khmer they drop their voices and speak quieter ... Older people and single mothers don't want to take advantage of the programs and services because they don't want to be treated with haughtiness. (personal interview, 1994)

In several Ontario communities, Cambodians complained that Khmer-speaking service workers were 'rude' to them and didn't talk 'respectful' to them over the phone.[2] What many Cambodians did not realize were the difficulties Khmer service workers had in making the transition from face-to-face social encounters to the impersonal telephone voice. A non-Khmer government worker who dealt with Cambodians in the 1980s commented:

There are so many gender bias, social class bias, and hierarchical divisions in the language. There are fourteen or fifteen different ways of referring to the other 'you' and as many for self 'I.' It all depends on status. Therefore, if you don't know the proper term for age and class, this offends people. Nuances are lost on the telephone and in the younger generation who don't know how to address people. It is seen as an issue of politeness. (personal interview, 1994)

Notions of class were exacerbated by the kind of employment Cambodians were able to obtain, impacting social relationships. A Khmer man explained:

Here in the Cambodian community there are many groups and no communication. This is based on class and job distinctions, that those in better-paying jobs don't associate with lower-class ones. Those here with unskilled jobs and no education feel that they have nothing to give and never feel confident to speak ... Now they are looked down upon because they are in unskilled labour. (personal interview, 1994)

Until recently, there have been very few Khmer professionals in Ontario.[3] Several men had worked in the UNHCR refugee camps as medical technicians, dental assistants, and teachers, but were unable to continue with this work without access to retraining programs. The one Khmer doctor who practised in Ontario retired in the late 1990s. Another Khmer physician was unable to renew his licence and returned to Cambodia in 2000. In the mid-1990s, there was one male Khmer nurse in Ontario who worked in geriatrics. Increasing numbers of second-generation Cambodians, however, have now completed post-secondary education, specializing in nursing, social work, psychology, business, and community development.

The few Cambodian businesses in Ontario are identified as being owned primarily by Sino-Cambodians (Chinese ancestry). Businesses tend to be family-run stores or services (grocery, currency exchange, flowers, sewing/alterations, bakery, laundromat, restaurant) and food franchises, particularly Subway and Coffee Time Donuts. Although there are several Cambodian-run restaurants in Ontario, few are identified as Khmer and most advertise their food as Thai or Vietnamese. Only the pictures of Apsara dancers or the Angkor Wat on the restaurant walls indicate a Cambodian connection. An exception is the Angkor Khmer Restaurant in Toronto. As one woman explained, Khmer initially lacked the capital, expertise, contacts, and confidence to establish small businesses:

It is not very common for people to switch from paid work to being self-employed. Most Cambodian people are afraid to make such a big jump. For one thing, you usually need a lot of capital and the other thing is, owning your own business is very stressful and time consuming. Most people would rather have the security of knowing they will have a stable income. The first few years of the business are very difficult and some months you might not even make a profit. You also have to be very sure in your abilities in order to open up your own business. People who open up their own business usually know how to speak English well and have had some sort of education. Most Cambodian people lack confidence in their abilities to open up a business. They are afraid of failure and losing all the money they have worked so hard for. They feel that they do not have the skills to make the business successful. They'd rather work for someone else and get a paycheque at the end of the month. (Vireak Ly interview, 2003)

During the early years of resettlement, lack of confidence and limited social contacts resulted in difficulties to access programs.[4] Cambodians expressed frustration over these lost retraining opportunities, as one man from Ottawa pointed out:

I had dental skills as an assistant from the camps in Thailand but I couldn't find out how to do it here. ESL teachers could only advise on courses, not how to get money to go to school. I didn't dare go to the government because we were very shy when we collected our money. We didn't ask questions or didn't speak unless we were asked. The government never offered any information on job retraining and people were too shy to ask. Cambodian workers were expected to find these things out and pass them on to Cambodians but they were too busy and didn't know.

It took three or four years before I found out about adult high schools. Most of my friends are cleaners, dishwashers, landscapers because they don't know anything about school, how to get funding to go. At that time the government was supposed to teach at least a couple of people how to re-educate themselves. We didn't realize it is all right to borrow money and go to school. We thought that would be a bad thing. At that time everyone wanted to learn and get ahead and get goals and to succeed but we didn't know how to go about doing this ...

People are really frustrated that they didn't get the chance. They are now stuck in janitor jobs or working in factories together with other Cambodians, and this doesn't give them a chance to use English ... Now it is too late to go back to school. Families are larger and we are in jobs we are afraid to lose. This causes so much frustration among the young adult men around thirty to forty years old. We feel we have lost our chance. (personal interview, 1994)

Instead of receiving advice about vocational training or how to take courses designed to integrate them into more skilled, higher-paid areas of the labour market, Cambodians were encouraged by both private and government sponsors alike to achieve self-reliance as soon as possible after arrival. Unlike Quebec, where French language acquisition was emphasized through full financial support and accommodation for one year of study, Cambodians in Ontario were pushed into unskilled labour employment, often working in two low-paying jobs, pooling resources, and sharing rental expenses with other families.[5] Cambodians felt that their limited formal education and low level of English-language fluency severely restricted their access to both the job market and government-sponsored retraining programs.[6] Early employment for both men and women was at the expense of attending ESL classes or continuing education. A Khmer man from Windsor described his struggles:

When I came to Canada ... I went to high school for six months. I was government sponsored and they provided the assistance for me to go to school. I passed the high school, and then I had no money, because we had two kids and my wife wasn't working. So, then they tried to put me into the job to work. I needed the money to support my family, because we were on the assistance and I was only working part-time ... After school I would go to work, but sometimes I would only sleep three or four hours a night because I had to do what was needed ... I worked in a factory making steel wheels for cars, and then I tried to quit school because I needed the job more than school. I wanted the education, to get the degree to get the job but then I found a job and it was good enough. They wanted me to stay in school but I couldn't do both. That was my choice, if I went to school, I couldn't do my job, if I did my job, I couldn't go to school. (personal interview, 2005)

Since Cambodians could not access retraining programs, they remained locked into the bottom rungs of the occupational ladder (Neuwirth 1987). During much of the late 1980s and early 1990s, Ontario experienced a huge loss of manufacturing and unskilled labour jobs, resulting in high rates of unemployment in all Cambodian communities. Compared with the overall provincial unemployment rate of 8.5 per cent, Cambodians with Khmer as their mother tongue had 19.8

per cent unemployment (Statistics Canada 1991: Special Tabulations). In some Ontario cities Cambodian unemployment was at almost 30 per cent.[7] A Cambodian man from Toronto commented:

> It is very difficult to find a job, especially now because of the recession. When there are not enough jobs out there, people are laid off more. If we look at some Canadians who have worked for thirty to forty years, they are still laid off. They have enough skill, they speak English fluently, they have high ability, but they still have difficulty in finding a job. If we compare them with us, they are better than us in every aspect. We speak poor English with accent, often enough they don't understand. We don't have enough experience to work. We don't have good references. Therefore, we are losing to them in every thing ... When we could not speak English properly, they would not want to hire us. There are many people who speak fluently English, why not hire them, and why should they bother to hire us? (personal interview, 1994)

The Khmer physician in Toronto described the psychological damage of high unemployment:

> For the first two or three years in Canada it was a joy and relief [for Cambodians] to leave the camps and to get assistance from the government and to start over. This created lots of good feelings, 1982 to 1987. The majority came then and it was an economic boom. After a year of dependency, then more than 90 per cent were working. Although it was unskilled labour, they felt independent. Now at the present time the reverse is true. Economic depression, the housing shortage is very difficult. Now people have to share, for example, a three-bedroom apartment with two families with three or four children each. Eighty per cent of people who are packed together get into fights within six months of sharing apartments. A problem with Cambodians is that they don't speak out but internalize it until one day they explode. At this point, the people then call for help but the damage is done. (personal interview, 1994)

A high percentage of Cambodians turned to welfare for support. The high rates of welfare dependency and other public assistance in the 1990s were emotionally charged subjects among Cambodians, particularly concerning welfare abuse and its long-term effects. Some felt that reliance on government welfare was a viable solution to a 'no-win' situation. A St Thomas man explained:

> At present there are six families who make no attempt to learn English ... They do not want to look for jobs or go for retraining, but to stay on welfare. These six families have no incentive or hope, because if they got Grade 12, they could get a job ... But it would take ten years for them just to get Grade 12, and they can't see why they have to go to all that trouble if there is little hope that they will get a job. (personal interview, 1994)

In addition to welfare money (that included entitlements to paid medical and dental health care), some families worked informally, thus making more than those in low-paid labour positions. One Khmer service worker detailed the negative consequences:

> Cambodians who work are called stupid. Women see their government assistance money as free and easy. They have lots of spare cash and they can stay home and gamble. They say, 'What's the point of going out to work to make six or seven dollars an hour? We can even have the husband or boyfriend to live with us and work.' The interesting point is that what starts off as a pretend separation eventually results in a real breakup as the wife won't accept the husband's attitude because he doesn't support her. But the children suffer through the breakup, and fights, and lack of role models. There is an emphasis on short-term gains, no appreciation of the long-term investment in the children, either ethically or in education. There is the difficulty in distinguishing between those who have real needs and those who express the needs to get the benefits. The worker never knows the truth and people don't like to ask questions. This is also a reason for suspicions against service workers. Khmer people are afraid she will let the government know. (personal interview, 1994)

During this time, Cambodian people differentiated others as to who remained welfare dependant and who worked at any employment opportunity. From this division, a new social class of Cambodians began to emerge of those who considered themselves to be moving up in society by staying employed and eventually leaving subsidized apartments to become homeowners. This new social identification did not replace the higher pre-migration status of urban-based Cambodians or the professionally educated Khmer, but further marginalized those Khmer who stayed on government assistance.[8] In 1995, a public school vice-principal in the Jane-Finch area of Toronto observed that at least half the Cambodian families in her school had recently moved to Newmarket and Brampton, where there were numerous factories and new housing developments. These families began a pattern of upward mobility that became increasingly prominent among Cambodians.

In 1995, Ontario's newly elected Conservative government initiated a severe reduction in welfare assistance, restricting eligibility and requiring that all able-bodied adults either find employment or be actively enrolled in retraining courses. Rent controls were removed and cities became responsible for assisted housing costs. All this occurred at a time when record numbers of new immigrants and refugees were resettling in Ontario. By the latter part of the 1990s, Ontario's economy was no longer in recession and employment opportunities began to grow in the manufacturing and the service industries. The majority of Cambodian men and women were able to obtain full-time employment once again, albeit in factories and food-processing plants. One Cambodian woman commented on her inability to look for other kinds of work:

> I am lucky to have the job working at this factory today. I have been working here for many years. Back then it was not so hard to find work [in a factory], but now it is very difficult to find work and companies want more qualified people. They want people to speak English well, who have graduated from high school, or even college or university. These days when you apply for a job, you have to go through an interview and you also have to pass a series of tests, you have to have fairly good reading and writing skills to pass these tests ... I would probably not be able to pass all these tests today to get the job that I have now.
>
> When you do not speak the language it is very difficult for you to find work. This is why you find most Cambodian people do not often change jobs, they usually stick to the job they have because they are afraid that they might not find another job. The only time people change jobs is when they are forced to, for example, when they are laid off or they move somewhere far ... Many people are worried that if they are laid off they will not have what it takes to compete with other people who can speak English and have an education. (Vireak Ly interview, 2003)

Cambodians are recognized as valuable and hard-working employees, and companies tend to hire them in large numbers.[9] Their substantial migration from other parts of Canada to London and Newmarket indicate that they seek job opportunities with companies that already employ Cambodians. One woman described how jobs are obtained through friends or family:

There are several areas in which a lot of Cambodian people work, in Newmarket, near the Jane and Finch area, and in Hamilton. Usually if one member of the family or a friend works at a company, they try to help get those people a job within the company also. That is why you get a clustering of Cambodian people in certain areas ... If someone in your family or a friend who works in a specific company knows that the company is hiring, they will let you know about it. Most people find work through word of mouth. It is not uncommon to see the whole family work for a specific company, the mother, the father, and their children. (personal interview, 2003)

For some Khmer men, factory assembly work has led to management positions:

After the unemployment time was over, I got the job I have right now. At first, I was an assembly worker, [then] a quality assembler, then I applied for the lift-truck driver, got the licence for that, and then they put me into propane training, for the propane truck. I did that for two years and then I applied for the senior assembler, and I had that job for a year. Then I applied for the team leader. I have been doing this for the last year and a half. I just tried to learn more about the environment there, about what I can do. We have the manager, then the supervisor, and then team leader. I am after the worker, I have to take care of all the workers, all the problems, all the machinés, whatever happens. I have to report to the supervisor who reports to the manager. The skills learned on the job, about managing things at work have helped with what I do at the temple. Some people – their minds or their ideas are not good for [being a] team leader. You have [to take] a lot of responsibility, and to care about things. (personal interview, 2005)

As full-time employment opportunities increased and home interest rates declined, many Cambodians became first-time homebuyers. Wanting to live close to their workplace, and since many factories are located on the outskirts of the city, Cambodians relocated from the city core and concentrated areas of assisted housing to newly developed residential areas. In 2002, the interim executive director of the Cambodian Community Association of Ontario (CCAO) noted that about half of the five thousand Cambodians from Toronto had moved and, despite the geographical isolation of these new neighbourhoods, they developed innovative ways to keep connected with one another:

Families have moved to new subdivisions in Bradford, Maple, New-market, Brampton, Keswick, and Woodbridge. Maple is a popular area because of its closeness to the temple ... New housing in general is more attractive because the houses can be custom-made to people's likes. Shopping is still done in the older locations, such as the Keele and Sheppard Asian food specialty store or those along Jane Street.

Although the community is scattered in the new neighbourhoods, they still maintain connections with one another. A popular mechanism is through potluck 'rotation parties.' One week a party is held in one house, then the following week in another, and so forth. Sometimes friends help out with the cooking but often people will bring food and drinks. Because the houses are bigger, with large basements, karaoke and dancing is very popular. A problem with the neighbourhoods is that children need school bus transportation. Seniors are especially isolated due to language barriers and lack of transportation. Also, seniors are expected to help out with the child care and other family responsibilities, such as cooking and cleaning. On weekends, families have to drive the elders to the temple, also on the new and full-moon days. (personal interview, 2002)

Unemployment continues among widows and single parents (primarily women), and those whose health problems prevent them from working.[10] Beiser and Hou's (2001) ten-year study demonstrates that depression is also an important predictor of employment. Among Cambodians who returned to the workforce in the late 1990s and gained significant upward mobility, several noted that a return to chronic unemployment and poverty is only an injury or illness away.[11] Their employment situation is similar to what Ong identifies for Cambodians in California: 'They are marginalized as the kind of people that industry has no need to invest in because they can be replenished by newer, more desperate immigrants. The perception that new immigrants are good enough only for poorly paid, labour-intensive, and often unpleasant jobs (such as food packing) also helps to shame them as laboring subjects who, despite their best efforts, are highly vulnerable to the shifting tides of dead-end jobs. Market volatility itself becomes a form of labor regulation, requiring parents to work long or irregular hours as long as a job lasts. Such precarious employment and income conditions among adults add to the problems of undersupervised teenagers as the family daily searches for cash' (2003: 232–3).

Chan divides Cambodians in the United States into three groups (2003: 36–7). The first, referred to as 'elites,' are middle-class professionals and people who have established their own businesses. They comprise about 5 per cent of Cambodians. The second group, about 40 per cent, are lower-middle-class people who live in medium-sized or small cities in states that have relatively small Cambodian populations. Although they earn low wages, families often consist of several wage earners, thus enabling them to buy homes of their own. The remaining 55 per cent of American Cambodians are made up of those who live in inner-city neighbourhoods, relying on welfare for survival, and identified as physically or mentally disabled, or single-parent households. While Ontario has a similar small number of 'elites,' the proportion of family households with multiple wage earners is much higher than in the United States. In 2005, Ontario community leaders estimated that about 60 to 70 per cent of Cambodians were lower-middle-class, and the less than 30 per cent of families on welfare or in subsidized housing are in steady decline. Depending on the health of individuals and Ontario's manufacturing industries, however, these proportions are subject to change. The uncertainty of steady employment may be a reason why the number of Cambodian-owned businesses in the Greater Toronto, Ottawa, London, and Windsor areas are increasing every year.[12] Many of the newer businesses reflect the growing influence and skills of the second-generation Cambodians, especially those with post-secondary education.

Three different employment patterns have emerged among second-generation Cambodian youth. After finishing high school, the majority of them do not continue with post-secondary education but tend to find employment in local factories where other friends or family work. Marriage, family pressure to contribute to household costs, lack of support from others, no interest in a career, poor grades, and a lack of money are several of the reasons given. In comparison, Cambodian youth who left school early (at age sixteen) encounter enormous difficulties in finding full-time employment beyond minimum-wage service jobs. With time on their hands, and a tendency to 'hang-out' together, many are accused of being in gangs. The smaller numbers of Cambodian youth who go on to college or university are more likely to work in offices, in skilled professions (social work, nursing, engineering, computer science, pharmacology), or to start their own businesses (video production, real estate, investment counselling, insurance). These educated youth are steadily increasing the levels of social capital in their families and communities. The subtle, but distinctive, class identities based on education and professional skills that now appear among second-generation Cambodians are overriding the pre-migration class or ethnic identities of the first generation.

Ethnic Differences among Cambodians

Ethnic ancestry and language is also used to differentiate Cambodians. Canadian census data in 1991 indicate that 16,940 individuals claimed Khmer ethnicity and 1,675 claimed multiple-ethnic identity. According to Employment and Immigration Canada (1980–92) statistics, of the 18,602 refugees who arrived from Cambodia between 1980 and 1992, more than three thousand claimed a Chinese dialect rather than Khmer as their native language. Interviews with Sino-Cambodians, however, indicate that many who retain a Chinese dialect still tend to self-identify as ethnic Khmer, or Khmer speakers. Only a small number of Cambodian refugees identify themselves as ethnic Chinese, clearly stating that they are not Khmer and will have nothing to do with the Cambodian community. In the 1990s, very few Cambodians in Ontario would admit to having Vietnamese ancestry, although in smaller cities such as Hamilton, London, and Windsor this has changed in recent years. A few Cham Muslim families are said to live in Toronto, but no one interviewed had personally met them.

In the mid-1990s, several Khmer with Chinese ancestry stated that even though they spoke only Khmer and felt a hundred per cent Cambodian, they were often labelled by others in the Cambodian community as not being 'real Khmer.' This labelling would be used especially when the individual engaged in a non-traditional activity or behaved differently from others (such as starting a business or working towards specific career aspirations). Some of the female Cambodian community service workers in the 1990s who had Chinese ancestry were told that if they were real Khmer women, they would not be doing that kind of work. As more Cambodian youth continued on in post-secondary education, however, these negative attitudes have declined. Today, Sino-Cambodians in Ontario are clearly identified with owning the majority of all small businesses. This association is consistent with other studies on Cambodian communities in the United States, reflecting their previous economic expertise in Cambodia in retail, trade, and import/export businesses (Ong 2003: 241–2; Kong 2003: 87; Chhim 2003: 57). Because of their financial skills and greater involvement with bureaucratic procedures, Sino-Cambodian business owners in Ontario are often encouraged to join the board of directors of Cambodian associations and to help organize large community events and celebrations. They are recognized as patrons and frequently invited to weddings and to participate in fundraising events. Sino-Cambodian business owners respond by being generous in their donations to support Buddhist temples in Ontario, helping to rebuild temples and schools in Cambodia, and contributing to ad hoc relief work.

The label of not being 'really Khmer' has also been directed towards Kampuchea Krom. Kampuchea Krom are ethnic Khmer who have lived in Vietnam for generations in an area that was once part of Cambodia. The December 2001 Kampuchea Krom Federation (KKF) population statistics list five hundred Kampuchea Krom in Canada; a thousand in Australia; three thousand in France; thirty thousand in United States; over one million in Cambodia; and seven million in Vietnam. In June 2002, the director of the Kampuchea Krom National Association of Canada (KKNAC) stated that about 130 Kampuchea Krom families, comprising about five hundred people, live in Ontario, with most residing in Toronto and Hamilton. Kampuchea Krom in Ontario readily acknowledge their status is different from those born and raised in Cambodia. Most speak Vietnamese as a second language and are said to have a distinct Khmer accent. Due to their historical situation of being an ethnic Khmer minority in Vietnam, Kampuchea Krom developed an ethnoreligious based nationalism to help them resist overt Vietnamese assimilation efforts. Kampuchea Krom have merged political and social activism, a rigorous adherence to Thervada Buddhism, and Khmer culture into a distinct discourse that is now globally activated and maintained. Although they continue to identity themselves as ethnic Khmer, they are considered to be a distinct part of Ontario Cambodian communities. Few Kampuchea Krom have connections with other Vietnamese nationals or Vietnamese community groups. The Khmer Cambodian suspicion of Kampuchea Krom is rooted in the centuries-old aggression and mistrust between Cambodia and Vietnam, and the recent Vietnamese involvement in Cambodian politics. In Hamilton, they have chosen to distinguish themselves from the larger Khmer Cambodian community by renaming the Khmer Buddhist Temple of Hamilton as the Khmer Kampuchea Krom Buddhist Temple.

A significant difference between Khmer from Cambodia and the Kampuchea Krom is that the latter were not subject to the genocidal regime of the Khmer Rouge, and never experienced the powerlessness, unrelenting fear, horror, and hopelessness associated with it. Although some Kampuchea Krom did reside in Cambodia, most lived in Viet-

nam until the late 1970s and do not manifest the psychological trauma
and distrust of one another that is common among Khmer from Cambodia. Some Cambodian leaders in Ontario have questioned how, if
Kampuchea Krom cannot fully understand the extent of depression,
torture-related trauma, and extensive cultural and personal bereavement of those from Cambodia, can they relate to the majority of Khmer
living here or become Khmer community leaders?

Kampuchea Krom tend to remain marginal to Ontario Cambodian
community networks and associations, especially keeping a low profile when in leadership positions. They have, however, been prominent in Buddhist activities by sponsoring Khmer-speaking monks
and facilitating the purchase and support of new temples in Toronto,
Hamilton, London, and Windsor. All Kampuchea Krom adults and
older youth in Ontario are members of the World (International) Kampuchea Krom Association. It is the largest transnational organization
of Kampuchea Krom, involving Buddhist monks, political leaders,
professionals, academics, and sympathetic individuals. Ontario Kampuchea Krom actively participate in and help produce Kampuchea
Krom media broadcasts, websites, magazines, videos, and CDs, and
dragon boat races. Their extensive political advocacy for the recognition of Kampuchea Krom is evident in the financial support they gave
to a Kampuchea Krom delegate to accompany President Bill Clinton's
visit to Vietnam in 2001. Ontario Kampuchea Krom also participate in
global organizations such as the Unrepresented Nations and Peoples
Organization (UNPO), which represents over fifty peoples, including
the Tibetans, Taiwanese, and former East Timors (personal interview
with the director of KKNAC 2002). One proactive Toronto leader urged
all Kampuchea Krom in Ontario to attend a 21 June 2005 demonstration at Lafayette Park (behind the White House) in Washington, DC,
to protest against the visiting Vietnamese prime minister. Kampuchea
Krom youth from Ontario maintain their own websites and network
with other Kampuchea Krom around the world. Along with adults and
Buddhist monks, Ontario youth diligently attend the World Convention of Kampuchea Krom, held every four or five years in Cambodia,
Vietnam, or one of the Western resettlement countries.

Community and Leadership Dynamics in Ontario

Among the larger numbers of Khmer from Cambodia in Ontario, there
are only a few individuals with the necessary leadership and organiza-

tional skills to help establish and maintain a Cambodian community centre or related mutual aid associations. The absence of Cambodian teachers, administrators, medical doctors, professionals, traditional healers, and Khmer Buddhist monks in Ontario reflects the continuing legacy of the Khmer Rouge regime. Cambodian refugees have not only lost families, homes, possessions, social identity, and status, but also a sense of trust in one another, what Giddens (1990: 140) refers to as 'ontological security.'

In Cambodia, most community social institutions or groups were an extension of the family. Cooperation, identification, and the sharing of resources and experiences remained within these small networks. Cambodia did not have a tradition of associations, volunteer groups, trade unions, or other common purpose organizations (Bit 1991: 49). In Ontario, community groups tend to involve fragments of the larger Cambodian population in a particular city, often consisting of extended-family networks and relationships among friends. The larger expressions of a Cambodian community only become visible when people gather together for annual New Year's celebrations, Buddhist ceremonies, or to attend performances of Cambodian music and dance. Smaller groups come together based on other types of allegiances, interests, or agendas. Cambodian people can maintain several different activities and interests simultaneously, easily shifting from one group to another. Even groups that identify themselves as a specific city community association will not necessarily be representative of a large portion of the Cambodian population living there. Cambodian associations that are maintained through volunteer groups tend to be small. Their activities are oriented to specific tasks such as cooking for parties, arranging advertising for visiting celebrities, fundraising, or organizing an event such as a guest lecture or New Year's celebration. Many associations throughout Ontario have either ceased to exist or remain dormant until a specific need arises.

Cambodian networks and relationships beyond family and friends remain weak, due to the past conditions of distrust, miscommunication, and power conflicts. Throughout the Khmer Rouge regime, people were forced into 'volunteer' work groups and associations; attendance at political meetings that propounded new 'revolutionary' values and codes of conduct was compulsory (Ebihara 1985). During the early 1990s in Hamilton, Cambodian people so distrusted the term 'community association' that the leadership changed its name to the Khmer Buddhist and Cultural Community. A Hamilton man explained:

I have been one of the members of the Cambodian Association in Hamilton since 1983. The big problem is that Cambodians have gone through many difficulties and terrified experiences. Normally, those bad things always haunt them and make them frightened to come out to get help from something called The Association. (personal interview, 1994)

Likewise, people do not like to hear the terms *Krom Srey Smakchith* (women's volunteer group) or *Krom Boros Smakchith* (men's volunteer group) and remain hesitant to attend any function identified as a 'meeting' or an 'association.' Cambodians in Ontario are also suspicious and critical of anyone aspiring to or already in positions of authority. Bit explains: 'Surviving the Khmer Rouge onslaught required a heightened sense of suspicion of everyone and everything, for life itself hung in the balance ... At the community level, social cohesion suffers from a continuing atmosphere of distrust between individuals and between leaders and their followers' (1991: 87).

The competition for leadership positions highlights divisions based on class, religious, political, and generational differences. Among older first-generation Cambodians in resettlement, superior and inferior social ranking continues to be one of the primary reference points for social relationships, within family, among friends, and in formal community settings (Ledgerwood 1990). They use distinct verbal forms and behavioural mannerisms to communicate with those of higher and lower status, and to acknowledge particular sociopolitical positions. Khmer-based leadership tends to be characterized by these traditional concepts, and deference to authority. Potential community leaders, especially younger Cambodians, have found their access to necessary social networks dependent upon these hierarchical social relations. In traditional Cambodian society, individuals excluded from positions of power were those with low education, rural people, youth, and women. Although Khmer youth and women are increasingly assuming leadership roles in Ontario, they face numerous obstacles. Women, youth, and those with low education tend not to challenge those of a higher status position, even if their own personality, understanding , or networks would contribute to more effective community leadership. In the mid-1990s, it was rare to find a woman or young person involved in leadership positions. A female Khmer service worker commented:

Because women leaders are so young, it is assumed that they can't read and write Khmer. Their knowledge is suspect because of their age and being a woman, and they get no respect from men or the elders. The most critical are the middle-aged men. Few women ever speak because they get no encouragement from anyone. Lots of subtle criticisms, for example, no help or public expression of support for ideas. As a married person, I am seen as outside the acceptable role. It is not acceptable for women to go to school or go to social activities or workshops ... Canadians are respected though, but not Cambodian youth.

This brings up the idea of young being expected to follow older people. This is a problem especially with middle-aged Cambodian men who are traditionally cast as 'leaders,' even if they are not bilingual or educated. Only a small number of these men have trouble adjusting to the leadership of youth, but they have a big effect. This is a big problem in the community. The two age groups don't come together. Until this gap is bridged, the touchy issues cannot be broached. Middle-aged leaders are not willing to play any role in community development. This affects funding because it is scarce and who decides who is a 'legitimate' leader? Young leaders want to cooperate but middle-aged don't. When older middle-aged [people] speak, the younger listen, but these older ones won't even listen to the new ideas of the youth, they listen politely but they ignore. The middle-aged are clinging to the 'old idea' and their experiences under Pol Pot have made them very scared and afraid to change. (personal interview, 1994)

Years later, a young Cambodian man described similar difficulties in attempting to get a youth group started at the local temple:

One day when speaking with [my friend], we discussed the idea about a youth group and I shared the idea with my dad. During this time, [another friend] who was a monk for three months, also became involved. At first, we just wanted to have the group affiliated with the temple, but for a variety of reasons it wouldn't work out. The elders wanted and needed to be acknowledged for leadership roles; the older people resisted the idea of the youth group because the youth weren't organized yet; the older people had too much of their old way of thinking and had specific ideas; and there was no immediate support for the youth ideas, it was just, 'No, it won't work.' So, it seems the process with the elders is to have the youth prove themselves first and only then will they actually look. At this point, people at the temple are very comfortable, and they don't want to see any change. They don't see any new level of interactions, or the need for them. (personal communication, 2002)

Past and current community divisions reflect the cultural conflicts between Khmer and Canadian concepts of leadership. In some Cambodian associations during the 1980s and 1990s, the Canadian democratic principles of electing leaders and following due process became formalized in order to get charitable status and funding. The traditional Khmer patron-client relationship, however, characterized the associations' internal dynamics. Leaders provided some degree of security, protection, and service provision, but withheld audit statements, minutes of board meetings, and bylaws, and ignored electoral procedures. People in the community were aware of the leaders' shortcomings and wanted changes, but their loyalty, sense of obligation, and lower status prevented any verbal or electoral challenge. While the authoritative behaviour of community leaders created this dichotomy, their English-language skills, level of education, and overt displays of leadership provided a semblance of community stability to funding sources and mainstream institutions.

The Khmer reluctance to engage in confrontation or behaviour that could be labelled as aggressive and competitive helped to avoid overt leadership disputes (Ebihara 1985: 139). One American Khmer explained: 'Americans like to argue, even among friends. It's this argumentative, confrontational style that seems to be the way they like to do things ... This is not possible in Cambodian culture. If we had such a blowup, we would avoid that person for such a long time, perhaps for life! We would not look that person in the eyes again in the same way. Why, even our next generation might hold a grudge on behalf of our name – out of respect for us. Cambodians will avoid any hurtful situation if at all possible. They will look the other way, turn their back, maybe even walk away' (Tenhula 1991: 29).

The lack of models for negotiated reconciliation to resolve disputes has had serious consequences for individual and community participation. Numerous misunderstandings and long-standing personalized conflicts arose between individuals, and between the people and community associations. Several Cambodian associations throughout Ontario ceased to function because people would not take part in elections or meetings. Their absence was a strong statement that community needs and concerns were not being effectively addressed. Innovative styles of leadership that would actively involve larger sections of the community have been difficult to implement, as changes must be negotiated within the existing hierarchy. Given the extent of psychological trauma experienced by the first generation, it will take time for them to rebuild trust in themselves, and to trust the growing self-reliance and motivations of the second generation.

Leadership is an essential facet of a community's social capital that arises through trust and reciprocity. The qualities of trust necessary for community solidarity and social cohesion are most absent among those who experienced mistrust, fear, and broken relationships (Mehmet et al. 2002: 2336). Low social capital and limited social networks beyond the community also result in low levels of defence when collective interest is threatened (Woolcock and Narayan 2000). These characteristics, common throughout Ontario Cambodian communities, have negatively affected resettlement opportunities and integrative processes. Without community leaders it has been difficult to identify and implement culturally appropriate services and programs for social and health needs, organize cultural activities, undertake advocacy on behalf of individuals, deal with neighbourhood hostility, facilitate sponsorship of family members or Buddhist monks, and develop effective strategies to resolve youth difficulties. Strong organizational skills and consistent leadership are necessary to participate in the 'politics of recognition and difference' and actively negotiate factors involved in the construction and presentation of image (Taylor 1994; Ross 1988).

The Cambodian communities in Ontario that have been the most successful in developing effective programs, services, and rates of participation are those associated with non-Khmer who helped form cooperative and beneficial liaisons, thus increasing their levels of social capital. During the early 1990s, non-Khmer at the London Cross-Cultural Learner Centre encouraged Cambodians associated with their centre to participate in community development. A Khmer worker who had trained in participatory learning models while working with the Canadian Cambodian Development Program (CCDP) helped develop a series of workshops on negotiation skills. The training sessions emphasized community leadership for utilitarian and collective purposes, rather than status. This effectively strengthened the London community and helped it to achieve common goals, aspirations, and effective social action. A non-Khmer United Church minister in London helped Cambodians form a tenants association to combat discrimination and verbal racist attacks from one of their landlords. Three non-Khmer lawyers and a local high school principal also helped Cambodians to effectively deal with legal and social issues. The series of workshops and programs spread to St Thomas, encouraging participation and involvement there. A non-Khmer service worker commented:

In London, people were more willing to talk about leadership issues. They were more participatory. Small groups often met to discuss specific problems and to come up with solutions. St Thomas community members were natural leaders. They are young, open-minded, and helped to carry these meetings. Many Cambodians will not admit that they don't know something. But, the St Thomas people were open to learning about things and developing themselves. (personal interview, 1994)

Non-Khmer resettlement service administrators and government officials in St Thomas and London actively supported these programs. A non-Khmer service worker familiar with different Cambodian communities in Ontario summarized how this worked:

I compare the response of government workers in Toronto to London where people in the same position were familiar with community difficulties and were incredibly helpful to the Cambodians. The program's officer in London helped the Cambodians write their proposals for funding from Multiculturalism and Citizenship by spending the time with them to understand exactly what was needed in the community.

Government people would make a point of coming to community meetings, even if they were held on Sunday night. Secretary of State people were supportive also, although ISAP was not and cut funding. Most government people in London have really good insight into the Cambodian community and had good relations with the Cambodians, for example, [two people] from Secretary of State were really supportive to London and St Thomas Cambodians, and even helped with the Windsor community. The Windsor community has a lack of leadership skills, especially in their ability to implement or organize things, for example, with writing proposals. They couldn't get any support from people in Windsor. (personal interview, 1994)

In Ottawa, non-Khmer social workers with the Somerset and Carlington Community Health Centres provided programs for Khmer. A Khmer women's worker co-op was created that had connections to one in Cambodia. Khmer women in Ottawa made clothes from fabric provided by the women's co-operative in Cambodia, and held fashion shows for both Khmer and non-Khmer. The non-Khmer community development worker at Somerset secured a $30,000 grant from Ottawa Housing to create a Khmer community centre in one of the subsidized housing developments, and to turn the concrete backyards into gar-

dens. At Carlington CHC, another non-Khmer social worker success-
fully advocated for Cambodian concerns to be included in programs.

At the Cambodian Community Association of Ontario in Toronto, a
non-Khmer social worker hired in the mid-1990s developed youth outreach, parenting skills training, women's health promotion, community economic development, leadership skills training, and employment
and education training sessions. Her skill in writing funding proposals
resulted in the hiring and training of Cambodian youth and women to
develop and run programs. Youth initiatives included weekly sports
activities, social events, and academic tutoring. She effectively mediated between Cambodian community factions that were isolated and
hostile to one another, and petitioned non-governmental agencies, such
as the Jane-Finch Family and Community Services, to provide additional services.

The participation of non-Khmer was especially necessary in the first
two decades of resettlement, given the lack of Khmer capable or willing
to undertake the leadership positions necessary for community development and renewal. Khmer leaders tended to step down after one or
two years, and were difficult to replace. A community leader in St Thomas commented:

> The biggest problem with leadership is that leaders don't have enough
> time. They have their own jobs, family responsibilities, and they are so
> busy. At the beginning, leaders were really needed to talk about resettle-
> ment. But now, the need is about working, and because the leaders can't
> help people get jobs, they don't see people as often. This causes people
> to feel estranged and left out, and feeling that leaders are not interested.
> Communication is now more difficult and what used to take one week,
> now takes longer. (personal interview, 1994)

In the United States, the hopes and status of the Khmer community
were focused on the younger refugees who were less than ten years
old when they arrived (Ebihara 1985: 142). In Ontario, it is the second
generation, born and raised in Canada, who are providing models of
Khmer achievement in business, science, and the arts. The leadership
and youth programs developed during the 1990s in Toronto, London,
and Hamilton have had enormous positive effect. The growing presence
of Cambodian youth in colleges and universities, and their employment
in professional positions, replaces the social capital that was provided
by non-Khmer for community building, development, and cohesion.

The pattern of delayed progress and the slow rise of Khmer social capital during the 1980s and 1990s reflect the extent to which Khmer adults and older Khmer youth were handicapped by trauma and educational disruption. One Cambodian woman who had arrived as an older youth observed:

> There is not much opportunity for people out there who do not speak the language and do not have a degree. When you immigrate to a new country, especially if you are older and have responsibilities, it is very difficult to learn the language and get an education because you do not have the time or the resources to do so. The first thing you do when you arrive is to find a job because you need to work in order to survive and provide for your family. For the moment, most Cambodian people hold blue-collar types of jobs. They mostly work in factories, but hopefully we will begin to see some changes in our children. They have the opportunity to go to school, to get an education.
>
> In Canada, you are taught from a very young age to believe in yourself and that anything is possible. I tell my children that all the time, to work hard because it takes hard work to achieve your dreams but it will all be worth it in the end ... The younger generation have the ability to get better jobs than we can get, they can work in nice offices and get those white-collar jobs that we are not able to get. (Vireak Ly interview, 2003)

The pattern of limited education is difficult to break, however, especially when buying a house necessitates that all members of a Cambodian family contribute financially. Even though educational status is connected with community recognition and leadership, Cambodian youth are still being encouraged to find work as soon as they are old enough to leave school, or when they have finished high school.

Political Differences

While unfolding political events in Cambodia are a constant subject for conversation, personal political allegiance, past or present, is one issue that Khmer do not like to discuss. Until the late 1990s, a common insult to demean other Khmer was to accuse them of being Khmer Rouge. Most often, these remarks would be made by an urban-educated Khmer. As an insult, the Khmer Rouge label was likely utilized as a representation of class, indicating a rural agricultural background. In several Khmer communities, certain residential clusters of Khmer were said to be 'mainly Khmer Rouge' who live there. The *Toronto Star* (28 February 1988) ran two articles on the presence of Khmer Rouge in Canada, detailing their continued harm to Khmer communities here. Some second-generation youth have commented that their parents were Khmer Rouge and have spoken to them about their experiences, but they did not want to discuss details. Among the first-generation Khmer, individuals would sometimes identify a specific Cambodian, who lived in their same Ontario community, as being a former Khmer Rouge cadre. During interviews they would give details concerning that individual's acts of torture, violence, even killing, against themselves and members of their families. Telling their stories revealed the hatred, anger, and rage still present. One man from Ottawa spoke of a Khmer Rouge cadre living in the same apartment building who regularly taunted him by reminding him that he had had control over his life and labour during the Khmer Rouge years. Other Khmer named individuals who also boasted about their past Khmer Rouge activities and how powerful they will become when the Khmer Rouge take over Cambodia again.

For those intent on developing social cohesion within their communities, past political allegiances are viewed as something best forgotten. A Hamilton Khmer man stated:

> Our lives in Canada should be sufficient to prove that Cambodians like making peace by forgetting the past and let time have a chance to heal wounded memories. There are about 40 per cent of Cambodians living in Ontario who used to serve actively in the Pol Pot army and social structure. Now, we forget everything in the past, we socialize together, talk to each other, treat each other as long-lost friends. (personal interview, 1994)

The past, however, is never forgotten. In the 1990s, media attention given to each new Khmer Rouge atrocity acutely reminded people of past trauma, and of the strong presence and power of those who committed the crimes against them. People also expressed concern about the increasing factionalization of political groups in Cambodia and the influence of the communist Vietnamese. Following the May 1993 elections in Cambodia, several middle-aged Khmer men in Ontario spoke about returning to Cambodia to resume previously held positions of military and government authority. At some community gatherings, controversies would arise between individuals who argued over which one would receive a particular governorship in a specific region. Ten years later, interviews with some of these same individuals revealed their disappointment at the lack of welcome and support they received when they returned to Cambodia to run for political office, and their frustration with the overt political corruption and nepotism. In the 1990s, the large Cambodian political parties, such as FUNCIPEC (Prince Sihanouk's Royalist Party) or KPNLF (led by Son Sann, a Khmer Kampuchea Krom born in Phnom Penh), had extensive representation among Khmer in Ontario, but now, support is given to the popular Sam Rangsey Party and new Buddhist-based political parties. Khmer tend to agree that the war crimes tribunal should be expanded, but they are cautious about its success since former Khmer Rouge leaders now play a 'legitimate' role in Cambodian politics.

Despite the recent economic growth, growing stabilization, and the rapid expansion of tourism in Cambodia, Khmer in Ontario continue to express concern for relatives and friends in Cambodia, and for the future of their homeland. As the first generation ages, some with secure pensions are considering a return to Cambodia to live. Some have already begun small businesses, or have bought a house and land there for when they retire. The relative security of Cambodia and its increasing prosperity provide opportunities for reconciliation with the troubled past and hope to reclaim lost identities, both of which give constructive meaning for Khmer resettlement struggles in Canada.

4 Re-creating Cambodian Buddhist Temples and the Significance of Tradition

Religious identities among Cambodian refugees are influenced by their experiences of war, seeking asylum, refugee camp life, involvements concerning sponsorship and resettlement, and the long-term process of dealing with the demands of adaptation and integration into Canadian society. The means and the extent to which they adapt, re-create, transform, or change their religious identities and traditions in the Canadian context are tied to these pre-migration and resettlement experiences. Cambodians in Ontario have had to put great effort into maintaining traditional Buddhist religious identities and practices. During the early years of resettlement when religious and cultural bonds would have done much to mitigate the suffering of Cambodian refugees, they were noticeably absent. Struggles to establish and maintain Buddhist temples in Ontario have been exacerbated by the extreme politicization and disruption of Buddhism in Cambodia, and the chronic shortage of Buddhist monks, most of whom were killed by the Khmer Rouge.

Since the eleventh century, Cambodian society has been shaped and influenced by Theravada Buddhist beliefs and monastic institutions (Keyes 1994: 44). Buddhist monasteries structured religious events and practices within every Cambodian village. Buddhist morality, based on the doctrine of kamma/karma (causation and effects), and a pervasive belief in animistic spirits, permeated the daily lives and thoughts of people (Ebihara 1966: 175). Laypeople acknowledge their Buddhism through the taking of refuge in the 'three jewels': Buddha, Dharma (his teachings), and Sangha (community of monks). They follow five basic precepts (to avoid killing, stealing, sexual misconduct, lying, and consuming intoxicants), support monks and temples (*wats/vats*), and participate in a variety of ceremonies and rituals. The traditional village

monastery or temple provided a recreational centre to celebrate Buddhist festivals and play traditional games, and gave support to elderly
Cambodians, orphans, impoverished people, and the mentally ill (Boua
1991: 227; Harris 2005: 74). Individual households and groups were
often identified according to their support of specific temples (Kalab
1976: 138).

A traditional Cambodian village was represented by an *achaa (achar)*,
who was a respected layman familiar with Pali chants and Buddhist ceremonial ritual. Most *achaa* are pious older men who were once monks
for a temporary period, and learned the appropriate chants and rituals through oral repetition and observation (Douglas 2005: 130; Harris
2005: 77). Known for financial trustworthiness, *achaa* are responsible for
the general management and maintenance of the temple and its prop-
erties, especially for the collection of donations (money, grain, building
materials, kitchen supplies, etc.); they act as spokesman on behalf of
the monks and the temple, and they help organize ritual ceremonies
and festivals (Harris 2005: 77). The position of *achaa* is recognized as
one of high social and spiritual standing, and it embodies considerable
informal power (Ebihara 1966: 185). The a*chaa* have pivotal ritual roles
in wedding ceremonies: the tying of threads *(cong dai)*, cutting pieces
of hair from the bride and groom *(kat saq)*, and honouring or calling
the ancestral spirits *(saen/pren cidon cita)* to participate. Although Buddhist monks will provide blessings at weddings, they do not perform
the ceremony. It is the *achaa* who provides a Buddhist interpretation of
the ritual objects and activities. *Achaa* are the liaison between monks
and laypeople, arranging meetings and visits at the temple or home.
They lead lay recitation in chanting (e.g., the taking of refuge or the
five precepts) before the monks' ritual chanting; they ritually invite the
monk to deliver a sermon, formally recite prayers during novice ordinations, play a pivotal role in healing activities, and act as astrologers
(hora) (Harris 2005: 77).

The concept of making and earning merit *(bon)*, on behalf of oneself
and others, is a central facet of Cambodian Buddhism, linking people's
past lives with their current class and status. Mortland (1994: 79) notes
that suffering is believed to be caused when one does not recognize or
follow the law of karma, thereby enabling bad actions to give rise to bad
consequences. In contrast, making merit, particularly through actions
that involve a Buddhist-related expenditure of large sums of money
and energy, 'sows the seeds of good actions' that lead to favourable
consequences (Harris 2005: 78). Douglas describes how Cambodians in

the United States make merit: 'The elderly often spend a great deal of time in the temples, earning merit to improve their status in their next life. Good works produce *bon* (merit) and bad works produce *bap* (evil or sin) ... Because men are viewed as moral superiors to and authorities over women, according to this principle men must have earned more merit than women in their previous incarnations. Women's behaviour is believed to reflect *bon* or *bap* onto their male kin, enhancing or detracting from the men's reputations. *Bon* and *bap* can also be accumulated by groups of people, such as entire families or communities. Merit can be passed on to others, by women to men and by the living to the dead, the latter especially by ritual acts performed by monks to assist deceased souls. Surviving family members can also engage in activities that will accumulate merit, such as fasting or chanting, and monks can send this merit to the deceased to help them in the afterlife' (2005: 128).

Ceremonial practices that involve giving food, clothing, lodging, medicine, and other necessities to monks enable laypeople to make merit. Monks are regarded as 'fields of merit' since they are believed to emulate the ideals of Buddhist belief and practice (Keyes 1994: 45). Through their personal cultivation, sermons, and ritual acts, monks are expected to help others seek the path to enlightenment. As 'fields of merit,' monks are accorded supreme respect by laypeople who treat them with deferential attitudes and behaviours. This deference is characterized by proscribed etiquettes when speaking or referring to monks, handing them objects with respectful gestures (using both hands), dressing and sitting modestly before them, and in restricting female interaction with them. Cambodian Monks perform ritual services, particularly crematoria, funerary, and memorial rites, as well as provide advice on domestic and business affairs, agricultural and financial matters, and spiritually based medical treatments.

Prior to 1975, Cambodian monasteries were active in giving both traditional Buddhist and modern education, primarily for males (Kalab 1976: 162). During the 1930s, Buddhist institutions of higher learning played a significant role in the development of Khmer nationalism (Keyes 1994: 45–7). Thommayut (Dhammayut) trained Kampuchea Krom monks and *achaa* were recognized as key leaders and architects of Cambodia's nationalist movement, founding the first Khmer-language newspaper and holding important positions in Buddhist and government administrations (ibid.: 49). In 1942, a group of four thousand monks took part in a well-organized demonstration against French colonialism (Boua 1991: 229).

The political dynamics in postcolonial Cambodia and the escalating hostilities in neighbouring Vietnam throughout the 1960s challenged traditional attitudes towards, and expectations of, Buddhism. The head of government, Prince Sihanouk, attempted to modernize Cambodia by reorganizing it as a socialist state supported by new concepts of Buddhist morality (Keyes 1994: 53). Initially, Sihanouk supported the communist Khmer. He favourably contrasted their actions as liberators and patriots with those of the unproductive monks, who in 1969 numbered 65,062 in 3,369 monasteries (primarily Mahanikay) throughout Cambodia (Boua 1991: 228). Sihanouk's emphasis on Buddhist socialism, his attempt at neutrality, and his extensive critiques of U.S. aggression led to his overthrow on 18 March 1970. By this time, the traditional Mahanikay monastic hierarchy and established village system had become increasingly disrupted, especially in areas controlled by the Khmer Rouge, whose power and control increased exponentially in response to the massive American bombing missions over rural Cambodia. Throughout the early 1970s, Khmer Rouge took over village temples and persecuted monks who were non-compliant with their ideologies and actions. Thousands of monks fled to urban temples. By 1972, the Khmer Rouge claimed about two-thirds of the country's rural territory, renaming these areas 'liberated zones' (ibid.).

In government-controlled parts of Cambodia, the monastic population expanded rapidly. Part of the increased interest in monastic ordination and educational training was fuelled by associated advantages in military rank and the possibility of avoiding military conscription (Kalab 1976: 167). The growing concentration of monks in urban monasteries exacerbated the politicization of Buddhism. Lon Nol, head of the Khmer Republic, actively supported the large group of mainly young urban monastics in the hope of reinforcing his own regime. The Khmer Rouge made a clear distinction between monks living in the liberated zones (identified as 'base' or 'patriotic' monks who supported the communist revolution) and those living in the city (Boua 1991: 230). Each side used monks and Buddhist activities to further its own interests. Simultaneously, the Khmer Rouge forced young monks to disrobe and curtailed laypeople's participation in Buddhist festivals and meritmaking activities, especially the feeding of monks or giving donations to them (ibid.). Between 1970 and 1975, the combination of war and bombings resulted in the destruction of more than one-third of the rural temples and thousands of monks and novices were killed, disrobed, or displaced, representing a significant portion of the more than half a million people who died during this time (Keyes 1994: 55).

Following the Khmer Rouge victory in 1975, all temples and monasteries throughout Cambodia were closed, and Buddhist activities and rituals were forbidden, including those concerned with burials and commemorating the dead. Many monasteries became Khmer Rouge compounds used for administrative purposes, torture and execution centres, food storehouses, or animal stalls (Harris 1998). Temple buildings were dismantled for building materials, their libraries destroyed, and Buddhist books burned with their pages used for rolling cigarettes and as toilet paper. The Khmer Rouge smashed shrines, beheaded Buddhist images, chopped up statues, or riddled them with bullets. By the end of 1975, Buddhism was declared to be a 'reactionary religion' and monks regarded as useless parasites (Keyes 1994: 56). Khmer Rouge especially targeted learned monks for 're-education,' which was a euphemism for execution. All urban monks, classified as 'new monks,' were forced to disrobe and were evacuated to rural areas to do hard labour (Boua 1991: 234). Eventually, the 'base' monks, who had earlier supported the Khmer Rouge, were also forced to disrobe. Any evidence of Buddhist practice, such as chanting, lighting incense sticks, shaving the head, or meditating, became cause for reprimands or even execution (ibid.: 235).

Following the defeat of the Khmer Rouge in 1979, estimates suggest that fewer than two thousand monks survived out of the more than sixty-five thousand, most of them having died from starvation, heavy labour, or execution (ibid.: 239). Harris (2005: 45–6) compares the situation immediately after the Khmer Rouge period to that of 1846, when Cambodian Buddhism also suffered massive temple destruction and monastic decline. The institutional and cultural re-establishment of Buddhism at that time provided a precedent and model for rebuilding in 1979.

The Vietnamese communists established control in Cambodia using former factions of the Khmer Rouge. The improvised government tentatively supported the re-establishment of the monastic ordination genealogy and the resumption of traditional rituals. Kampuchea Krom monks from Vietnam were brought in to re-ordain former monks, temples were reopened, and a factory was started to manufacture new Buddha images (Keyes 1994: 61). Measures were also implemented to restrict ordination opportunities to those over the age of fifty; consequently, by 1982, there were only 2,311 monks in several thousand temples (ibid.: 62). After 1988, when the ordination restrictions were lifted, ordinations increased rapidly, rising to 16,400 by 1990, including 6,500 novices (ibid.). The severe shortage of Khmer Buddhist texts and the virtual absence of experienced Buddhist scholars, however, continued to undermine the quality of religious education in Cambodia. A further difficulty has been the extent to which all the Cambodian political leaders (Vietnamese-backed People's Republic of Kampuchea in Cambodia, Coalition Government of Democratic Kampuchea in exile, and current officials) engage in conspicuous acts of Buddhist piety in order to bolster support and legitimacy from both the Cambodian people and international observers. Although much of institutional Buddhism was re-established in the 1990s, the old tensions returned regarding monastic traditionalism, Thommayut expansions, and modernists within the Mahanikay (Harris 2005: 130).

Cambodian refugees who resettled in France, the United States, Canada, and Australia have played pivotal roles in re-establishing Buddhism in Cambodia. Khmer in these countries have financed numerous programs for temple reconstruction in Cambodia in both urban and rural areas. Their donations provide essential support for the health and welfare of monks, the refurbishing of statues and *stupas*, and programs to replace scriptures. They have also contributed to re-establishing Buddhist institutes for higher learning, encouraged Buddhist social activism, and expanded opportunities for monastic scholarship in both Western and other Theravada countries.*

Re-creation of Cambodian Buddhist Beliefs and Practices in Ontario

The demand for qualified and experienced monks to meet the needs of Cambodians resettled in the West has far exceeded the supply (Smith-Hefner 1998). During the 1980s, few monks were available for sponsorship from refugee camps. Most of the monks sponsored from Cambodia during the 1990s were quite young, and potential sponsors were concerned that these young monks had joined the order as a path to education or as a means to escape impoverished conditions. The conditions that affected Buddhism in Cambodia have had serious consequences for Cambodians in Ontario. Several Ontario communities have only recently established their first Buddhist temple with a resident monk, almost twenty-five years after initial resettlement.

Until November 1999, there were only two Cambodian Buddhist temples (*wats*) in Ontario, one in Ottawa and one in Toronto. Three new temples, under the direction of Kampuchea Krom monks and the support of Kampuchea Krom lay leaders, have been established in Hamilton (Wat Khmer Krom Buddhist Temple, 1999), London (Khmer

Buddhist Serey Sousdey Temple, 2001), and Windsor (Wat Khmer Santivararam, 2005). Khmer Buddhist temples outside of Ontario include one in Edmonton under the leadership of Reverend Chea So, the Montreal-based Pagode Khmer du Canada under the guidance of Reverend Hok Savann (one of the highest-ranking Khmer monks in North America), and the Wat Pothi Preuk, also in Montreal, but without a resident monk.[1] The Ottawa temple, known in English as the Ottawa-Hull Cambodian Buddhist Association, was founded in the early 1980s and, currently, is under the direction of a Khmer-speaking Thai monk.[2] There are smaller Cambodian Buddhist associations throughout Ontario, but without a monk or temple.

The Toronto Cambodian Wat, founded and governed by the small Khmer Buddhist and Cultural Community Group, was first organized during the early 1980s. The majority of members were ethnic Khmer, but they also included Sino-Cambodian and Kampuchea Krom.[3] Until 1996, the Toronto Cambodian Wat did not have a permanent Cambodian monk, although one or two *achaa* would be available as well as several *duan chee* (elderly nuns), who daily attended the shrine and recited prayers. One monk who resided at the temple intermittently between 1983 to 1995 was an elderly Kampuchea Krom associated with the Pagode Khmer in Montreal. To provide Buddhist ceremonies, the Toronto temple had to bring in guest monks from Cambodian communities in Montreal or the United States, or use the services of Laotian monks in Toronto, when they were free from their own ethnic community's obligations and responsibilities.

In April 1995, the Toronto Cambodian Buddhist community purchased a large house in Maple (York Region), just north of Toronto, and converted it into a monastic institution.[4] A Chinese shrine was installed on the front veranda, giving Sino-Cambodians the opportunity to offer incense to Kuan Yin and other protector deities. Whereas the original Khmer Buddhist temple in Toronto was within walking distance for many Cambodians, the Maple temple is several miles away from most of their homes and accessible only by car and public transit. With more families moving into the Maple, Vaughan, and Newmarket areas, having a temple within walking distance is no longer anticipated. Initially, neighbours of the Maple temple were hostile to the Cambodian Buddhist presence. For several years, one neighbour used various strategies to reduce the temple's effectiveness: accusing the temple of possible zoning by-law infractions, advocating against temple renovation plans, making complaints about parking, and expressing animosity towards monks. In response, the temple restricted the number of people visiting at any one time, which effectively prevented the holding of communal festivals or children's activities. Additionally, traditional outdoor recreations were modified to prevent outdoor noise, and much of the temple lawn area was paved over for parking. Cambodians were eager to accommodate to the neighbour's requests in order to avoid further misunderstandings, and to demonstrate their willingness for multicultural adaptation. Consequently, the temple hosts only smaller celebrations and ceremonies, such as *Tngay Sil* (observance) days of *Penh Bo* (Full Moon) and *Khe Dach* (No Moon), or smaller group gatherings, such as the *Krom Satrei Shmer Samaki* (Khmer women's group) anniversary. Since Khmer participation in annual ceremonial activities has always been strong, the larger ones continue to be held at rented locations.

Buddhism remains the primary expression of the traditional Cambodian way of life for many Cambodians in Ontario. Much of the traditional culture found in family rituals, cuisine, and language is influenced by Buddhist beliefs and practices. Older Khmer people continue to address each other with *Sompeah* (placing the palms together in a Buddhist gesture of greeting and respect), and annual cultural celebrations and festivals remain linked to Buddhist ceremonies. Whenever possible, Buddhist events are held on auspicious *Tngay Sil* days. The traditional Khmer Buddhist ritual calendar begins with the observance of *Bun Chaul Chhnam* (Cambodian New Year) in mid-April. In Cambodia, this event is a three-day observance, during which family members make every effort to return to their parents' house and to pagodas where their ancestors' relics are stored. On the third day of the celebration, parents are honoured as *Preah Ros* (living Buddhas) and offered money, food, flowers, and a ritual water blessing. Cultural ceremonies, celebrations, and religious observances would always be held at the local Buddhist Pagoda. In Ontario, since the temples are too small to accommodate the large numbers of Khmer (up to 1,500 or more) who attend culturally significant ceremonies, most communities rent a hall or school auditorium for the day.[5] Following the religious portion of ceremonies, meals, popular songs, dances, and fashion shows may be provided. Another reason to hold the festivals and ceremonies in rented locations is to enable the use of loudspeakers for announcements, amplified prayers during monastic chanting, and amplified music as a background for cultural performances, without ensuing complaints from neighbours.

For Cambodians in Toronto, the most significant New Year's observance was held in 1996 to celebrate the purchase and establishment of the Maple temple, and the first successful sponsorship of three monks from Cambodia. Thousands of people attended the morning religious ceremonies (conducted by four Khmer and one Laotian monk), and six hundred tickets available for the evening's entertainment were sold out in advance. Following the religious ceremonies, Khmer children and youth were delighted and many were awestruck by their first exposure to live performances of traditional Cambodian culture. A classical Cambodian dance in beautiful costumes, accompanied by the playing of traditional instruments, was followed by a village folk dance with dancers, drummers, and two huge scarecrows parading around the rented hall. Many young adult Khmer recalled seeing such a folk dance in their early youth in Cambodia; and older people, some with tears streaming down their faces, excitedly told others that the dance brought back memories of the happy times in Cambodia before 1975. The Cambodian Association and the Buddhist community had worked together to present the dances, demonstrating the effectiveness of close cooperative bonds. The Maple temple received the money raised from the ticket sales plus donations given during the religious ceremony.

As most Cambodians in Ontario have neither parents nor memorial relics, they feel that a large part of the New Year's celebration is missing. To alleviate this loss, they get together with as many friends and family as possible. At the 2005 New Year's celebrations in Windsor, about sixty families held a traditional *Preah Ros* ritual, honouring all the community elders as symbolic parents.[6] This innovative ceremony reinforced the teaching that elders, as parents of the community, are manifestations of the Buddha. If monks are available, private *Preah Ros* rituals are also held in people's homes, where family and friends gather to participate in the expressions of honour and respect. Sarorn Sim's 2005 video, *Memories: Celebrations of Remembrance*, depicts a *Preah Ros* ritual in an Ontario family home honouring the mother and father.

After the New Year's celebrations, the next major ceremony is in May to commemorate the birth, enlightenment, and death of the Buddha. This is known as *Visakh Bochea (Bocie or bauchea in* Ebihara et al. 1994*)*. A ceremony at the beginning of the three-month monks' retreat in mid-July, *Chol Preah Vassa (Chaul Vossa* in Ebihara et al. 1994), marks an intensive period of learning and meditation, as well as the preferred time to hold monastic ordinations. Following *Vassa*, community festivals are then held to offer gifts and clothing to the monks. These festivals often feature 'flower money-tree' (*bon pgah*) ceremonies in order to raise funds for the temple.[7] (See Sarorn Sim 2005 video.) A larger flower festival known as *Bun Katin* (*bon phka* in Ebihara et al. 1994) is held in November. The Feast of the Dead or commemoration of ancestors, known as *Prachum Ben* (Douglas 2005; *Phchum ben* in Ebihara et. al. 1994), is held in September or October (see Sarorn Sim 2005 video). In Cambodia, *Prachum Ben* traditionally lasted two weeks and memorials for deceased ancestors took place in people's homes and at local *wats*, each characterized by prayers, chanting, and offerings of food, drink, gifts, and money. Douglas provides a description of a privately hosted *Prachum Ben* in the United States that is similar to those held throughout Ontario:

> An elderly *achaa* oversaw the Prachum Ben commemoration, and the guests, after initially greeting the host and family, went straight to the *achaa* and presented him with money ... Near the *achaa* was a temporary outdoor shrine, incense burning and bundles of gifts wrapped in colored cellophane lying there for the monks. The gifts included coffee, sugar, toothbrushes, and other personal items, the standard package given to monks during Prachum Ben. Those donating the gifts are earning merit for good karma, and the monks would later chant and sprinkle blessings of rose water over them and the other guests. Though this event lasted all through the night and into the next day, most people came and visited for an hour or two before leaving. Only the *achaa* and the host were present for the entire event. (2005: 132)

The nature of the Cambodian Buddhist ceremony, albeit condensed and loosely structured within the North American context, continues to function as both a religious and social event combining Buddhist prayers, communal feasting, adult socializing, and children playing. Before each event, the *achaa* sit at a table near the entrance to collect donations, bless the money, list the amount given, and record the name of each person or family. If the ceremonies are held in a rented hall, people will bring their own mats (*kantel*) to sit on. Before the ceremonies begin, ritual accoutrements such as the Buddha image, incense, and flowers are set up where the monks will sit, either on a stage area or a raised platform built for the occasion. At every festival and ceremony, Cambodian and Buddhist flags are prominent, as is a large banner (in English and/or French and Khmer) identifying the event (see Sarorn Sim 2005 video). Taped Buddhist ceremonial music is often played before and after the monastic chanting. Sometimes musicians will perform traditional music in the *areak ka* and *pin peat* ensemble styles (Sam 1994: 40). The *achaa* lead people in reciting Homage to the Buddha and the Three Refuges; then the monks chant a series of Pali prayers, give blessings, and recite the five precepts to the laypeople. During some celebrations, tables are placed on the lower level in front of the monks and covered with dishes of food. Some are specially prepared Khmer dishes that are only served during special celebrations, due to their cost, scarcity of ingredients, or preparation time. *Ansam* (sticky rice cooked in banana leaf), for example, is traditionally made for *Prachum Ben*. Common food dishes include rice, salads, sweets, and curry or noodle dishes made with chicken, beef, pork, or seafood. Any offerings are acceptable, including fruit, store-bought cookies, donuts, potato chips, or takeout Chinese food. Prior to the religious service, monks ritually bless the food and offer it to the ancestral spirits. When ceremonial observances are finished, the food is first offered to the monks for their own meal, then redistributed for the lay participants as part of their communal feast. During the redistribution, some communities include a cultural program that may feature Cambodian classical and folk dances and singing.

The cultural festivities that accompany traditional ritual celebrations of the New Year are difficult to re-create. April weather in Ontario and limited space inhibit outdoor water festivities, games, feasts, and theatre. Rented halls are set up for religious celebrations, but most cannot accommodate the playing of Cambodian games. Without the games, Ontario youth find it difficult to appreciate or to understand the traditional songs about rice production, buffalos, or Cambodian courting rituals, all of which embody elements of Khmer identity and history. Many of the Cambodian children in Toronto, Hamilton, London, and Windsor have not experienced these games and, therefore, do not associate the Buddhist temple or ceremonies with such pleasurable activities. In Ottawa, when New Year's celebrations are held at the large Foster Farm Community Centre, outdoor Cambodian games can be played in the afternoon after religious ceremonies and the communal feast are finished. The Montreal temple, with its large courtyard and activity rooms, has held these games since the early 1980s. According to elders, the games in Cambodia enabled Khmer teenagers to interact with others of the opposite sex, and flirtations would often lead·to marriage proposals. In Ontario, the games are played mostly by married adults and younger children; only a few teenagers are interested.[8]

At cultural and religious celebrations in Ontario, young and old women wear the traditional Khmer dress of *sarong* (skirt/top) and *krama* (a long scarf) in radiant colours and lustrous fabrics woven from cotton or silk. Older men tend to wear suits and ties, while younger men are casual in shirts and jeans. Some older men who do temple maintenance during the summer may be seen wearing traditional *sampots* (a long wraparound cloth). Buddhist festivals and ceremonies allow people to express traditional Khmer identity. They earn religious merit through their contributions of organizational involvement, attendance, and donations; renew community and friendship ties; and exchange information either privately or through amplified announcements before ceremonies begin. Buddhist events provide an opportunity to showcase Khmer culture to non-Khmer guests, such as local politicians, service workers, friends, and researchers. For many guests, it may be their first experience of traditional Khmer food, music, and dance. The close relationship between traditional Cambodian cultural heritage and Buddhist services, practices, and ceremonies does, however, alienate those who have rejected Buddhist or ancestral beliefs, including Cambodians who converted to Christianity.

Relationships with Khmer temples and monks are both personally and family centred. People come to the temple to make offerings (*Bun Phka*) that celebrate special events marking rites of passage (marriage, birth, death) and auspicious events (finding lost family members). Monks provide healing rituals (such as *p'dah kruoh*, an exorcism and purification ceremony) and blessings for individual needs (*Sang Khatean*) upon request, either at the Buddhist temple or when invited to the home.[9] In Ontario, it is rare to hear anyone speak negatively about Khmer monks, although in the United States, where more monks are available, criticisms are common, particularly concerning their deviations from traditional monastic behaviour (Tauch 2003: 219; Douglas 2003: 164; Smith-Hefner 1999: 25–7). Monastic modifications, however, are deemed necessary for monks in Ontario. Some monks are given a car to drive to school, to reduce their reliance on laypeople and to avoid sitting too close to women on public transit. When engaged in monastic business, such as a visit to someone's house to perform a ceremony, they are still driven by the *achaa*. Because of the harsh Canadian weather, monks wear long underwear, socks, sweaters, shoes or boots, and coats, in addition to their three basic robes. The community also recognizes that the daily alms begging (*Pindabatt*) in Canadian residential neighbourhoods is not practical. The scarcity of monks makes them a valuable resource, and older Khmer particularly are grateful for their presence. A Khmer man from Windsor noted the importance of the presence of monks:

In 1988, we didn't have New Year's, and I didn't even know when New Year's would be … because when we came here we lost all the calendars. We had no dates for Cambodian culture, so we didn't know what time, or what month, or what day … Without a temple or monk, we just prayed with the elder, an *achaa* for the wedding, for the memorial. We have three *achaa* in Windsor now. The *achaa* could lead the prayers. People would have liked to bring in a monk for special occasions but that was difficult. The first time I saw a monk in Canada was in 1998, ten years later. That was the monk from Hamilton, the Venerable Tach Dhammo, the first monk I saw. We invited the monk for the New Year's celebration. After that we got a connection with him. At that time he stayed in Toronto, at the Cambodian temple …

Since then, once people knew there was a monk in Toronto, people started to invite the monk up here. They made the flower money tree, and made the celebration to bring it down to the temple in Toronto. This was a tree special from the people in Windsor. We went around asking for $10 or whatever you can give, and we got all the names, before we went to Toronto. This helped us to start to really know one another. This was in support of Venerable [Tach] Dhammo. Whatever he said, or whatever he did, people really paid attention …

In Windsor, since 1988 we wanted a temple, but the problem was not being able to get a monk. We wanted a temple in our hearts but we could not get the monk, it is hard to get a monk. It is even hard to sponsor a monk on a visitor visa. (personal interview, 2005)

Although some laypeople view the monk's life in Canada as an easy one, most affirm the importance of the monk's role as a spiritual symbol and for performing rituals.[10]

Much of the necessary support required for monastics in Ontario is provided by the *achaa* who do the monks' personal shopping, arrange interviews, drive them to appointments, and handle any *dana* (donations) given to monks or to the temple. The efforts and commitment of the *achaa* is crucial to the daily administration of Ontario Buddhist temples, holding Buddhist ceremonies and rituals, and helping to facilitate people's understanding of Khmer Buddhism. Douglas (2003: 163) notes that one *achaa* at the Khmer temple in Tacoma, Washington, has raised thousands of dollars for building additions to the temple there. Each Cambodian temple in Ontario has at least two full-time *achaa* and several who participate in activities as needed. The position provides these men with venues for intensified Buddhist practice and comes with a highly regarded community leadership profile. *Achaa* are especially respected for their essential role in temple organization, administration, and financial accounting, and for teaching people about Buddhism, guiding them in chanting and proper temple behaviour. They are actively involved in Khmer Buddhist rituals associated with *Tngay Sil* ceremonies, funerals, memorials, exorcisms, blessings, healings, life transition rituals, and fundraising events. Their presence is essential for traditional Cambodian weddings, which in Canada may be held over two days, involving different ceremonies and several changes of clothing.[11]

In Cambodia, the temple served as a combined community and religious centre, providing the space and focus for significant life transition celebrations, ceremonial and social events, and agricultural festivities. Rural temples were a crucial part of children's lives, being the primary institution to give them (especially boys) a rudimentary school education. Monks provided the necessary religious training to shape young men's moral and ethical development. Before a young man was considered eligible for marriage, he was expected to become temporarily ordained as a monk for a short time (usually three months). Although significant as an expression of gratitude towards one's parents, this period of becoming a monk is relatively rare in Ontario. Khmer parents in Ontario continue to rely on temples and Buddhist monks to provide Buddhist education and Khmer cultural classes to youth, but few organized programs are available.[12]

Public forums combined with cultural programs provide an alternative way to involve Ontario Cambodian youth with Buddhism. At the 1997 Cambodian Youth Educational Development Conference in Hamilton, Ontario, guest speakers included the Venerable Hun By, abbot of the Maple temple; Dr Chanthan Chea, vice-president of the Cambodian Buddhist Association in San Diego; and Dr Pheng Kol, founder of the Pannasastra Buddhist University of Cambodia. The Venerable Hun By's opening address reiterated the strong link between Buddhism and Khmer cultural and social identity:

> All Cambodians are influenced by Buddhism. The role of Buddhism is to educate and to assist in the society for people to become good. Buddhism educates people, families, women, and children to know the proper ways to behave through the five precepts (*Sal Prom*). What is right for the individual is right for society. As individuals you have to think about your feelings and that of others. You are not to lie and you need to obey parents and elders. You need to find the right way to educate the younger genera-

tion to preserve the history and the heritage of Cambodia. You are the first generation here to create this. As such, you need to understand the consequences of your actions, this is Buddhism. Buddhism is for the families, to make people aware, to be cautious at all times. In a family with children, Buddhism teaches the proper role, the respect. This is the main purpose of Buddhism, to show the good way ... Thank you to all the Cambodians who have worked so hard and still continue to make this education. The youth are the future of the nation, so please preserve our culture and heritage for a long time. Please preserve for the next generation to come. (Cambodian Youth Educational Development Conference, 1997)

In support of the Venerable Hun By's comments, a young Khmer man noted that Buddhism has helped him to understand the multifaith context of Toronto:

Buddhism is a religion to find the truth, the peace. It is located not just in the temple, but everywhere. It also teaches you that others may have their own religion but this is also part of what Buddhism teaches, that you need to educate yourself about others. (personal interview, 1997)

Although relatively rare, ordination ceremonies provide an opportunity for younger Khmer men and boys to engage in structured religious activities with Khmer Buddhist monks and the temple. Temporary ordination entails a young man's sacrifice for others, and this ritual marks an important stage in the Cambodian community's ability to recreate traditional Buddhism. Douglas and Mam note that ordination is also used to lessen negative influences, such as gangs and violence, that young men may encounter (2005: 63). Montreal has held ordination ceremonies since the early 1980s, and over the years several young Khmer men from Ottawa have participated there. The first Khmer ordinations in Toronto took place in 1995. The location was on a large rented boat that toured the harbour, similar to Ontario Lao ordination events (Van Esterik 2003). Subsequent ceremonies have been held at the Maple and Hamilton temples. Some young men take ordination with the aspiration to make a serious, long-term commitment to monastic life, but their difficulties in learning Pali prayers and Buddhist rituals and adhering to Vinaya precepts cause them to leave after a few months. Older Khmer men who wish to leave lay activities (employment, marriage) tend to have an easier transition to monasticism, and they are found in several Ontario temples.

The Kampuchea Krom Buddhist Temple in Hamilton held an innovative ordination ceremony that included females. Over a two-day period (6 and 7 July 2002) during *vassa* (the traditional rainy season), ten young men and four young women participated in an ordination ceremony under the direction of five Khmer monks and one Caucasian monk. The Venerable Hok Savann was invited from Montreal, and two Khmer monks came from Washington. The young men undertook the ten precepts required of novice monks, and the young women took eight precepts as *duan chee* (committed religious women). The ordination ceremony concluded with the male novices being given begging bowls, monastic robes, and detailed instructions on how to adhere to the ten precepts and to follow seventy-five monastic rules. They were reminded that their new *samanera* (novice) status made them worthy of respect and differentiated them from ordinary laypeople. Most of the youth were ordained only for a few days, but some of the young men stayed several weeks until they returned to school in September (one staying even longer). In the few weeks following the ordination ceremony, the male novices visited the Theravada Sinhalese temple in Mississauga and the Venerable Hok Savann's temple in Montreal. They were also taken on public outings (e.g., walking in downtown Toronto) to raise awareness of Cambodian Buddhism, since non-Khmer tend to be curious about the young monks in their robes and will ask questions of them. The young female *duan chee* were not included in these activities. They did not receive alms bowls, and their duties were not to act as *samaneras*, but to provide service to the monks at the temple through cooking and cleaning. When asked why they chose to be ordained, the young men and women indicated that part of their wish was to 'pay back' their parents who had done so much for them.[13] A young Toronto man who took temporary ordination as a Buddhist monk in 1997 stated he did so because he was engaged to marry a woman in Cambodia and his ordination would show respect for his mother and future in-laws.

Women's Involvement in Buddhism

Khmer girls and young women are generally not encouraged to seek Buddhist education or training at the temple. The representative decision making, and positions of secular and sacred authority remain firmly with men. Women's participation is limited to worship, temple caretaking, and domestic service for religious celebrations, such as preparing and offering food to monks and ancestral spirits. During

Khmer Buddhist ceremonies in Ontario, women and girls participate in merit-making rituals, listen to Pali prayers and blessings, and recite the precepts. While the women and girls sit on mats during the monk's prayers and sermons, younger men and boys are usually elsewhere in the temple (or rented hall) playing or just standing around waiting until the religious observances end and the communal feast begins. Unlike other Buddhist women in Ontario, few Cambodian women have developed new concepts of self-expression, service to their community, or leadership opportunities in Buddhist contexts (McLellan 1999). One middle-aged woman in Ottawa is so familiar with the different types of chanting available at the temple, and the monastic and lay rules governing *achaa* activities, that several Khmer have suggested she serve as an *achaa*. She would be willing to assume the duties, but is concerned about the negative attitudes and perceptions of others towards her if she did move into a traditionally male role.

The low status of Khmer Buddhist women limits their ability to access or create innovative educational, cultural, and spiritual programs. Theravada Buddhist monks traditionally view women with apprehension because females are potential temptresses who may lure monks from their vows of chastity (Ebihara 1974). In Ontario, Cambodian monks are still forbidden to be alone with a woman, to touch women casually, or to even engage in social conversation with them. Only elderly women are able to establish close ties with monks. At local Buddhist temples many elderly women engage in spiritual opportunities beyond that of merit-making contributions, for example, attending meditation retreats during the time of *Chol Preah Vasa*. When their last child marries, older women in Ontario often become ordained as *duan chee* (also referred to as *yeay chee*). As committed religious women, *duan chee* follow eight to ten precepts, wear white robes, and live in or near the temple. Although referred to as nuns in English, they are not considered as *samaneras* or novice *Bhikkhunis*. In exchange for domestic duties, *duan chee* receive Buddhist teaching and meditation instruction from the monks, and are given the chance to establish a peaceful life for themselves within the temple. Most retain close ties to their families, frequently tending grandchildren and returning home during traditional Buddhist celebrations or for longer periods of time. Through their dedication to Buddhism and conscientious practice, *duan chee* earn considerable respect. They are acknowledged as wise women, and trusted to avoid slanderous gossip and being judgmental of others, enabling other Khmer to turn to them for advice and to share emotional difficulties. The several *duan chee* associated with the Toronto and Ottawa Khmer temples are said to be of great benefit to those Khmer women who still face the emotional problems of grief, trauma, loss, isolation, and family difficulties. Because most *duan chee* are elderly and illiterate, however, many educated Khmer and youth raised in Canada feel that the *duan chee* cannot offer the level of mental health counselling or family and social advice that they need.

Importance of Traditional Religious Beliefs and Practices for Positive Mental Health

Many Ontario resettlement agencies did not provide services to Khmer in ways that were culturally familiar. An exception was the Somerset Community Health Centre in Ottawa, which utilized the local Cambodian temple to provide an educational program for older Khmer women who felt comfortable being there. Ontario's separation of its service provision from culturally familiar venues is in sharp contrast to the close cooperation between Quebec's Communauté Khmere du Canada (Khmer Community Association) and the Pagode Khmer du Canada (Khmer Temple) in Montreal; a closeness also observed in Quebec City (Dorais 1991). With the majority of Cambodians in Ontario being Theravada Buddhist, more culturally familiar services could have facilitated long-term adaptation and integration, and enhanced levels of community trust and support for service providers and agencies (Canda and Phaobator 1992). In the absence of support services, Buddhist temples become more important as religious, cultural, and community centres, especially in assisting with mental health concerns.

Intertwined with the morality and ethics of Theravada Buddhism, first-generation Cambodians hold strong beliefs with regard to astrology, the supernatural, and a complex array of spirits. Spirits include the *tivoda* (Hindu deities assimilated into the Buddhist pantheon), *hau pralung* (wandering soul spirits also referred to as *hav praloeng/hau bralin*), and a variety of guardian *neak ta* and ancestral *meba* (Harris 2005: 59; Men 2002: 224). Nineteen *pralung/bralin* soul spirits are said to animate the human body, but they tend to wander. Thompson (1996) refers to the *Hau Bralin* (Calling of the Souls) as one of Cambodia's earliest vernacular texts that is recited during ritual celebrations to call wandering souls back into the body of their proper owner. The *hau pralung/braling* ritual is especially necessary during periods of personal transition, rites of passage, and illness. It also plays a crucial role in reconstructing individual and communal Khmer identity after someone has stayed in a foreign land. Through the ritual, any wandering spirits are invited back and reintegrated into their proper seat within the body (Harris 2005: 59). *Neak ta* spirits can be solitary individuals (*cah srok*),or hierarchically organized into families. They can include guardian, ancestral, territorial, and animistic categories, all of which can be benign or malevolent. *Neak ta* are also dynamic spirits, capable of being created and able to shift their place of residence (ibid.: 52–3; Men 2002: 230; Smith-Hefner 1999: 40). Rituals associated with *neak ta* may be simple blessing vows, formal ceremonies, or the monastic recitation of protective verses (*parittas*) to counteract serious difficulties (major illnesses, famine, accidents).

Many *neak ta* invocation rituals 'raise up the ancestors' (*loeng neak ta*), and are oriented towards general protection, health, community welfare, and happiness (Harris 2005: 55). Ancestral *neak ta* (some of which are referred to as *meba*) are considered to be spirits of the dead, usually from specific deceased persons. They are regularly offered food and drink, especially during Buddhist ceremonies, death day memorials, and life passage events (such as naming days or weddings) to watch over living members of the family and intervene during difficult times. If ancestral *neak ta* are not given the proper deference and consideration, or have been offended, they can also bring illness and other trouble (Men 2002: 230–1). Personal health is an inseparable aspect of maintaining one's relationships with family members, both alive and dead (Ong 2003: 104). In Ontario, older Khmer from rural backgrounds attribute their illnesses or misfortunes to angry ancestral spirits, and their fear of arousing this anger remains strong. They explain that their physical symptoms of malaise, lack of energy, and little interest in oneself or others (classic symptoms of depression and post-traumatic stress) are manifestations of spirits who deprive them of their vital life-sustaining essence. Their life failures or ruptures in personal social networks are also considered to be symptomatic of this spiritual dis-ease.

Ritual specialists called *Krou/gru Khmer* have traditionally used herbal remedies, astrology, fortune-telling, magic, sorcery, and talismans to both access the *neak ta* spirit world and to provide protection from it (Harris 2005: 59). Since many *Krou Khmer* in Cambodia were also Buddhist monks, they were regarded as spiritual healers who could divine the cause of a person's illness or misfortune and provide treatment through prayers, blessings, or mediation with spirits (Eisenbruch 1992). In resettlement, *Krou Khmer* are distinct from Khmer monks but continue to provide spiritual and medical treatment based on *neak ta* principles (e.g., preparing special amulets or blowing on the body). Reynell (1989: 162) notes that these traditional Khmer healers were predominant in treating stress and anxiety disorders within the refugee camps. To cure disease or emotional problems, *Krou Khmer* healers metaphorically enter the world of the patient's distress, identify the spiritual and somatic causes, then drive the spirits from the body (Eisenbruch 1992). Men (2002) notes that in America more elaborate healing rituals are not performed due to the absence of ritual specialists, performers, and musical ensembles. Due to the traditional relationship of *Krou Khmer* and Buddhist monks, however, older Cambodians continue to associate spiritual healing and medical treatment based on *neak ta* principles with Buddhism and Buddhist temples. Many Ontario Khmer from rural backgrounds have had Buddhist prayers and animistic symbols tattooed on their bodies to enhance mental and physical health. There are only a few practising *Krou Khmer* in Ontario Cambodian communities (one in Hamilton and two or three in Toronto), not enough to meet the needs, especially of older Khmer. For consultations, Cambodians in Ontario must travel long distances at considerable costs in time and money. In the United States, *Krou Khmer* do a flourishing trade, attending to sick people who simultaneously use Western drug therapy (Ong 2003: 110). Spirit mediums (*mnuh chaul rup*) and astrological specialists (*a krou teay*), distinct from the *Krou Khmer*, are also said to be active in American Khmer communities (Smith-Hefner 1999). Since these specialists are rare in Ontario, Cambodians consult with their local *achaa* to determine suitable astrological dates for planned special events (weddings, house/business moves, commemoration ceremonies).

In the mid-1990s, many Ontario Khmer stated that the diverse somatic complaints that troubled them (headaches, dizziness, stomach pain, fatigue, joint aches, and general pain – *chheu*) were related to *neak ta* (McLellan 1995). The pain is often associated with emotional anxiety regarding conflicts in social and interpersonal relationships or stressful situations (Marcucci 1994: 132). Eisenbruch (1991) identified these pervasive ailments as *chii kbaal*, and considered it a Cambodian sickness specific to resettlement. Another common *neak ta* affliction is the experience of *sramay* (ghost haunting), caused by the visitation of spirits (*kmauit or khmoch*) of family members or other loved ones who were murdered and not given proper burial rites. During the Khmer Rouge regime, numerous Khmer witnessed the death or disappearance of family members, and were forced to abandon sick and starving relatives during their many evacuations. Bodies were left out in the open, by the side of the road, thrown down wells, or placed in mass graves, instead of being cremated. The Khmer Rouge did not permit funerals and death rituals, crying or displays of grief were severely punished, and there was no food to offer the deceased spirits. A Hamilton Khmer man commented:

> When our parents and family members died, there was no time to do funerals. They died then like cats and dogs. Here we only have one annu- al memorial day celebration to send prayers and merit, and we can only afford to bring in one or two monks. Some people have gone back to Cam- bodia so they can do a 'formal' funeral service with at least four monks. Without this there is still much suffering. (personal interview, 1994)

Cambodians have said that when they dream of dead or missing fam- ily members they believe the ghosts are angry at them for their neglect and will punish or possess them. The psychological disturbances caused by spirits are difficult for Cambodians to convey to non-Khmer doctors, especially when most Western mental health practitioners are trained and regulated by the norms of American psychiatry based on the Diagnostic and Statistical Manual for Mental Disorders Categories and Measurements (DSM). When *neak ta* symptoms are left untreat- ed through the lack of *Krou Khmer* mediation or the ritual prayers of Buddhist monks, people's emotional and spiritual suffering manifest in physical ailments, social withdrawal, and mental anguish. Regrets, depression, guilt, and grief weigh heavily on the minds of many Cambo- dians in resettlement (Eisenbruch 1991; Mollica et al. 1987; Kinzie 1988; Rumbaut 1991; Tenhula 1991; McLellan 1995). There are striking simi- larities between the symptoms of chronic, unresolved grief and those of post-traumatic stress disorder (PTSD) (Boehnlein 1987). Responses to these emotions (denial, preoccupation, or acceptance) become part of an individual's mental health. For Cambodians, however, the term 'mental health' is not easily understood. As Tenhula notes, emotional or psychological problems are seen as essentially private issues: 'Talking about them indicates a lack of discretion and taste. Because hardships and suffering are considered as givens that are part of everyone's life, there is no point in complaining. To do so is a sign of weakness that denotes a lack of character. If in the end help is sought, it should be from a close relative, never a stranger. "For a Cambodian to talk with a psychiatrist about such personal problems," said former professor and judge Phat Mau, "is unthinkable, it just does not happen. That is strictly a Western thing to do"' (1991: 86).

In the mid-1990s, Cambodians still felt that it was culturally inappropriate to talk with an outsider about such personal problems. The only Khmer worker for Hong Fook, an Asian mental health clinic in Toronto explained:

> The majority of Cambodians have mental health problems. But every time I ask about flash-backs or depression, there is a flat denial, people don't want to talk about it or even admit it. My biggest problem is that I am identified as a 'mental health' worker. People deny that they have mental problems. This is an area for shame and no one wants the label of being associated with 'mental health.' In Cambodia, the focus on mental health was always a focus on negative, worst-case mental illness. I try to ask people how they deal with stress and the factors associated with stress. People are afraid to admit they have stress. People don't want to receive attention from Hong Fook. Even when I am called in by the school, people don't want to admit. People only come with crisis situations, but even then when the crisis is not so intense, they back down again. There is no long-term resolution of problems. People just say everything is all right, even when it is obvious there are lots of problems. (personal interview, 1994)

In Cambodia, there is no tradition of mental health services, and mental health problems were hidden in families. If healing or behaviourial consulting were required, people turned to Buddhist monks and *Krou Khmer*. In London, a Cambodian service worker commented:

> Here there are no Buddhist services for Cambodians to help them express their fear or deep feelings of mental problems. If Cambodians do come to an agency for mental help, be aware that they must be really low or depressed, in a crisis, to even begin to try and share. (personal interview, 1994)

Even in Asian-centred mental health clinics, talking, or group therapies based on Western psychiatric models have not been effective (Eisenbruch 1991; Mollica et al. 1987; Kinzie 1988; Rumbaut 1991; Tenhula 1991). As Ong notes: 'Cambodians had survived war, labor camps, and flight by becoming masters in the contest between self-willed silence and forced confession ... Silence and opacity became a shield of defense in the face of authority ... Thus in practice, treatment often entailed a struggle between silences and truths' (2003: 107).

For most Khmer, talking of past traumas is considered culturally appropriate only between those close relatives and friends who form part of their immediate social support networks. It took several years for a small group of Khmer women at Hong Fook to form close bonds with one another. For many older Khmer in Ontario, traditional healers and monks remain the only trusted source of wisdom and knowledge to explain the causes and cessation of suffering in their life. But, the lack of Buddhist monks and traditional Khmer specialists meant that few were able to access this culturally significant system of healing, guidance, and support. There has been little sensitivity to their psychological needs, as one Hamilton man pointed out:

> There are no programs here for our sleeplessness, tears at night, or awareness of the starvation that killed our families. There is no understanding by health care workers of our emotional or cultural needs. (personal interview, 1994)

The lack of professionally trained Khmer mental health counsellors to assess the personal and social consequences of excessive trauma reduces the possibility to provide culturally sensitive programs (particularly effective religiously based therapeutic interventions). It also creates further misunderstandings of psychological concerns presented through somatic symptoms. The one Khmer-speaking physician in Ontario was a Christian, and several Khmer noted their reluctance to discuss *neak ta* complaints with him. In California, Dr Chhean Kong, community services coordinator of the Long Beach Asian Pacific Mental Health Program and abbot of Wat Khermara Buddhikaram (Cambodian Buddhist temple), states that almost 90 per cent of their Cambodian clients still have recurrent nightmares about their time under the Khmer Rouge and continue to seek spiritual intervention (2003: 75). In Ontario, Khmer psychological disturbances remain largely untreated.

When emotional and spiritual suffering and chronic grief are unresolved, pervasive anxiety is created that permeates through families into the second generation (Boehnlein 1987; Terr 1989). Younger Cambodians raised in the West tend to be dismissive of spirit-based concerns, further alienating themselves from understanding or appreciating traditional cultural frameworks of meaning that would help them to deal with their parents' anxiety or lingering grief. In recent years, clinics in California, Oregon, Minnesota, and Massachusetts, have observed an increasing number of younger Cambodian clients, some of whom were traumatized in childhood, but more who grew up in households with adults who had experienced atrocities and transmitted their PTSD to the second generation (Kong 2003: 67). To date, the only attempt to address the consequences of stress on the mental health of Cambodian youth in Ontario has been through the combined efforts of the Toronto Cambodian Association and the Hong Fook Mental Health Clinic. They produced a fifteen-minute video in 2005 called *Life beyond the Rain* that highlights current generational and gender issues and promotes positive mental health through Hong Fook counselling sessions. The lack of Ontario medical and mental health professionals to study and treat Khmer concepts of well-being, and Khmer somatic idioms of personal and social distress, means that culturally sensitive systems for healing, guidance, and support may eventually be lost to the younger generation.

Boehnlein (1987) identified a new concept, *sateh aram* (moral sickness), that particularly affects Cambodian refugees in America. When asked, Cambodians in Ontario did not identify the concept as such, but did acknowledge a decline of traditional ethical and moral attitudes and behaviour within families and throughout the community. Many felt the decline was due to the absence of Buddhist monks during the first fifteen years of resettlement when they were left without a traditional model of high moral development to emulate or seek advice from. Cambodian women, especially, lamented their limited opportunities to do meritorious deeds on behalf of their loved ones, living and deceased. Without an easily accessible monk or temple, the shared rituals of Buddhist practice that could help to integrate individuals with the community and reinforce Khmer social ties were not available. Payne (1990: 3) found that the lack of opportunity for sharing in communal celebrations increased the social withdrawal common in people who have undergone extensive trauma and loss. Cultural and personal bereavement was significantly greater in Khmer resettlement communities that did not participate in traditional Buddhist ceremonies (Eisenbruch 1991: 674).

Kong (2003: 68) presents the Buddhist temple as the most conducive environment to help Khmer cope with their past, preserve their cultural heritage, and adapt to the present, as they discuss conflicts or problems faced in their new society. At the Wat Khemara Buddhikaram in Long

Beach, California, there are several monks who provide counselling services through Eastern psychotherapy, prayers, meditation, and group discussions, creating an environment where 'depressed, distressed, frustrated, and sorrowful people [come] to receive blessings and relief from their burdens' and thereby enhance their mental health (ibid.: 70). The abbot encourages Cambodians who meet at the temple for meals or events to talk about their trauma experiences and their memories. It has become more acceptable for Cambodians in small groups to discuss intensely personal issues when they gather together there. They share experiences about their forced march into the countryside, about separations from family members, about walking over the dead and dying, about witnessing violence, murder, torture, and horrific cruelty, about starvation and deprivation, and they talk about the things they did to survive (ibid.: 73–4). In contrast, at the Maple temple in Ontario, only the abbot, the Venerable Hun By, has the knowledge and experience to discuss these issues with people. Older Khmer highly appreciate the opportunity he provides to participate in monastic daily prayers and temple activities. As one fifty-year-old woman noted:

> When I have trouble sleeping, I often come to the temple to help out with the daily chores, such as grocery shopping and tending to the garden. In the summertime I usually come to the temple on the weekends for six to eight hours a day. (personal interview, 2003)

Most other temples in Ontario have monks who are either too young to understand the complex mental health and community issues, or who did not experience the Khmer Rouge regime.

Challenges in Monastic Leadership

From the mid-1990s, Cambodians in several Ontario communities have actively worked towards sponsoring and retaining monks from Cambodia. Because many Cambodian monks are relatively young, however, there are problems. Some are not skilled or experienced enough to deal with people's personal issues, and others give up their monastic vows ('disrobe') shortly after arriving in Canada, to seek employment or marriage. During the early 1980s, the Montreal temple sponsored five Khmer monks from Thai refugee camps, and all of them disrobed within their first year. In 1994, one of two monks sponsored from Cambodia by the Khmer Buddhist and Cultural Community of Toronto disrobed soon after arrival, as did another monk in 1997. Younger Cambodian monks currently in Ontario (whether on visa or sponsored) are encouraged to learn English and attain higher education. This enables some to obtain their driver's licence if a car is made available for them. During evenings and weekends, they assume full-time duties as monastics. Ontario community leaders note that an educated or knowledgeable Khmer monk willing to address people's difficulties and engage in a process of community advancement is considered·an embodiment of community well-being and a powerful symbol capable of pulling people together. These Buddhist monks are given enormous respect and trust, and Khmer people will listen more to their views and opinions than to those of any other community leader. Leaders from the Toronto Cambodian Buddhist community consider themselves fortunate to have such a monk in the presence of the Venerable Hun By. A community leader from Windsor discussed his community's concern with finding a similar kind of monk:

> With our people, we know a lot about the monks' rules, and we pay attention to that. We need to have the monks who are experienced. If we have the young monks we cannot learn too much from them, because they have just started. We need the monks who have been a monk for about ten or fifteen years, who have the experience. They have to know about the religion, about Buddhism, about the problems of families. A young monk doesn't know what he has to do. When you get older, you have more experience, and you understand about working hard, about taking care, about maintaining things. The more someone does, the more thinking they have to take care of things ...
>
> Even from the [Thai refugee] camps, if there were monks, it was really hard to get them out. Now it is not much better. The monk here is from Hamilton, and is just at Windsor temporarily, but he is still in the process of being sponsored. When we sponsor, we have to ask for a specific monk. We can find out the name of a good monk because we have family and friends back home and can get information on who to search for to come to Canada ... Also he must be a good monk, and be willing to stay here and work for the community, not just for their own personal. The monk must put the community first.
>
> Finally, we found some monk who will be good for the community. We are communicating with him for the last three years ... The monk we are in the process of sponsoring is from Cambodia, but has Kampuchea Krom parents. (personal interview, 2005)

As Van Esterik (2003: 55) notes among resettled Lao Buddhists, choosing, attracting, and supporting a monk in a North American city is a complex process, fraught with practical and political problems. Immigration selection procedures within Canada regard potential monastic candidates as unskilled and therefore problematic immigrants in their potential for future dependence on government support (ibid.: 57). In Ontario, the process for sponsoring Khmer monks from Cambodia became even more difficult with the Thai refugee camps closing in the early 1990s (emphasizing repatriation rather than resettlement), and the continuing absence of a Canadian consulate in Cambodia. All Ontario applications must now be vetted through Thailand, a country that community leaders throughout Ontario say continually rejects their sponsorship applications for Buddhist monks from Cambodia. It is felt that the Thai officials involved do not have any understanding or sympathy for their applications and actively work against them. Some leaders note that they were pressured to sponsor monks from Thailand instead of from Cambodia. A monk from Hamilton commented on some of the difficulties he has encountered:

The only monks from here are myself and [monk's name], who came from Battambang about three years ago. We are in the process of doing his residency application. We still have problems with sponsorship, even just for periods of extended study. I went with [a Caucasian monk from Hamilton] to Thailand to help process the visas, but this didn't work. So the monks went to India to study. In London, for example, there is only one monk to meet the ceremonial and spiritual needs, but this is not enough. Despite our explanation that these monks are needed for services, it still doesn't help. Even we asked [former MPP], but she also said it was difficult. (personal interview, 2005)

Temporary measures continue to prevail: inviting monks from Cambodia to visit for a year then applying to extend their visa, bringing monks in on a short-term visitor visa for one or two months, or borrowing monks from other cities to facilitate major Buddhist celebrations and other ritual necessities. In contrast, the United States has an extremely supportive sponsorship program to bring monks from Cambodia. The large community populations that settle around a Buddhist temple illustrate the extraordinary importance of both Khmer monks and Buddhist practices (Chan 2003: 36).

The few Cambodian monks in Ontario are faced with constant

demands. They administer to the needs of lay members, conduct a range of ceremonial and ritual services, do community outreach, are available for consultation, undertake their own educational pursuits, and engage in spiritual cultivation. Community expectations of monks remain high, perhaps unreasonable. While initial adaptive and integrative concerns of unemployment, illiteracy, welfare dependence, language, and educational difficulties are being resolved, widespread psychological and emotional distress continues and is particularly manifested in family tensions and intergenerational dynamics. Khmer monks in Ontario are under enormous pressure to heal traumatized individuals, fragmented families, and community distrust. Although they may be well trained in Buddhist monastic liturgy and ritualism, many monks have no training in family counselling or community development. Yet, they are still viewed by many first-generation Khmer as the most culturally familiar means to address their needs in resettlement. Cambodians in Ontario greatly value the presence of young monks from Cambodia, but continually worry that expectations from the community may be too much of a strain and cause them to disrobe. The monks are under pressure to perform miracles and to overcome people's concerns that they will somehow fail.

In contrast to monks from Cambodia, many of the Kampuchea Krom monks in North America are well educated and speak English as well as Khmer. The educational and linguistic abilities of Kampuchea Krom monks make them attractive candidates for Cambodian communities in resettlement. Kampuchea Krom are especially sensitive to the difficulties that religious and cultural minorities face in trying to maintain traditional language, culture, and religion in an unsupportive environment or social system designed to eliminate it.[14] The three newest temples in Ontario (Hamilton, London, and Windsor) have all been established through the efforts of Kampuchea Krom individuals and their transnational associations.[15] The monks presiding in each temple are all Kampuchea Krom (either from Vietnam or Cambodia), as are the majority of directors and the *achaa*. It is feasible that the successful strategies employed by Kampuchea Krom to preserve an ethnic Khmer identity in Vietnam could be utilized by ethnic Khmer from Cambodia to help develop and maintain their Buddhist identity in Canada. The Kampuchea Krom model of resistance could support the relevancy of Buddhist religious beliefs, identities, and practices among the second and succeeding generations of Khmer, especially against secular and material alternatives.

Unfortunately, while Kampuchea Krom recognize the important role of Buddhism in helping to retain a Kampuchea Krom minority identity here for their own children, they seem to be less willing to organize and work together with Khmer from Cambodia.[16] One reason may be that the roles and activities of Kampuchea Krom temples and monks are different from those in rural Cambodia. Monasticism among the Kampuchea Krom is seen as a long-term vocation providing an essential support to help their people retain identity. In contrast, the majority of Buddhist temples in Cambodia are not seen as 'progressive' or 'modern,' and young men are usually encouraged to become monks only for a short phase in their lives. One Kampuchea Krom monk felt that these differences were related to the Kampuchea Krom's significant affiliation with the Thommayut (Dhammayut) modernist approach to Buddhism. Harris notes that the Kampuchea Krom were a significant part of the Thommayut (Dhammayut) reformers in Cambodia who attempted to break the connection between the practice of Khmer Buddhism with its agrarian environment (2005: 75). Hansen states that the Dhammayut identified more with the 'pure' expressions of Khmer culture and authentic aspects of Theravada Buddhism, particularly its moral values and teachings (2007: 14).

The Ontario Kampuchea Krom monks are part of a tradition that has encouraged monastics to go overseas for secular and higher monastic education, and to become acquainted with modern media technology to retain links with Kampuchea Krom outside of Vietnam (director of the Kampuchea Krom National Association of Canada, personal communication). Kampuchea Krom monks in Ontario are active in the United Association of Kampuchea Krom Buddhist Monks and regularly attend annual transnational meetings in Australia, France, the United States, Canada, Cambodia, and Vietnam. They also actively participate in interracial and interfaith forums in Ontario to help raise the profile of Khmer Theravada Buddhism and Kampuchea Krom concerns.

Differing expectations regarding the activities and leadership in Ontario Buddhist temples arise between Khmer from Cambodia and Kampuchea Krom. At the London temple, for example, although there are three Kampuchea Krom monks available to provide traditional religious services and rituals (blessings, prayers, memorials, purification ceremonies, New Year's celebrations), there are no youth or children's programs for Khmer language instruction and cultural activities. Khmer from Cambodia have noted that the majority of financial support is from non-Kampuchea Krom members, and some feel that Kampuchea Krom monks have little concern with the local Khmer community and their needs (other than the provision of Buddhist ritual services). It is recognized that Kampuchea Krom do not share the same collective memories and experiences, and that their underlying reasons for establishing and developing Buddhist temples are different. Some Khmer note that Kampuchea Krom monks and laity prefer to remain active primarily within their own institutional networks and political concerns, and to maintain close affiliation with the Kampuchea Krom temple in Hamilton.

During interviews, Kampuchea Krom monks and leaders spoke extensively of their activities with other Kampuchea Krom and with the situation in Vietnam. They gave little attention to the resettlement difficulties that Khmer from Cambodia face: for example, struggles in re-creating community bonds and networks, and maintaining Cambodian healing traditions. If the Kampuchea Krom monks' intense involvement with their own associations and agendas continues to leave them less aware or concerned with the specific needs of Khmer from Cambodia and their Canadian-born children, future developments in several Ontario Cambodian communities could include challenges to leadership (monastic and lay) and the administration of local Buddhist temples. Thach (2003: 262) notes the court case concerning the ownership of a temple in Tacoma, Washington, where the majority of Khmer members from Cambodia are attempting to remove the Kampuchea Krom name in favour of a more generic Khmer profile, and to introduce a more democratic style of leadership. Khmer from Cambodia have already raised questions concerning the name of the Khmer Kampuchea Krom Buddhist Temple in Hamilton, especially when the majority of Khmer who attend are from Cambodia, and only the monastic leadership and executive directors are Kampuchea Krom.

Generational Tensions

Older Khmer in Ontario hold traditional views regarding the activities and involvements of monks. Their focus is on a monk's exemplary role as spiritual and ritual specialist, his adherence to the Vinaya (monastic discipline/rules for deportment, eating, etc.), and a carefully regulated participation in the affairs of secular society and with laity. Concerns arise among the first generation when monks change or expand their roles in the community, particularly when interacting with the second generation, thus bringing into question whether the traditional system of monks and temples can be sustained in Canada. There are tensions between the conflicting needs of the generations. During a private 2002 meeting, a small group of Cambodian young men raised various issues about their participation and relationship with the local temple:

First youth: Youth here are concerned that only old people are coming to the temple and wonder what will happen in ten years.
Second youth: The idea is that the temple should be more close to the community, to keep in touch; to have the monk more active in the community. Young people don't know why they go to the temple and why they participate in the ceremonies. After ten years, they all seem the same.
Third youth: When [one of the youth present] was a monk in Montreal, he played badminton with the kids and they loved it. This is what the monk needs to do, to become more involved with the youth.
Fourth youth: We don't have a meeting place, no space for youth activities.
Fifth youth: We suggested a meditation class, but there are no books, no teaching. Also the monk did not think that people would come, and he said that he was too busy.

Cambodian youth want more active monastic involvement in their lives, modern teaching formats, and more personable monks to whom they can relate. The older generation tend to have lower expectations on the quality of the monk's personality or ability to interact socially, being more grateful for the rituals, blessings, and religious presence. In return, they show traditional forms of respect to the monks. Some youth expressed a fear of interacting with the monks because they do not know how to behave properly. One young man noted his difficulties in approaching the monks at the temple because of this:

I've never been able to talk to the monks. I just never had the opportunity to talk to them because I'm afraid I might do things that might upset them. When a monk passes by you, you have to bow your head down, and put your hands together. And I don't want to offend them by any way of not doing it right. And some of my words may not be acceptable to them, because the monks have different words for everything. Right now, I am hesitant to approach the monks. I am concerned about not knowing the right behaviour.
    This concern plays a big role in why a lot of young people don't talk [to] or connect with the monks. For instance, you want to thank the monk and you touch his hand, I believe that it is wrong, because, I don't know, I just

think it's wrong. And if I was to do that in front of all these adults, they would be like, 'Oh, why are you doing that, you can't do that!' The older adults are very critical, even the friends. When a monk comes by, you have to behave, unless you are really old or something. (personal interview, 2005)

A youth leader actively involved with Buddhism in his community, discussed his concerns that youth needs are not being recognized by existing temple elders:

At first, we just wanted to have the group affiliated with the temple, but for a variety of reasons it wouldn't work out. The elders want and need to be acknowledged for leadership roles. Older people resisted the idea of the youth group because the youth weren't organized yet and the older people had too much of their old way of thinking and had specific ideas. There was no immediate support for the youth ideas, just 'No, it won't work.' So, it seems the process with the elders is to have the youth prove themselves first and only then will they actually look. At this point, people at the temple are very comfortable, and they don't want to see any change. They don't see any new level of interactions, or the need for them. (personal interview, 2003)

Several Ontario Khmer youth noted that all the Buddhist ceremonies seem similar, with the same things being said and the same format. Many admitted that they don't know why they go to the temple or what the ceremonies mean, and that they can barely recite the simplest prayers. One youth explained:

When I go to the temple, or to the celebrations, no one tells what it is for. I just show up. Every New Year they always have a monk bless the community and stuff like that, but I wasn't interested in it. I am not a strong Buddhist because I haven't been exposed to it much. It's just a heritage, just what the family does, and I really don't know why they do it, but it's there. (personal interview, 2005)

Yet, others long to have more intense connection with the monks, as expressed by two youths:

I would never consider shaving my hair to be a monk, even for a short time. I really like my hair and I kind of like my girlfriend, but I would be willing to do the training. I wouldn't mind getting trained by the monks, to listen to them, to talk to them ... Basically the younger people want this. We want to interact with the monks too. When I say we, I am speaking for my friends too. They would love to have that kind of connection. Even with the language issues, I believe we would do fine and we would ask a lot of questions. I would prefer the talk to be in English, but the monks have their own dialect. They speak in big words that I can't even imagine ... I don't really understand what they say. But I would be interested in coming to the temple if they had a translator. My friends would too. I want the monks to interact with the youth too. (personal interview, 2005)

I want [to find out about] their teachings, their ways of life, their philosophies, their discipline, things like that. I believe finding out about meditation would come afterwards, because monks can provide support for youth, and help them move on in life. I believe a monk can change anyone, because their words are so powerful, yet so kind. I would like to have these teachings even once a week. Because at the temple they have a program to teach the young children how to read and write Khmer, but I don't believe they interact with the monks. Once a week at the night, or any time when there is a bunch of youth and the monks, just come and teach them, because they are the future generation. Without them, Buddhism could be destroyed, especially the Cambodian community, because not many people go to the temple. Youth rarely go to the temple. (personal interview, 2005)

A common youth ideal is that the temple should be more closely connected to the community, and that monks should play a more active role with Cambodian youth. One young man noted his considerations of a good monk for youth:

A Khmer monk from Thailand visited for one year. He was very open-minded and visited the Cambodian houses, but the other monk did not think this was appropriate. Yet, this monk from Thailand wanted to talk to the children and their families about activities in Cambodia, to get news from the Internet. He was very interactive with the community and when he spoke, he was speaking in ways which the young people liked. He made jokes, and he smiled. In comparison, the head monk is more reserved. The head monk is really knowledgeable about Buddhism, but is reserved with social interaction ... Another young monk from Cambodia, now in Montreal, used to want to visit, but was not encouraged, we don't know why because we liked him. (personal interview, 2003)

Another youth noted the important role the temple could play in preventing youth problems:

We figured one of the best ways to get the kids off the street is to have a centre of activities for them at the temple. We don't want to see kids dropping out of school. Here, there is a great drive for material success. In the families there are two parents working hard to make money, but neglecting the kids, and the kids turn to one another. Or each kid has his own computer and spends too much time on the Internet. There is a lack of communication in families. For some families, there is too much social service dependence. There is a lack of activities for Cambodian kids to be together, other than New Year's and the parties, but these are good for fundraising and not good for social interaction.

The [local] Cambodian association does not promote Khmer culture. For example, the last fashion show was five years ago. We suggested having a library in the temple, just a small space in the basement even, some shelves to put books for the children, but the monk and the directors said no, there was no room. The monk is the founder of the temple and he is the total authority. He doesn't seem to want to spend money for the community here ...

We are planning for the April 12 New Year's. There will be a morning religious ceremony from 9 to 12 noon, followed by a meal. The hall is rented until 4 p.m. and we want to have a cultural event with traditional dancers, local singers, and traditional games, but the head monk says this is not a good idea. The association head thought it was a good idea, but then changed his mind when the monk said no, so we are still trying to figure out what to do. The community really wants the cultural events, especially the youth. (personal interview, 2003)

Some youth leaders question the way current temples are being run, especially the enormous power in the hands of the abbot. One youth group raised the idea that the monk should be restricted to rituals and religious issues, while lay administrators run the temple, but the larger community felt this suggestion was too contentious to consider. Instead, youth are advised that they should adjust to the situation as it is and not have expectations. These restrictions, however, inhibit the youth from spontaneously seeking religious connection, as noted in the comments of a young Cambodian man:

> I was at the temple on Saturday, but I didn't get to pray to the Buddha there. The monks were doing a ceremony. I was at the temple because of the picnic, but I wanted to pray inside too, but I couldn't because the monk was doing something. Do you think I could sit with the monks and the elders, like the elders just sit with the monks? I asked one man and he said no, it was not 7 p.m. yet, when they [the monks] do their prayers then, and people can go there. He didn't want me to go and disturb them before this time. (personal interview, 2005)

To help bridge the generational gap and to address adaptive changes, some Khmer monks have developed innovative strategies for outreach to the Cambodian community and increased communication with non-Khmer. During the Samleng Khmer Ontario radio program, heard every Saturday and Sunday (11 a.m. to 12 noon) on CHFT AM1430, the Venerable Hun By discusses various aspects of Buddhism. In Hamilton, the Venerable Thach Dhammo has held Vipassana retreats for both Khmer and non-Khmer, assisted by a young Caucasian monk living at the temple.[17] The monks at the Hamilton Kampuchea Krom temple also modified the daily alms round of *Pindabatt* to suit the specifics of their mixed neighbourhood.[18] In Hamilton and Ottawa, monks and members of the Cambodian temples regularly join with other Buddhist communities to engage in intra-Buddhist activities, such as *Wesak/ Vesaka*, and participate in multifaith summer celebrations. These activities highlight the presence of Khmer Buddhism and its role in Canadian religious diversity.

Challenges to the Centrality of Buddhism as a Marker of Khmer Identity

Ontario monks continue to face the disillusionment that many Khmer have towards Buddhism, especially concerning its political appropriation, or the leadership capacity of ritual specialists. Older Khmer men who were involved in political activities in Cambodia and younger Canadian-born and -raised Khmer who attend college or university question the long-term role of traditional Buddhism for Cambodian communities in Ontario. As Bit notes: 'Buddhism has been used by every ruler in the modern times, from Sihanouk, Lon Nol, to Pol Pot and the present regime to legitimize their political control. In the process, the integrity of Buddhist principles as the spiritual foundation of Cambodian culture has been sacrificed. Buddhism's role as a socializing and acculturating force has been compromised and distorted into a secular force which instead encourages factionalism' (1991: 35).

Factionalism among Cambodian community leaders, compounded by class, status, generational, and ethnic differences, has been a major obstacle for Ontario Buddhist temples. Conversely, the close relationship of Cambodian culture with Buddhist services, practices, and community events has also alienated those Cambodians who no longer share Buddhist religious beliefs. In some Khmer communities, religious differences have led to community divisiveness and tension. Throughout the 1980s and 1990s, certain small Khmer evangelical Christian groups in Ottawa and Toronto isolated themselves from Buddhist Khmer and would not participate in or support Buddhist cultural ceremonies, particularly the merit-making offerings. This also occurred in Kingston and St Thomas, where the majority of Khmer converted to Christianity. Religious differences restricted the shared community leadership needed to organize annual cultural celebrations and to advocate for familiar forms of mental health healing. Yet, because traditional culture and health could not be disengaged from the Buddhist ritual context, religious differences exacerbated the difficulties Khmer had in their ability to connect with, or trust, one another. As a result, community bonds and networks that could have enhanced social cohesion were limited.

Buddhist and Christian Khmer each have distinct attitudes towards the value of traditional cultural identities and in addressing the lingering psychological trauma. Christian churches in Ontario link Cambodians with non-Khmer people and institutions, encourage rapid cultural integration into Western ways of life, and support new roles and expectations in being Cambodian-Canadian Christians. For Cambodian Buddhists, the temples and the monks represent traditional beacons of clarity, calmness, and solace, providing a refuge for prayer, blessings, offerings, healing, and hope. Khmer Buddhism in Ontario provides tangible evidence of their pre-migration way of life and cultural identity and is used to connect the past, present, and future. Most Buddhist households contain at least one Buddha statue and/or ancestral shrine. Cambodian stores and businesses often have places for small shrines with offerings of artificial flowers, incense, and food. The Maple Cambodian temple is planning to build a special room, the *cheat dain* (sacred ground), where ashes of the dead will be stored. This traditional temple room will allow families to bring the remains of their parents from Cambodia, and to place the ashes of those who have died in Canada. The presence of *cheat dain* enables Ontario Khmer to properly hold the twice-yearly memorial services, and to further satisfy their need to expand realms of meaning and connection between the living and the dead. Regular temple attendance is not an obligatory requirement to demonstrate Buddhist piety. Many Cambodians who consider themselves devout Buddhists only attend two or three larger community Buddhist events a year, and visit the temple or monks when needed.

Both Christian and Buddhist religious beliefs and practices strengthen individuals, families, and group cohesion. The presence of permanent monks and an active cultural cooperation through temple activities, however, has been the most effective means of revitalizing Cambodian communities in Ontario. In scholarly and popular works on Khmer diasporic communities and individuals, it has become commonplace to 'place Buddhist definitions of self and community squarely at the centre of the articulation of what it means to be Khmer' (Hansen 2004: 41). Yet, in Ontario, some Khmer Buddhists today no longer believe in the saying, *'khmae preah putesasna'* (to be Khmer is to be Buddhist).[19] When asked, Khmer people were hesitant to equate their identity in Canada with Buddhism as the main component. Instead, they gave clear acknowledgment that people change through resettlement and that the cultural context of Canada has influenced people's attitudes and expectations. They noted that there are now numerous ways to reflect Buddhist beliefs and practices, and that conversion to Christianity, secularism, and materialism all challenge the traditional Khmer/Buddhist identity.

Similar to other groups and communities in diaspora (Leonard et al. 2005), religious beliefs and experiences among Ontario Cambodians have expanded beyond traditional forms. Their complex resettlement experiences reflect adaptive and integrative necessities. When Cambodians in the United States were asked about religion, they 'invoked key words associated with Western subjectivity: choice, freedom, self-identity, and personal responsibility, reflecting not only their evolving religious beliefs but their induction into American society as refugees' (Douglas 2005: 125). Ontario Cambodians use comparable language, especially when they emphasize the openness of Buddhism and its ability to coexist with other religions and secular facets of North

American society. In recent years, these attitudes, combined with common concerns to retain Khmer culture (particularly through heritage language and classical and folk dances), have downplayed religious divisions. There are now more incidences of Cambodian Buddhists and Christians working together to help organize and participate in cultural programs held at the Buddhist temple or other venues. When Ontario Buddhist Khmer were asked about differences between Buddhism and Christianity, they noted that both provide positive teachings on morality, gender roles, and family stability. Their acceptance of the value of both religious traditions is similar to Khmer in the United States (Ong 2003; Douglas 2005). For the Long Beach and Seattle communities, however, this complementary attitude is maintained 'in the face of pressures from Christian leaders who asserted that a synthesis between the two religions was at best unlikely and at worst an anathema' (Douglas 2005: 124). In Ontario, only the evangelical Christian groups support this restrictive view.

Generally, distinctions between Buddhism and Christianity have become relaxed to the point that Cambodians who became Christian are feeling more confident and secure in their welcome when they attend Buddhist festivities and ceremonies. While Khmer Buddhism still retains its role as a significant personal and community marker of Khmer ethnicity, it is no longer the 'defining identity' for diasporic Khmer. The emerging Khmer identities that Ontario Cambodians are constructing reflect new and syncretic religious beliefs and practices. The second generation is particularly concerned with reconfiguring traditional Buddhist relationships (especially between monastic and lay). New ways of expressing ethnic identity, technological engagement, and personal connections with Cambodia and other communities in diaspora are shifting the primacy of traditional patterns. Generational contrasts and conflicts particularly express and shape these new identity constructions, as do the small, but significant, number of Kampuchea Krom. Cambodian Christians also retain a strong Khmer ethnic adherence and homeland linkages, but without a Buddhist framework.

5 Cambodian Christians in Ontario

Conversion Processes

The conversion themes, values, and aspirations of Cambodian Christians who resettled in Ontario have similarities to those of new Christian converts from elsewhere in Southeast Asia and Asia Pacific. Miyazaki (2000), Hefner (1993), and Schieffelin (1981) indicate that Christian conversions in Indonesia, Papua New Guinea, and Fiji reflect transitions from traditional lifestyles to those of modernity, new moral systems of support and reciprocity, and different opportunities for upward mobility and social hierarchy. Among Hindu Javanese, for example, youth who were active in the new Christian church became the best educated and most cosmopolitan (Hefner 1993: 115). They not only easily deserted the ways of their ancestors, but also displayed hostility towards traditional leaders and religious patterns. These characteristics and attitudes were found among young Cambodian Christian converts in Ontario, and in the United States (Smith-Hefner 1994; Mortland 1994: 74).

Before the Khmer Rouge regime, village religion in Cambodia had been communally based, highly ritualistic, and organized around the hierarchical authority of the village chief and the Buddhist monks (Ebihara 1966; Kalab 1994: 60). When some Cambodians fled to Thai refugee camps, they had already rejected Buddhist religious beliefs and practices, particularly in regard to their soteriological effectiveness, traditional hierarchy, and forms of communal mediation (C.M. Coleman 1987: 366; Vickery 1984: 12). These Cambodians became attracted to the Christian belief in a heavenly salvation, new religious dynamics that represented different types of power and authority, and Christian explanations for what they had experienced. Among Seventh-day Adventists, Evangelical Christians, and the Christian Reformed Church, a profoundly personal experience of Jesus and/or God was presented to potential converts. Following the common pattern of Asian conversion, intense and committed prayer and Bible study was emphasized, with the conversion experience expressed through narratives 'fitted to the peculiarities of their own life experience' (Hefner 1993: 116). Unpublished testimonies from two Cambodian Christians who resettled in Ontario reflect this experiential dimension:

> About one week later [the worker with] Youth With a Mission came to Rangsit looking for me. She told me the Gospel: 'From the beginning God created the world. On the cross before He died, Jesus said: "Father, forgive them; for they do not know what they are doing."' His Words touched me and I was converted ... His death on the cross when He forgave those who crucified Him although He had done no wrong ... Jesus could forgive his enemies by His power and I could forgive the Khmer Rouge. The miracle happened, God changed my heart. The bitterness and hatred has been replaced. (Cambodian woman from Ottawa, no date)

> I remembered, too, the ancient legend of the Cambodian people that some day a god called Se a Matrey (The Head of Love) was going to come to save people from sin, suffering, and death. I wanted to believe that the old man's story from the Bible [John 3: 16] was true. I wanted to accept Jesus as my Saviour ... One day I met face to face with the soldier who had tied me up years before in Cambodia, intending for me to be shot. When he first met me he was frightened because he, too, remembered the incident. He was now a refugee also, having deserted the armed forces and fled to Thailand. But God had set me free from hatred and bitterness inside, so I said to him, 'Don't be afraid. I have become a Christian. God has forgiven all my past sins. I am a new man, so I too have forgotten the wrongs of the past.' What a joy he told me, 'I too am a Christian now!.'..
>   The Lord tested me further by allowing severe sickness to strike my wife ... When I finished praying I looked down at her and she moved ... She said to me, 'I saw a boat filled with people dressed in white, with a fire in the middle of the boat.' ... I said to her, 'The people in white were the angels of God, and the fire represents the Holy Spirit in the Bible. He healed you!' (Cambodian pastor from Hamilton, no date)

Both testimonies were written in English so they could be distributed to others for inspiration. Smith-Hefner (1999: 23) also found that experiences of previous trauma in Cambodian Christian testimonies are reinterpreted to provide opportunities for 'teaching God's message' and to offer 'spiritual comfort to those in distress.' As Schieffelin notes, building upon their experiences in the conversion narrative, the 'drama and rhetoric of the evangelical process' becomes a testimonial witnessing to the power of God, and a moral force to convert others (1981: 150).

Although conversion to Christianity did not overtly imply a rejection of Khmer heritage, it did involve an active adherence to new social and moral commitments. In placing oneself first and foremost as a Christian, other things, activities, or involvements not in accordance with 'God's will' or 'truth,' as mediated and understood in the particular Christian group, must be left behind (Hefner 1993: 118). Cambodians who became evangelical Christians were told to repudiate and avoid those aspects of the Khmer cultural tradition embedded within and supported by Buddhism and popular spirit beliefs, especially the practice of making merit on behalf of one's ancestors and offering food to the spirits. Cambodian Christians were encouraged to cultivate moral sobriety, self-discipline, and economic worthiness. Once resettled in the United States, Cambodian Christians were advised to quickly insert themselves and their children into the ideals and practices of American capitalism (Ong 2003: 197–206; Douglas 2003; Smith-Hefner 1993; Hopkins 1996: 119). Similar behavioural and economic patterns were found among Cambodian Christians in Ontario.

Large-scale conversion of Cambodians first emerged in the refugee camps. A Christian identity increased the opportunities to participate in Christian-sponsored educational and vocational training, medical and social services, or resettlement opportunities (Smith-Hefner 1999: 23; Mortland 1994: 75). These beneficial byproducts of conversion reflected the Asian phenomenon of 'rice-bowl Christians' (Tapp 1989; Van Esterik 2003; Akcapar 2006). Cambodian women, especially, invested time and effort in building patronage relations with relief workers, acquiescing to Christian discipline, and attending religious classes in order to obtain preferential access to goods and services (Ong 2003: 62). They received clothes, food, money, and regular visits to their homes by church workers sympathetic to their family circumstances. These non-Asian 'Christian friends' provided Cambodian women with critical social capital. A primary task of many of the aid agencies run by American church groups was to find local American sponsors for refugees seeking resettlement abroad (ibid.: 52). World Vision International and other Protestant Christian groups used relief supplies and promises of prompt resettlement in 'Christian' countries to induce Khmer Buddhists to convert (Gosling 1984: 61–2).

The contextual dynamics of power, dominance, and gift giving resulted in various depths of religious devotion, commitment, and belief. These depths range from Vickery's (1984: 12) assertion that Khmer refugees were actively seeking an alternative to Buddhism to Douglas' (2003) observation of one young woman who converted because Christian meetings were a pleasant diversion from refugee camp life, providing her with opportunities to sing and dance with others, and a safe place to interact with young men. Hitchcox (1990) identifies several forms of missionary Christianity in Southeast Asian refugee camps, each asserting its own style of what Ong (2003: 52) calls 'compassionate domination.' The motivations of Christian agents, the personal and psychological impact of proselytization, and the different aspirations and responses of those who converted produce a complex, and at times, contradictory depiction of Cambodian Christians. Kang Kek Ieu, for example, the Khmer Rouge chief administrator of the horrific torture and extermination centre (S-21), became a born-again Christian when charged with genocide by a Cambodian court, declaring that his life is now in 'God's hand' (Chan 2003: 19).

For many Cambodians, conversion had as much to do with the traumas induced by war and flight as with reaching salvation (Ong 2003: 204). Christian missionaries promised Cambodian refugees they would find peace of mind if they entrusted themselves to God (Smith-Hefner 1999: 23; Himm 2003: 106). Interviews with Cambodian Christians in Ontario and reading their testimonials show that many converted because of psychological need. Conversion provided them with a mechanism to come to terms with their past actions, their enormous hatred and thoughts of revenge against those who perpetuated so much violence and suffering, and to move beyond debilitating depression, despair, and hopelessness. Several Cambodians stated that conversion was their opportunity for 'forgiveness,' receiving God's forgiveness first, then developing their own towards others. Forgiveness enabled them to continue to live. One Khmer man from Ontario recounted his struggle for forgiveness:

> How could I ever forgive those who killed my family? Do I need to forget before I can forgive? What does forgiveness mean to me? I struggled with these questions, but in time I discovered that forgiveness opens a chan-

nel for real spiritual work in my life; a power which brings healing and wholeness.

First of all, does forgiving mean forgetting? I don't think so. By forgiving those who killed my family, I haven't erased the painful experiences from my heart and memory: they will always remain. The images are always with me: the baby being clubbed and butchered; my father being knocked into the pit, his body slashed; the head of a younger brother axed into two pieces; the stomachs of another brother and sister torn out; my mother as she was dragged to be killed ... When I first became a Christian, I realized that forgiveness was an important part of the Gospel, so I tried to find out about it ...

Since God had forgiven me, it was right for me to forgive them, even though it seemed impossible to do so. Forgiveness has been a special gift from God in my life ... I needed a power outside myself, and that power was the love of God. (Himm 2003: 120–6)

A Cambodian pastor in Ontario spoke about his conversion during a time of acute desperation and hopelessness when he no longer wanted to live:

I wanted to commit suicide and a friend approached me about inviting Christ to be my Lord and Saviour, who could direct my life and give me a purpose for living. The friend said I need forgiveness for the salvation of my soul. After that, I went to the big church in the refugee camp but didn't want to go inside. I was not sure.

While I sat outside the building, I heard the sermon being taught by one of the Cambodian pastors and his voice was so powerful. He spoke about who Jesus is and why he came to visit us, and why he died on the cross and how people can get salvation. This pastor invited all those who wanted to be saved to come to the front of the church. I was so moved, I went to the front and this pastor read the scriptures and prayed for me, and I repeated the words after him. When we prayed, I felt a kind of conviction to God grow in my heart. It was very emotional and I cried many tears, out of a sense of gratitude, of joy, it's hard to say in words. After that, I felt the power of the Lord to start working in my life. The thing that was working was inside of me, drawing me, giving me a sense of purpose in the area of forgiveness. I really needed to learn forgiveness. I began to see that the people who were against me were no longer my enemies, but were all part of the Lord. My wife had died of starvation at that time and it was hard to forgive. I had so much anger and now I tried to see these people as objects

of love. Even particular people who ruled during the communist time I
had to forgive.

And also, I had lost my trust in everything. It is hard to get back that
trust after what we went through. (personal interview, 2002)

A young woman from Ottawa illustrated how she was drawn to the
church:

I was first attracted to church in the refugee camps, because I heard the
beautiful music and I wanted to go into the church. The music really
moved me, especially one missionary lady who sang Amazing Grace at
sunset, and it was so beautiful it made me have tears run down my face.
This lady was reading from a big red Bible and she had a beautiful voice.
I was so moved by her singing that people said I should go to the church.
So I joined the choir but I still wasn't giving myself to God.

But during this time things were really bad with my family. It was so
difficult and people were mean. I was so sick, so depressed, at one period
I tried to kill myself with so many pills that they took me to the hospital
and pumped my stomach. My sister said I should go to church. My sister
had become a Christian but her husband was abusive, and I said to God,
'Please don't let me have this kind of marriage.' One experience I had
at church, the words were so powerful that all at once I realized I was
standing outside the church. I don't know how I ended up standing there,
I don't remember anything, but all of a sudden I am outside. Later that
week, another sister saw a fire above the church and didn't understand.
The church was not on fire, but had this light above. (personal interview,
2003)

Conversion was often an attempt to put the horrors of the past
behind them, wanting to achieve what Martin (1990: 23) refers to as
'free space.' One Ontario man wanted to be free from the Buddhist concept of the karmic law of cause and effect, especially the consequences
of his actions, since he felt karma held him responsible for the misery
and suffering he had experienced (Himm 2003: 101, 131). Conversion
enabled some people to attain a sense of autonomy and separation from
Cambodian social ties, authority, history, and from their recent experiences under the Khmer Rouge. Rejecting this legacy allowed them to
begin new identities and/or a sense of purpose to their lives, providing
them a clear expression of being 'born again.' In consequence, Buddhist
Khmer viewed conversion as evidence of a person's desire to adopt a

new, non-Khmer identity (Smith-Hefner 1999: 33). One Ontario Khmer woman, who converted in the camps through Youth With a Mission, recounted how her suffering under the Khmer Rouge made her want to lose her Cambodian identity:

I assumed my religion was Buddhism since it is part of being Cambodian, but I was a student at a Catholic school. The school had really nice desks and books and was air conditioned. During the Khmer Rouge time, my mom died along the roadside, and I was taken from my father and sisters to work in the farms. Two years later, I did not know where my family was. By 1977, I so wanted to find my family and I constantly questioned who I was and where I came from. I remembered the teaching at the Catholic school on people being descended from apes, but I still questioned what our origins were as humans, and who created the world. Before this, I always thought God and Christianity were just for the whites, the European people. I also questioned about Buddhism and could not understand why the people were offering food to the spirits in the forest when they were starving.

Also, around this time I was forced to marry against my will and I refused. When my wedding day came, I still refused, so the Khmer Rouge came to kill me. I was tied with handcuffs behind me and placed in the car and driven to a temple where they killed people. In my mind I saw how they were going to dig a hole in the ground for me and then smash my head. Instead, they took me to the prison with about six other women. We were searched for hidden gold or whatever. That night and every night, I was placed in the stocks. This first night I was left there for three days and then they took me to torture. The asked me questions and didn't believe I was in the jail because I didn't want to marry. They put electric shocks on me, placed plastic bags over my face, and used swear words and said very hurtful things to me. They continued this for four months. Finally I began to lie, but they still beat me all over, and I was so black and blue and in pain. That night, I realized Buddha could not help because the Khmer Rouge destroyed all the statues in the temple and I started to believe that God would see my tears.

Soon after, they took us women to another jail in Battambang. Out of about twelve of us, there were only four or five left. One woman, she was really kind to me and was a wonderful person. Her husband was also in the jail, and she always tried to find out about him. She was killed, and when they took us to the other jail, her husband was asking about her and we told him she was killed, it was so sad. This jail was better because at night we were not placed in the iron stockade. Also at the second jail they fed us rice and we stayed there one month. Then we went to another, where we worked in the rice fields day and night. We slept on the ground outside.

When the Vietnamese invaded, I escaped and on the road I met my father and sisters. We all cried. One by one, we escaped to Thailand. I was the last one to go, with my father. I swore I would forget Cambodia and that I didn't want to associate with Cambodians. (personal interview, 2002)

This woman has also written a testimonial that describes these same experiences.

Through conversion, Cambodians formed new relationships among themselves, with the foreign missionaries, and with their Christian sponsors in resettlement. Several scholars note the powerful influence Christian sponsors had in converting the Indo-Chinese refugees whom they had helped to resettle in the United States and Canada (Nagata 1989; Routledge 1985; Tapp 1989; Van Esterik 2003; Winland 1992; Zhou and Bankston 1994). Christian churches and their members provided refugees with critical social capital that facilitated their resettlement needs of accommodation, employment, cultural mediation, and advocacy. One Khmer pastor in Toronto converted to the Christianity of his sponsors because he liked their ideals of self-reliance. Another Khmer pastor from St Thomas noted he was attracted to the church's emphases on self-dignity and not being a burden to society:

My early experiences in working with the Christian churches showed me the process of how the churches employ training to help people grow and take control. This is my basis for being a Christian. The message of Christianity is good for Cambodians to hear, especially about peace and to serve each other, rather than for the Cambodian method of retaliation and aggression. It is good that many Cambodians came to the church to help sponsor friends and families. (personal interview, 1994)

Church premises provided a ready-made place where refugees were able to extend social networks and receive social support beyond their ethnic community. They could hold traditional celebrations there, such as New Year's, thereby retaining cultural forms of food, music, and dance. Churches provided an established space for weekly meetings and services that helped refugees strengthen their ties with one another, especially when held in their own language.

Cambodians expressed the subtle reciprocities and obligations of patronage towards their Christian sponsors. A Khmer woman from Kingston explained:

People from the church met us at the airport and were good to us. Cambodians are very grateful people, and because they have done good for us and looked after us and kept us very well, we must do good for them. This is why we keep going and every year we donate to the church. It would betray them if we didn't go. This is what our Buddhist culture and background taught us. We can never turn away from them, it would not be right. Because we are good Buddhists, we become Christians here. Inside we still hold many Buddhist ideals, but we don't tell them or say anything because this would make them sad. Buddhism teaches us that we must be flexible. (personal interview, 1995)

Ledgerwood notes that sponsors were identified as 'patrons' and refugees became their 'clients,' reflecting an exchange-basis relationship: 'The critical method whereby Khmers obtain assistance in times of need or accomplish tasks which require effort beyond their own resources is to enter into personal relationships with those more important and powerful than themselves ... Both patrons and clients are providing services to one another. Patrons possess superior power and influence that allows them to assist and protect clients. The clients, in return, contribute loyalty and personal assistance, thereby increasing the patron's power' (1990: 141).

As clients, Cambodians felt obliged to express loyalty to those who provided financial and other forms of assistance to them. A Khmer woman from Kitchener expressed her experience in the refugee camp:

We started with Christianity in the camps. We had to depend on a French missionary lady [Seventh-day Adventist] for help to pay somebody to pick up our daughter left in Phnom Penh. To pay her back, we started to go to church to make her happy. (personal interview, 2003)

When the Christian Reformed Church sponsored Cambodian families, they assigned them a 'friendship family' from the church. Cambodians treated them like pseudo-sponsors with the same sense of obligation. One woman explained how she had to attend church every Sunday, even though it was not conducive to her mental or physical health:

We met the friendship family in 1983 and they helped us find an apartment, took us to the doctor, and helped us in whatever way we needed. They invited us to visit the church and then asked us to come to church every Sunday. Every Sunday, they came by to take us to church and I would want to hide, but I couldn't. It really made me sick to drive in that car. And I didn't understand any English, so I would sit there and feel really sick and so tired. Sometimes I just said I was too sick to go.

In our culture, we try to hide our feelings, what harms us. Because they are so nice to us, to help us, we didn't want to disappoint them. So I went … This gave us a lot of hard time because nobody speaks Cambodian … Every three or four months, another Cambodian family would be brought in through sponsors and they, too, were pressured, like us, to go to church. (personal interview, 2003)

Several Ontario Cambodians stated that their conversion to their sponsor's religion was more out of a sense of obligation and/or subtle coercion rather than a genuine interest. Similar pressures were noted among Cambodians who resettled in the United States: 'Hillside Church served a social, rather than religious, function for the Cambodians. For them, it was primarily a helping agency, and they sought a patron-client relationship with it. For a time they attended as bidden, but as the patrons slowly withdrew services, the Cambodians' participation also ceased … There was some conflict over loyalty. Some of the refugees were sponsored by other churches and felt obligated to those churches and more specifically to individuals at those churches who had helped them at the beginning or were continuing to do so; but some members of Hillside felt they were doing more for the Cambodians, so all the Cambodians should attend there' (Hopkins 1996: 118–19). Marcucci (1994: 139) observes that while Khmer affirmed their Christian affiliation, they continued to hold Buddhist rituals in secret, hidden from Americans. Beiser et al. (1989) submits that the emphasis Christian sponsors placed on conversion was an unnecessary source of stress for Vietnamese Buddhist refugees that negatively affected their mental health. Ong (2003: 73) suggests an underlying agenda of Christian sponsors was to replay the same 'civilizing mission' that church workers first directed at defeated Native Americans; to transform Cambodian refugees' attitudes, habits, and goals to a 'process of ethnic reformation, erasure, and cleansing in order to become more worthy citizens.' A sponsor from Ottawa, however, noted a much different attitude from Catholic parishes there:

As distinct from some of the more evangelical churches, Catholic parishes were told not to proceed with any attempt at conversion or trying to get Cambodians to come to church. This was very important to us. We encouraged and assisted in bringing a Buddhist monk here in 1980. The Bishop of Hull, Adolph Proulx, offered the hall of the Cathedral Church for Buddhist ceremonies ... Out of all the Cambodians sponsored by the Catholic parishes, only one family and one individual became Catholics. (personal interview, 1994)

Although Cambodians participated in Christian services and events, there was little understanding. Several Khmer noted that it was only through television and radio programs that they began to learn enough English to recognize what was being said in church. Few were fortunate to have a Cambodian pastor or Khmer university student to teach them scripture study from a Khmer Bible. In Ontario, the conversion of Hmong from Laos was similar. Except for the Hmong religious leaders, most Hmong did not understand their Christian sponsor's doctrine, rituals, and distinct Mennonite identity from other Protestant denominations (Winland 1992: 106). Sponsors also expressed doubts concerning the Hmong's motivation for conversion, and the impact this conversion would have on their own church (ibid.: 102).

As Cambodian families prospered, their patron-client relationship began to change. One woman felt that when she no longer needed assistance, some people in church looked at her family 'like we were too successful, being refugees, coming here from nothing.' She stopped going to church to move beyond their image of her as a dependent refugee. Another woman also stopped going to her sponsor's church:

I didn't need to go to church to be a Christian because I felt that God was everywhere, but I only went to church to please the sponsors. By about 1997, I had to stop to go to church because I was really depressed and it was too hot and crowded and it really made me sick. But I still believe in God. (personal interview, 2003)

While conversion may have been undertaken through a sense of obligation or convenience by some Cambodian adults, Christianity became a more primary aspect of their children's identity. A Cambodian man in Kingston commented:

When I come to Canada, before, I was Buddhist, but now I am a Christian,

so I am half and half. My background is Buddhist, but the children go to
church every time and they have no Buddhist teaching, so they are more
Christian than I am. (personal interview, 1995)

Christian churches provided social capital to Cambodian children
through non-Khmer support networks, acculturation with non-Khmer
playmates and church events, and interested non-Khmer adults who
wanted Cambodian children to succeed in resettlement (Hopkins 1996:
119). For poor Cambodian youth in America, churches represented
dominant institutions that, when turned to, would provide them a way
to gain majority white acceptance and articulate new Western identities
and signs of success (Ong 2003: 197).

There are fewer than five hundred Cambodian Christians in Ontario.
These include Catholics, Mormons, and Seventh-day Adventists, but
the majority are evangelical Protestants. Although small in numbers,
Christian Cambodians have had a significant impact on the larger communities. The strong Christian orthodoxy that they are taught, with
clear delineations of beliefs and acceptable behaviours, is often at odds
with traditional Khmer cultural and religious practices. One Khmer
man noted that as Christians, 'We don't smoke or drink so the other
Cambodians feel uncomfortable with us' (personal interview, 1995).
Other Cambodian Christians also voiced this sentiment.

Most of the approximately twenty Cambodian Christian churches
across Canada are affiliated with several evangelical Protestant denominations, some of which are involved in national and global networks
of faith. The Cambodian Evangelical Fellowships in Ottawa, Hamilton,
London, and Toronto belong to the Cambodian Christian Network of
Canada (CCNC) and to an international organization called the Cambodian Christian Services. An annual summer conference of the Federation of the Cambodian Evangelical Churches in Canada has been held
in Ontario for over ten years. For more than twenty years, most Cambodian Christian churches received financial and organizational support
from larger Christian bodies. This support usually lasted a year or two,
at which point the congregation was expected to be self-sufficient. As
a funding source dried up, some Khmer churches changed the name
and affiliation of their church to access another available source, reflecting a fluidity of denominational identity or commitment. Other Khmer
churches developed strong ties with their funding source, and Khmer
men quickly became elders, with some sent for ministerial training.

Christian congregations with Khmer-speaking ministers try to preserve a Cambodian atmosphere during services and celebrations by reading from a Khmer Bible, singing Khmer songs appropriately reoriented for a Christian message, serving Khmer food, and sometimes encouraging Khmer dance. A Khmer Christian woman commented on the innovative way her church retained traditional tunes, but changed the words from an inherent Buddhist meaning to now carry the Christian message:

> The [in another city] Cambodian Church has not allowed the traditional Khmer songs into the Christian tradition because it is non-Christian. Here, we don't worry. Our hymn book has two parts. There are the old Khmer tunes with new Christian words, as well as English hymns which are also sung in Khmer, so people can sing together in both English and Khmer. (personal interview, 2003)

During one Sunday service at the Cambodian Evangelical Fellowship in Ottawa, the singing of Khmer hymns was accompanied by Khmer youth playing guitars and a non-Khmer man playing the piano. The Khmer pastor explained:

> We encourage the children to keep their culture and their identity. The church runs a Cambodian language school on Saturdays, 10 a.m. to 12 noon, to learn reading, writing, and speaking. The purpose is to expose children to Cambodian literature we have brought from Cambodia, the same books that children in Cambodia use. Some of these stories help the children understand their culture. We retain Cambodian cooking and keep New Year's celebrations and play the Cambodian games then. We sing the traditional Cambodian songs, but also have the hymn books in Khmer with the cover featuring traditional instruments. The first part is English hymns translated, and the second part is based on Cambodian tunes. Some Cambodian Christians in Montreal have trained the children in the Khmer classical dance, but here we don't have anyone to teach the children. For special celebrations such as New Year's, the women wear the *sampot*. We teach the children about Cambodian culture and history, and when finances are available, parents like to take their children back to visit Cambodia. (personal interview, 2002)

As noted earlier in some of the Cambodian conversion narratives, music created an atmosphere conducive to attending Christian services. Music has special missionizing appeal as well as liturgical value, integrating people into the service and emphasizing teachings from the Bible (Sandos 2004: 129). Cambodian melodies, as well as simple and repetitive words, can have an emotive effect, moving people to devotion.

Christian churches tend to encourage Cambodian integration to Canadian norms. Ontario Khmer pastors advocate for steady employment, strong marriage commitment, educational achievement, reduced reliance on welfare, and avoidance of drinking and gambling. For one Khmer pastor in Toronto, these Christian ethics and attitudes are a more meaningful model for behaviour in Canada than the retention of Cambodian cultural traditions:

> We try to build the Christian community up as part of a family. The values of a Christian family are different from those of non-Christians. I emphasize three priorities in a Christian family: One, the priority of the Lord, to be close and follow the teaching. The second priority is to think of the family and help one another, and to love and give forgiveness, to learn how to work problems out. The third priority of the parents is to value education. For example, parents need to make time for the children after school, to talk with them, to help them with homework if you can. Parents need to make the children feel valued in the sight of God and in the family. Encouraging education is an expression of the value and care. The kids are so smart and they know they are being loved and this love gives them strength and power to move forward. One way is moving forward through education. (personal interview, 2002)

Several young Cambodian refugees who converted to Christianity through their own inner convictions became so extensively involved in church activities that these associations comprised their primary social events. Older individuals, who were isolated and lonely, also found that Christian groups with an emphasis on communal prayer and Bible study provided critical social needs. Often, these individuals were women who had lost husbands, children, and parents, and felt marginal to others in the Khmer communities. One older Khmer woman with little moral, social, or economic support became a Mormon because she said they were the only people to consistently call on her and keep her company. During the early years of resettlement, Cambodian Christian churches were very successful in meeting their members' social and emotional needs, encouraging youth to remain in school, and teaching Western work ethics. An Ottawa Cambodian pastor described the activities of his church from 1984 to the present:

The church, early on, provided services to newly arrived Khmer. Transportation, translation, aid in helping them to apply for welfare, relating to schools, accompanying people to doctor visits, things like that. Many families were associated with the church at this time, but when they became more settled, and didn't need the services or being connected, they moved away. Now, we have about fifty adults and twenty children. We have Sunday school for the children according to their age, a Women's ministry every two weeks, home-study, Friday evening fellowship and Sunday worship. Once a year, we go camping for the weekend with the whole group. Families also socialize together and learn from one another, help support each other. People have different gifts so having fellowship together helps one another. (personal interview, 2002)

A Cambodian Christian pastor in Toronto commented on his commitment to providing resettlement assistance for church members:

I have no money, but I still need to outreach and provide services for Cambodians. I have to act as escort, go to court, counselling for family breakdowns (e.g., wife beaten because she doesn't show proper respect, children beaten for same [reason]), to organize clothing drives, toys. The church is independent and gets no financial support. Many times you want to give up. Communication is so poor, anger and upset is a common reaction. The majority of Cambodians who come here are rural poor people with no understanding of cities. Ladies are illiterate and men have learned only the basics from the refugee camps. (personal interview, 1994)

During the 1990s, members of the Cambodian Evangelical Fellowships in Ontario felt that their social groups were the most cohesive, that more of their youth were in higher education, and that they had the lowest levels of unemployment among Cambodian communities. Similar sociocultural phenomena were found among Khmer Christians in the Boston area (Smith-Hefner 1993). In California, young Cambodian converts to Mormonism were also provided with a path to moral discipline, higher education, and movement into white middle-class society (Ong 2003). In the early 1990s, Khmer Christian youth accounted for the majority of the small numbers of Cambodians who attended colleges and universities in Ontario. During interviews, several commented on the support they received through the established Christian networks for students (boardinghouses, social activities, transportation), and the guidance given them by non-Khmer members of their church. Their success was so noticeable that the larger Khmer Buddhist youth groups in Toronto and Hamilton began to emulate Christian examples of social organization and support, and actively worked to keep young Khmer in school. With some assistance from non-Khmer individuals, these youth groups developed sports clubs, Buddhist instruction classes, and after school tutoring. By 2003, the educational distinction of Khmer Christians was no longer evident.

In the early resettlement years, religious differences among Khmer led to community divisiveness and tension, and to innovative attempts to balance the conflicting traditions of Christianity and Buddhism. One private sponsor noted the difficulties that arose from the Christian conversion pressures:

> There was a push by evangelical groups to convert. This divided Cambodians because they were told by evangelical Christians not to go to the Buddhist temple or attend New Year's celebrations because they are the work of the devil. Even today, Cambodian store owners who have a small Buddhist shrine in the store have Cambodian Christians come in and rant about the shrine being the devil, etc. (personal interview, 1995)

A Christian Khmer man commented:

> The biggest difference in becoming Christian is that we no longer do food offerings and merit-making for the spirits of our ancestors. We now feel that it is important to tell Buddhist Khmer who have *neak ta* shrines in their homes and who offer food to appease spirits that it is wrong to invite the devil into the home. (personal interview, 1995)

Another Christian man recounted the difficulties in trying to honour both religious traditions during a wedding ceremony:

> My brother in Edmonton also married a Cambodian girl and he tried to have it both Khmer tradition and Christian. He first had a Christian wedding upstairs and then they went downstairs and had a ceremony with tying the string and cutting the hair, but this is already creating a belief in trying to ward off evil spirits from the couple's union. I don't think my brother realized this was tied in with traditional Buddhism. At our wedding [in France] we had Khmer music but Christian songs, and we wore traditional Khmer wedding clothes with seven changes. We struggled with the issue of drinking because in France everyone drinks, even

the Christians. But the Christian Khmer wouldn't drink anyway, so we didn't serve wine at the table, but we had a bar for the French guests and the Khmer who were not Christian. Yet, most people didn't drink anyway. (personal interview, 2003)

The Toronto Cambodian Association, which focused primarily on resettlement services, did not involve itself in Khmer Buddhist and cultural community groups until the mid-1990s. From 1988 to 1994, leadership positions at the Cambodian Association were held by Christians, who would not participate in, nor support, Buddhist ritual ceremonies organized outside the association. The absence of these Christian community leaders at Buddhist celebrations and ceremonies reaffirmed what Christian missionaries and sponsors had previously told Khmer people; namely, that Buddhism and its cultural expressions are not worth keeping in Canada. Similar attitudes were found in the American Hillside Church: 'They gave specific loans for specific needs, such as for college tuition or home purchasing, and would not have supported more traditional needs, such as bride price, wedding costs, bringing in a monk for a family emergency, support for the wat, or traditional medicine ... it [the church] was actually a major active force for social change' (Hopkins 1996: 118).

Khmer evangelical pastors in Ontario acknowledge that, in the 1990s, they were quick to denounce Buddhist beliefs and activities and those members who maintained ties to Buddhist temples or attended Buddhist festivals. Now they say they no longer speak about this. Buddhists have consistently stated they would welcome any Christian Khmer to attend and participate in a Buddhist festival, ceremony, or social event, yet when shared interaction would occur, some Khmer Christians remarked that they were accused of denying their cultural heritage and ethnic community. These different perceptions of one another are revealed in two quotes. One is from a Buddhist Khmer community leader, the second from a Christian Khmer woman, both from the same Ontario city:

Christians in Cambodia are open, but not the ones here. The Christian Khmer don't want to share celebrations with us. They hate that people are involved with Buddhism and don't want to discuss any community issues, what can be done for the community. There is no opportunity to discuss problems. I went two or three years ago to visit their place and they want you to join them. If you join, then they are happy, but only then will they want to talk with you. Otherwise, no. Buddhists do not ask this. It is up to yourself to make the decision, to believe or not. Sometimes you can come to the Buddhist temple, only once a year or twice or three times a year and this is okay. Buddhists don't talk about other religions, that this is bad or that is bad. Christians always say something bad about the other group. (personal interview, 2003)

The Christian Khmer get hassled all the time about why they are wasting their time going to church. One lady accused Christians of being 'brainwashed.' Almost every time Christian Khmer interact with other Khmer, they are poked about their Christian beliefs and sometimes what people say really hurts them. This is why they don't want to join with other Khmer. (personal interview, 2003)

Cambodian pastors in several Ontario cities have expressed dismay at the reduced numbers of committed Cambodian Christians, and they do not seem confident that the situation will change. They gave a number of reasons why people no longer go to church: the sense of obligation to sponsors/patrons has waned; there is yearning to identify more overtly with Khmer culture; churches no longer provide the social networks to find employment; and Cambodian youth no longer need churches to encourage them to succeed in school. One Cambodian pastor commented on the decline of a Christian group, different from his own affiliation, which began when a new Khmer pastor was brought in:

Although the new Khmer pastor spoke English well, the people don't need as much help from a pastor these days, help in translation, mediation with school or government officials. They can do things by themselves or get help from their children who have grown up here. From about thirty-five families who once belonged, now there are only five families. The sense of community continues but without going to church. Several families meet together often, for example, at weekly parties, to drink, dance, and eat together. Several other families have joined with Khmer to build a Buddhist temple there. This leaving the church indicates their motivation for joining was not a religious belief in Christianity but to get help. Also, why they move back to Buddhism is to fill a cultural part in their life.

Also, because 60 to 70 per cent of the Cambodian population were so poor when they came to Canada, they find that tithing is difficult. They don't have enough money with what they send back to their families in Cambodia. They want to get and keep as much money as possible so they don't want to lose time with church involvement and they don't want to give money to the organization.

They don't want to join the church because the no-alcohol is an inhibition. For Cambodian people, alcohol is the medium for socialization and people don't want to give up the social aspect. Cambodians are invited to the church for special events and people do come, but only for the day.

Cambodian culture is that if someone helps you, you help them back, for example, by going to the church which sponsored you ... After ten years, people felt they had paid their gratitude and they don't feel they need to go anymore to church. (personal interview, 2002)

Some Ontario Khmer who used to go to church on a regular basis also participated in Buddhist ceremonies and rituals. Once a local Buddhist temple becomes established, however, a significant 'reconnecting' of Christians back to Buddhism occurs, similar to the pattern in the United States (Smith-Hefner 1994: 24; Men 2002: 228). During recent interviews, most Christian and Buddhist Cambodians minimized the differences between the two religions, emphasizing their moral commonalities to do good by helping others and being generous, not to do harm by killing, stealing, lying, and not to engage in other inappropriate activities. Men also notes that Khmer returning to Buddhism use Christianity as an additional tool for moral teaching, enhancing the existing religious system (2002: 228). Cambodians in resettlement conflate religious boundaries to create new social and religious spaces for themselves. Their complex attempts to relate religious life to urban settings and override apparently contradictory religious affiliations and practices 'speak to their efforts to create new meanings in the context of their experience as refugees and their insertion into a particular form of American capitalism' (Douglas 2005: 125). Ontario Cambodians note that what is important is not the religion one has, but that Khmer cultural identities and practices are retained. These can include, participation in traditional ceremonies and festivities, making Cambodian food, wearing traditional clothing, supporting Khmer music and dance, speaking the Khmer language, honouring the ancestors, and maintaining an association with Cambodia. Cambodian Christians today feel that they can choose for themselves what to retain. Individual judgments are made as to when to go to a memorial service or not, depending on their relationship to the hosting family. New attitudes and meanings allow a greater flexibility in attending religious activities, both Buddhist and Christian, and in developing innovative syncretic practices.

Ontario Khmer Missionary Work in Cambodia

As the numbers of Cambodian Christians decline in Ontario, many of the Khmer Christian pastors and highly committed Khmer Christians are returning to Cambodia to do missionary work. They cite a great need in their homeland, and that people there are more receptive to their Christian message. In the United States, Cambodian youth are encouraged to work at odd jobs for non-Khmer Christians in order to earn money to participate in organized short-term summer missionary activities in Cambodia (Douglas 2003: 172). Among Ontario Khmer Christians, motivations to do mission work are more personal. A Cambodian woman from London who returned to Cambodia to work for a Christian aid agency explained:

> Many people ask why I do this work with so many struggles and demands and difficulties of the children, and my husband leaving his church-related job in Canada. But because I am a Christian, one believes that you are being called to serve. And it would be in my heart, too, to serve my own people at the same time. Even there in Canada, I also service my own people, too, it's just that it's different here. (personal interview, 2002)

A Khmer Christian woman from Ottawa has been returning to Cambodia since 1993. She explained that working there provides an outlet for her aspiration to strengthen the message of Christianity in women:

> In 1999–2000, I moved to Singapore to produce the *Women of Hope* program in Khmer as part of the Transworld World Radio Project. Project Hannah was the women's program and I translated and provided the voice with other Khmer women. By 2000, I was back in Cambodia to broadcast the program, specifically for women. It was a one-half-hour program with two parts. The first part was a lesson for life, based on education or health care; the second part was a lesson for the soul, spiritual encouragement based on the word of God ...
>
> Most villages have churches and most of the churches have a women's group with women leaders. When I visit the churches in the villages, it is to visit with these women. They ask me about areas of the Bible because they don't read and write. So I share the word with them through Bible study, and we listen to tapes about the Bible. The distribution of tapes was part of the Hannah Project. But this time, it will be on my own as I am no longer on contract with the Hannah Project. I have a good relation-

ship with the EFC [Evangelical Fellowship of Cambodia], Women's Cambodian Ministry. This ministry is for women who work in the church as volunteers. Women pastors do exist but they are still not really respected by the men so they have a hard time. Yet, the church is growing because of the women. (personal interview, 2002)

Cambodian Christian women in the United States are said to be active contributors to church services, with several significant public roles (Douglas 2005: 135). This does not occur to the same degree among Christian Cambodians in Ontario. For some Cambodian Christian women, fighting against the patriarchy of Cambodian culture is a critical feature of their ministry. This modernizing feminist stance, directed at the male Christian leadership who still assume spiritual authority and power over women is expressed by a Khmer Christian woman from Ottawa:

Christian teaching gives women a whole different perspective. In the church, the most active, focused work is from the women. The men pastors cannot 'lift up the women.' The way they speak to the women is in a way to keep themselves as the 'leader' and they put down the women. Some do not realize they do this and afterwards I tell them. Although the Khmer pastors are Christian, they still use the traditional terms for women and speak about women being there to serve the men. This is not right. The Bible says women are helpers, not servants.

The women are not stupid, but are bound to the society, to the culture, and the traditional Khmer culture is to keep women down. When the women grow in maturity, spiritually as Christian women, they can increase their standing. They have more self-esteem and care for themselves more. God wants us to be like Him and this brings us close to the spiritual, this is the grace of God. Women are afraid to say or do anything because they think they are weak, but I want to help them realize they are strong, and that is God's teaching. The value that God gave to them [the women] is high, it is not a value based on what men have given them. This is the word of God, the truth ...

The Christian women in Cambodia are so strong, they can stand up and talk. Even the government is recognizing the strength of the Christian women. I want to help the women to become effective leaders, to support them and give encouragement to them because they know their people best. Now, when I go back to Cambodia this time, I will be a partner with the OMF [Overseas Missionary Fellowhip], for fellowship and accountability. But I am free to do my own work with the local Christian station and with the village women. (personal interview, 2002)

In contrast, male pastors from Ontario tend to return to Cambodia to build churches. One pastor first returned in 1992 to introduce Christianity to surviving family and friends in his home village. His conversion attempts were so successful, he has returned numerous times since:

All the friends and family were happy to see me and wanted to celebrate with food and wine, but I told them while we were eating that now I am a Christian, I don't drink, and I told them about Jesus. I showed a Christian film (video) to about four hundred people in the village and some made their commitment then. Fourteen young people made their commitment over the month I was there ...

During the month I stayed there in February 1994, a church was started and a child care centre. The child care is to help the parents work and to keep the older children in school by not having to quit to look after the younger ones when the parents work ... In August 1994, I went with my wife and with [another pastor] and his wife, to Taiwan for a ten-day orientation and then all four of us went to Cambodia to a village there for two weeks. My wife and my youngest son, then thirteen years old, decided to go back to Cambodia in 1996 for one year or more. We had to return to Canada in 1997 due to the political fighting, but then we returned in 1998 and stayed till 1999 December. The church in my home village expanded to seven churches in different villages, all in the same district. People came from distant villages, heard the Gospel, the message, and they became committed and built their own church. Not all churches have buildings, only two, while the other five meet in people's homes. (personal interview, 2002)

An Ontario Khmer pastor commented on the transnational connections of the particular Christian organization that supported his ministry in Cambodia, noting the various support services provided to converts:

In 1994, I returned to Cambodia ... to teach people in my village. I held the first baptism for two hundred people during this time. The village is 22 kilometres south of Phnom Penh ... When I came back, I reported on the baptism.

I made [a] connetcion with the Free Methodist Association in Asia, which involves missionaries from Canada and the United States. The Free Methodist Association in Asia is an organization of missionaries in nine Asian countries (India, Japan, Taiwan, Philippines, Hong Kong, and so on). The idea is to send people in these countries to other countries to open new doors. Cambodia is considered to be a 'new door' ... They [converts] get some financial support from the Free Methodist Church in Canada and the organization in Asia.

Missionaries from Hong Kong and Japan will make short visits to Cambodia twice a year, to those villages with churches, and will bring with them doctors, dentists, schoolteachers, nurses, and pastors. Over a couple of years, they will have seen all the villages ... These people make reports to the organization in Asia, then recommendations are made for what needs to be done, for example, to build a church, to dig a well, to build a school. In the village next to my village the Free Methodist Association in Asia built a school, but the Cambodian government provides the teacher. They also provide Khmer Bibles, Khmer songbooks, and literature. They also provide funding for Khmer pastor-training in the Phnom Penh Inter-denominational Bible School. The finances come through the Hong Kong office ... Women can also be trained as pastors. Many are also teachers and medical trainees. (personal interview 2002)

A non-denominational Khmer pastor returned to Cambodia in 2002 funded by, and in the company of, several Korean evangelicals from Toronto. Another Ontario Khmer pastor, associated with the Christian Alliance Church, regularly returns to Cambodia to assist with inter-denominational leadership training seminars, preaching in churches outside his own mission. He noted that more than a thousand Khmer Christians from this organization, mainly American, have returned to Cambodia as missionaries since the 1990s. The small Seventh-day Adventist Cambodian group in Toronto also maintains affiliations with other Khmer Adventists in the United States through annual camp meetings and crusades, providing money for conversion activities in Cambodia, and participating in a Cambodian radio project. These transnational connections provide important support for Cambodian Christians in Ontario, but it remains to be seen if they will contribute to the expansion of Ontario Cambodian Christian communities. Without providing details, Marston and Guthrie (2004: 196) note increasing evidence of some tension between Christians and Buddhists in Cambodian rural areas, and it is assumed that this, too, will effect continuing conversions of Canadian Khmer to Christianity, as well as the status of

Christian pastors from overseas communities. Poethig (2001) also finds this tension among Cambodian American Christians and their defence of new religious identities.

Initially, conversion provided a small number of Ontario Khmer with opportunities to reinvent themselves and fast-track into Western values of individualism and self-interest. The majority of Khmer, however, retained the conviction that the continuity of traditional Cambodian holidays, ceremonies, celebrations, and classical culture is closely affiliated with Buddhism. Participation in Buddhist festivals and events provides them with a significant expression of their Cambodian identity, even among those who, simultaneously, retain a belief in Christianity. The acceptance by first-generation Cambodians of a growing religious accommodation and syncretism reflects the abiding importance of personal and community connections through weddings, funerals, and honouring the deceased. The second generation's limited knowledge of both Christianity and traditional Buddhist practices and activities, however, has resulted in more expressions of confusion regarding the hybrid religious and cultural identities available to them.

6 Challenges and Concerns of Ontario Cambodian Youth

Family Dynamics and Cultural Continuity

As Zhou and Bankston have pointed out, 'children growing up in households headed by poor, low-skilled immigrants face uncertain prospects for moving ahead through school success. The parents, of course, have few of the economic resources that can help children do well in school. The environment does not help when neighborhoods are poor, beset by violence and drugs, and local schools do not function well. To add to this difficulty, immigrant children receive conflicting signals, hearing at home that they should achieve at school while learning a different lesson – that of rebellion against authority and rejection of the goals of achievement – on the street.' Meanwhile, both real life and television inculcate children with the consumer standards of Western society, and 'children come to expect more than their parents ever had' (1998: 3).

Second-generation Cambodians in North America have been raised within these kinds of competing value systems. Changing expectations of cultural behaviours and relationships have particularly affected both them and their parents. First-generation Khmer refugees experienced marital problems that reflected gender-specific difficulties in adjusting to a new society while attempting to retain traditional norms and roles (Krulfeld 1994; McLellan 1995; Smith-Hefner 1999; Ong 2003). The father's role in supporting the family and maintaining moral authority at home was especially challenged. As wives found alternative financial support through employment or welfare payments, many Cambodian women left their husbands (Ong 2003: 154). In Ontario, ongoing integrative and adaptive challenges to often hostile social environments weakened already-fragile family relationships. One young Khmer adult who had arrived in Canada when he was eight years old, recalled the impact that these challenges had on his family:

> At work, that's where prejudice really takes its steam, 'cause it involves adults. Part of it was the language issue. My Dad, he never drank, he was a hard-working farmer until he came here. And he started working and the only jobs he could get without the English language were a lot of farm jobs, agriculture jobs. Even then, he still faced prejudice and racism. He started working and facing this, and he developed a drinking problem because of the pain and the sheer pressure of just being what he was as a small minority. Not only did I encounter it myself, but I saw how it affected my family. When he had to face this on his mind every day, it took him away from the family, especially playing with the kids, me and my brother and sister. It totally just disbanded the family. He developed this drinking habit and it was just so sad. This really explains why I turned to the Cambodian [youth] group as a young man. (personal interview, 2005)

The consequences of family tensions often manifested themselves in domestic violence, men refusing to help out at home and who stayed away gambling and drinking with friends, women who refused to accept male authority, and parents who desired to make up for lost teenage years, seeking parties and fun (McLellan 1995). During the 1980s and 1990s, as parents attempted to balance their Khmer identity with the necessity of learning a new language and finding a sense of place within Canadian multicultural society, youth faced their own issues of self-identification. Youth found that Khmer cultural practices at home and within the community were often in conflict with the dominant Canadian culture that surrounded them. One young Khmer mother stated:

> In Cambodian culture we seldom call a person by their names as this is impolite or not showing respect. Respect is very important. This causes big problems with families. Children learn English and call their siblings and friends by name. The parents see this as a lack of respect. I advise my kids not to call Asians by names, but it is okay to call whites by Mr or Mrs family names. For [Cambodian] kids, it's not okay to call each other by names, but to put more emphasis on the general, like big brother or little sister and adults as grandfather or auntie. (personal interview, 2004)

Some Cambodian youth were pressured to change their Khmer names to common English ones, as noted in the comments by two brothers from Windsor:

Elder brother: We are still in contact with the actual church that sponsored us. The people there, the man became our godfather.
Younger brother: They're the ones that pushed us to have our names changed to English names. Before I went to school, that's when my name was changed.
Elder brother: For about the first fifteen years, we didn't say what our real names were.
Khmer friend: I didn't know what his Cambodian name was, just now is the first time I knew it. I always knew him as [Canadian name].
Younger brother: I was always called by a Cambodian name at home, and the Canadian name at school. My parents would know that when someone called and asked for [Canadian name], that was me.
Elder brother: They only changed mine, [my brother's], and my sister's name because we were the only ones that were going to go to school. My other brother, and my other sisters, they were expected to work so their names didn't change. Like [older sister], she changed her name by herself eventually, afterwards when she wanted to return to school. When we were initially going to school, it was [Canadian names]. I don't think today you would have to change your names to go to school. Today, you hear all kinds of names.
Younger brother: Now it's a celebration of diversity, there are so many different names. People just make up names for their child. (personal interview, 2005)

As Khmer children developed identities based on their experiences of being raised in Canadian society, they rejected more traditional forms of parental authority (social and moral). The generational conflicts that arose are similar to those found in other Cambodian immigrant groups (Berry et al. 2006; Rosseau et al. 2004; Zhou and Bankston 1998). Cambodian youth in Ontario identified several problematic intergenerational dynamics within their homes: parents being unable to help with school homework or participate in school-based activities; strong parental emphasis on Khmer-based models of social behaviour and showing respect; emotional restraint; demands of unquestioning obedience from children towards elders; and harsh reactions towards youth rebellion, especially in daughters. Parents and youth clashed over styles of dress, food preferences, types of entertainment, and socializing. A forty-nine-year-old Khmer woman with two daughters and a son in their teens and early twenties commented on the generational differences in her family:

There is a difference between the younger and older generation. When you come to a new country or when you are born in a country that is not the same as your ethnic background, you tend to try and fit in as much as possible. My children came to Canada when they were very young, and therefore, they pretty much follow or live more of a Western type of lifestyle. Their taste in music, clothing, and views on particular things are very different from mine. I try to preserve their Cambodian roots, but it is difficult to do so.

I speak Cambodian to them all the time so that they will not forget the language. I usually say something in Cambodian and they would respond in English. They can understand a lot of Cambodian, but they have a hard time speaking it. I usually cook Cambodian and Western foods at home; my husband and I prefer Cambodian foods, and my children prefer Western foods. There are only a few Cambodian dishes that my children enjoy. I actually prefer cooking Western foods because I find it to be a lot easier; there is usually a lot less ingredients and steps to go through.

The Cambodian youth of today want to be free. They seem to be very independent, they want to go out and live their own life. This is much different from when I was a youth, and we usually lived with our parents until we got married. When my children were younger, they used to go to the temple or Cambodian celebration with me, but as they got older, they did not want to go anymore. They do go once in a while if I ask them to go with me, but they do not stay long. I do not blame them because they are very busy and the celebrations are fairly long. (Vireak Ly interview, 2004)

In some American Cambodian families, generational conflicts were reported over the kinds of material representations within Khmer homes (Ong 2003: 169). Ontario Khmer youth did not regard Cambodian furnishings and pictures as contentious, but as recognizable features of Khmer identity. In describing their homes, Ontario youth stated that most living rooms included portraits of the Angkor Wat (wall paintings or on calendars); statues and/or large pictures of *Apsaras* (Khmer female deities); a shrine area for Buddhist statues, incense, and candles;

pictures of deceased ancestors and family members; karaoke, video, and DVD machines (usually to play Khmer music or Khmer, Thai, and Chinese movies); and in recent years, satellite TV to play Cambodian stations all day and evening. Other youth mentioned that the smell in the air (a merging of fish sauce, tamarind, and incense), taking shoes off before entering the home, and the use of a bucket and scoop for bathing would also identify the home as Khmer. Youth regard the smells, behaviours, and material representations as symbols of their cultural and ethnic continuity.

Distinct differences between older Khmer youth, who had arrived in Canada as pre-teens or teenagers, and younger Khmer youth, born and/or raised in Ontario, have added to the complexity of generational tensions. Rosseau et al. (2004) note that while Cambodian refugee youth initially expressed overcompensation in their efforts to succeed, overwhelming issues of mental health and family environment led to numerous secondary stresses in schooling and individual challenges. Many Cambodian families imposed two sets of behavioural criteria for their children. Older youth were expected to adhere to the traditional Khmer ideals of obedience to parents, restrictive gender behaviour, proper etiquette in speech patterns, and a willingness to accept arranged marriages. Younger youth, now in their teens and early twenties, however, have questioned and/or rejected these practices and associated restrictions on their freedom. Most oppose traditional expectations, especially regarding restrictions on dating and arranged marriages, and more aspire to careers and higher education. Achieving these aspirations has been particularly difficult for young Khmer women. In the mid-1990s, one twenty-two-year-old Khmer woman found solace in the fact that although she had been pressured into an arranged marriage and forced out of college, her fifteen-year-old sister would not be. Parental involvements in courtship and marriage are highly significant facets of traditional Khmer culture in resettlement. Their power to arrange marriages represents a key expression in preserving the moral reputation of daughters, especially when countering allegations of sexual promiscuity that may arise through casual dating or school-related activities (Ong 2003; Smith-Hefner 1999). One teenage Khmer girl in Toronto stated:

> It is not possible for me to date boys. My parents go crazy. There is no compromise in my family on this subject. You date and that means you marry. (personal interview, 1994)

Gender restrictions among Cambodian youth made it difficult for them to socialize with one another in public, or to make friends in school, since any male/female interaction could result in a forced engagement. Cambodian girls were not encouraged to participate in Cambodian youth association meetings or to become involved in youth activities, such as weekly volleyball play. At the Toronto Cambodian Workshop in 1994, the few Cambodian girls present were all accompanied by a parent. While many parents did encourage their daughters to finish high school, and showed pride in their accomplishments, moral reputations remained of greater concern. Cambodian girls who did not act in a traditional manner and wanted to go to out after school, have dates, a boyfriend, or multiracial friends were labelled 'bad' girls. This label prohibited them from having friendships with 'good' girls and reduced their chance of a good dowry. To avoid this label, or if a girl's reputation was being threatened, parents often insisted that she get married before her schooling was finished. They felt that in this way their daughter would at least become a respectable Cambodian wife, and being dependent on the husband, would concern herself with housework and raising children. The consequences of this clash were evident in the early 1990s, as noted by one young adult Khmer from Ottawa:

> The young girls here are rebelling and this is breaking up family structure. If parents get tough in discipline and in teaching girls to obey, for example, spanking or beatings, this is considered child abuse and youth know their rights. They report parents and youth leave home and collect welfare to go to school. The young girls say, 'It's my life.' Parents feel helpless to control girls. This causes a lot of frustration, and mothers feel even more depressed because they are blamed for not raising their daughters properly. (personal interview, 1994)

During the 1990s, younger Khmer youth expressed confusion about the value of their Cambodian identity, and were especially shamed by the ongoing conflicts in Cambodia. They did not understand why the traumatic events of the Khmer Rouge regime occurred or why the Khmer Rouge were continuing to cause suffering to their own countrymen. Khmer youth spoke of being taunted by other Southeast Asian youth about the genocidal tendencies of the Khmer Rouge and the helplessness of the Khmer people to resist either Khmer Rouge or Vietnamese control. Some youth wondered if there was something inherently wrong with Cambodians. These experiences, combined with the severe shortage of Khmer cultural and language programs and community role models or leaders, inadvertently encouraged youth to renounce their Khmer identity and seek alternatives to develop self-identity, self-esteem, and success. During the 1994 workshop for Cambodian refugees in Ontario, several of the youth participants were highly critical of Khmer culture, ridiculing the wearing of traditional Cambodian clothing (*sampot* and *krama*) in Canada, and expressing doubt that rural Cambodian values and traditions had any worth in urban Canadian society. Other youth passionately debated why wearing long hair and an earring should negate their identity as Khmer in the eyes of the community. Khmer youth expressed confusion as to what was involved in identifying themselves as a Khmer: Was it a matter of acknowledging Khmer ancestors, or must it involve an active participation in cultural traditions? Similar issues were raised concerning those Khmer youth whose families converted to Christianity and refused to associate with or attend Buddhist ceremonies and festivities. The pervasive difficulties and confusion confronting youth, however, gave rise to the emergence of youth leaders.

Youth leadership during the mid-1990s was primarily comprised of individuals born in Cambodia and who arrived in Canada as pre-teens or as older youth. The Khmer Youth Association of Hamilton (KYAOH) was the first Ontario youth group to form. A former leader from Hamilton recalled the development of the KYAOH:

In the early 1990s, we began networking with youth groups in Ontario through sports (basketball) and social events (parties, galas, mutual friends). Education was not mentioned because youth were not looking for learning. Once the network was in place, then education became a factor, not so much because we talked about it, but because of peer pressure. The youth noticed the examples of who was going to college, who were finishing school, and so forth. These examples pushed kids to take the extra step of keeping in school, of having dreams, and of getting higher education. Before, they didn't know people who had done this. This was a big influence on me when I was in high school and made me make the effort to go on to university. When the youth networks became more formal, this is when the leadership began. Leaders were looked up to as older brothers, as older youth who had accomplished things. This allowed the creation of the organization KYAOH, about 1993–94. This was also my first year of college.

KYAOH was narrowed to Hamilton youth, but word got out about the association and others liked what we were trying to accomplish, especially to get youth off the street into creative activities such as sports (swimming, playing ball), social ties, crafts. The Hamilton Police Youth Unit and the United Way were interested in us and provided funding. All activities were held at a Cambodian Drop-in Centre, rented from the YMCA. Of course, youth could bring their non-Khmer friends, but the emphasis was for Cambodian youth. Education was a silent theme merged in with all the other programs. When KYOAH was active, we saw a really positive response in kids going on to school. Some kids started post-secondary education only because they were supported and encouraged to do this. (personal interview, 2002)

Hamilton youth leaders developed a variety of successful strategies to address their concerns.[1] This association provided a model for other Ontario Cambodian youth groups to follow.[2] Youth associations provided positive models of educational success and utilized existing social ties between friends to expand peer networks. They connected youth with mainstream institutions, channeled youth into creative activities, addressed contentious family dynamics, and provided an environment wherein cultural and background experiences were understood and shared. Youth associations became a forum in which new leaders could be nurtured to participate in organization and future directions.

By the late 1990s, as the initial leaders of the Hamilton youth group married, began their own families, and became involved with careers, their involvement with the youth association decreased. The new generation of youth leaders continued to face challenges in encouraging post-secondary aspirations and dealing with restrictive parental attitudes towards gender. In addition, they increasingly contended with the lure of gang activities and changes in younger youth attitudes. A former youth leader from Hamilton commented:

From 1994 to 1997, the group was fairly strong and we brought a lot of people together and did many activities, most of which were fundraising events to keep the group going. Despite the strength of the group and the knowledge, once the leadership left, the group doesn't exist anymore. As a result of that association in Hamilton, when it existed, the youth who utilized the association benefited greatly from that. There was a surge of educated Cambodians, [both] male and female. After the Youth Association didn't exist anymore, until today, the education level I noticed is a lot lower than before. Now there are a lot of problems with drugs and other things in Hamilton. Just because they don't have anywhere else to go to. (Khmer Youth Workshop, 2005)

The Hamilton Khmer youth drop-in centre still has about two hundred participants, but the leadership has dissipated. Potential leaders are going to university and working full-time, leaving little time for community involvement. The newer youth associations formed within the last few years in Toronto, Ottawa, and Windsor tend to be more identified with Buddhism and emphasize cultural continuities as well as educational achievement.[3] Khmer youth leaders burn out quickly in the face of extensive youth needs, the lack of institutional support, and resistance from within the community. A former youth leader from Hamilton noted the traditional and current kinds of pressures facing youth leaders:

The gender gap used to be very distinguished, and the early activities of KYAOH attracted a male audience. It was very hard to attract females and still have community support, as the Cambodian community is not supportive for female participants. This problem continues, with the female youth mainly being the audience when the male youth play sports. Still, there are some female leaders who stand out for their leadership abilities. Yet, they run into the stigma of a community; for example, it is not acceptable that a female leader approaches a male participant.

Part of the continuing problem is that incidences did occur when there was male/female interaction. These problematic incidences only added to parental fears and gave parents actual examples of what they didn't want to see happen if the males and females participated together, so they used these examples of why they don't want their daughters to participate.

Unfortunately, these few bad experiences have given the second-generation youth leaders more difficulty to break through the parental/community suspicion. Now, young men are going off and creating their own gangs with gang-related activities (involved in narcotics, hanging out, getting into trouble with petty theft). Violence among the youth is also increasing, especially with weapons such as knives. The older youth had grown up with religious beliefs and respect for community knowledge (proper way to behave, listening to elders). This relieved some of the potential dangers of getting involved in certain activities. The older youth had a sense of consequences from the religious teaching [karma, cause and effect]. Now, the younger youth do not think about consequences, they just act out. (personal interview, 2002)

In Toronto, many of the newer youth leaders are second-generation. Cambodian women, several of whom have post-secondary degrees and work with the CCAO or Hong Fook developing leadership and community programs. Young Khmer women leaders' attempts to modify the older generation's expectations regarding what consti-tutes a 'good' Cambodian girl are slowly changing Cambodian gender dynamics in Ontario. They also state it is a continuous struggle to find a place for themselves as Canadian women with all of the opportu-nities, and still be considered 'good Khmer women' within the com-munity. This struggle begins to escalate in high school when issues of dating and close male/female relations arise. During the 2005 Khmer Youth Workshop, the young men and women spoke on gender issues. Participants included those born in Cambodia who came to Canada as young adults (within the previous ten years; a new first generation), older youth with some Canadian education (resettled in the 1980s; the 1.5 generation), and younger youth born and/or raised in Canada (the majority of participants). Comments during one group discussion reflect their different opinions and expectations, indicating that while change is imminent, individuals and families remain uncertain as to what those changes will embody:

Young Toronto man: Cambodian parents disapprove of girls having close relationships with another guy. That's how I see it in my family anyway.
Young Brampton man: My family is all male, but what I've noticed in oth-er families is that the women, the girls are not really allowed out, but the guys just do whatever they want to.
Young Toronto man: Some families are more Western now.
1.5 generation Hamilton man: I see the roles changing very much right now. Because of my age, I have a daughter, and it used to be that parents were very strong and the girls stayed at home. But right now she is work-ing and she has a boyfriend, and we don't expect the same things. Our attitude is that we can't expect that they will do like in the past. We have to be more open. Parents have to change over time.
New first generation Windsor man: Over there [in Cambodia], girls don't have much choice to have a guy friend, but over here they are more free. Myself, I have had a lot of friends who are girls, and we sneak around to just hang out and have fun. And slowly the parents realize that this is not really bad and they don't mind too much.
Young Toronto woman: If you come from a family that has strong Khmer

traditions, it's bad, it's really bad. It's bad for her to be seen in public; they're careful of the clothes. It's a little ridiculous 'cause when you come here, these things are okay. My parents are sort of okay, they accept me and compromise a little bit, but the curfew is really strict, like at 5 p.m. And sometimes when you come home, it's bad. It's really horrible. I think there's got to be a balance.

1.5 generation Toronto man: I don't think it's only Cambodian people alone who are strict on the girl. A lot of cultures, other countries are more strict on the girl. The guys can go out any time they want, but the girl – you've got to go in a group, and tell the parents the time, and where they go.

1.5 generation Toronto woman: It's very different now here. In Cambodia, the man is going out, he may be the breadwinner and bring home the money, and all the money he makes he gives to his wife. She manages it, and everything to do with the home. But here, that is changing. Women here also have a full-time job, and often she is doing the same kind of work he is doing, maybe working in the factory, in the office. She may work somewhere downtown and she has to go out. Also, she may be doing cooking for the temple. So here she has more responsibility, she has to make sure the kids do well, keep the budget. And if you buy a house, that's even more responsibility with all the cleaning. So, something is going on here and she has more responsibility and less power.

Young Windsor woman: I don't see it as power. We may have more responsibility in the household, but that has nothing to do with power or authority. What kind of power or control do you have in your life situations. For us it's more like, 'This is your role, this is your responsibility.'

Young Maple man: I think in traditional Cambodian families, the father's power is absolute, whereas the mom, even though she has more responsibility, she has no say what to do, the decisions of taking care of things. Even if she worked, the money goes to the father's account or to the father. She pays the mortgage, she pays everything but in the house the father's power is absolute. What goes on in the house is the father's choice. He can kick anyone out.

1.5 generation Toronto man: If you have the Khmer identity, if you dilute all the tradition and culture, then you're not being Khmer, you're just becoming Canadian. Because you're not true, that's how I look at it. I will have my children do certain things, certain traditions, that is, Cambodian traditions, that I will consider she's Cambodian. If she dates, or goes out, that's not Cambodian, so therefore she has the mentality of Canadian. That's not true, that's diluted.

Young Brampton man: We can't ignore the fact that there are certain traditions that might not be so righteous as you think. And to ignore that is just
being neglectful. There are certain things that really can't be changed, but
a little bit of change is okay. For myself, I see myself in a family where the
chores can be divided, both parents working. So it's not diverging too far
from the tradition but it's modified slightly. There are parts of the tradition
that can be improved, and this is not diluted, it doesn't hurt the identity
in any way.

Young Toronto woman: Yes, you can still preserve the culture and just
share the responsibility.

School Environments and Gang Associations

Generational expectations and confusion have affected Cambodian
youth involvement in education. Their levels and types of participation, aspirations, and scholarly achievements were associated with personal and family difficulties, disillusionment, and during high school,
with danger. Many Cambodian youth acknowledged that their parents
were not able to provide them with concrete guidance regarding school,
or the discipline to help them navigate competing demands of school,
work, and social activities. One young Khmer man recounted the effect
that this had on the second generation:

Some of the other issues going on with the youth were that a lot of people,
my cousin for one, they grow up with nice families, but they still end up
dropping out of school. I believe their parents were too nice. The parents
don't push the kids. But the parents have to struggle a lot, too, because
they don't know how Canadian children are supposed to grow up. We
grow up in the Canadian society, and the parents feel that they can't help
their children. They don't even know how to look over the report cards.
But that was in the 1990s. We don't see this in 2005. The [younger] parents
now, they know more what to do; they have been raised here; they know
how the Canadian life is. It is just too bad that we have had to go through
that. (personal interview, 2005)

A female youth worker explained the cultural background that contributed to the parents' attitudes towards school, particularly regarding
discipline:

The cultural expectation among Cambodians is that the teacher will help raise the children and teach them the proper way to address parents and elders, and to teach them discipline, saying, 'Your teachers are your second parents and you need to listen to your parents.' In Canada, the teacher is a regular worker and the value of education is just education. But in Cambodia, there is a higher value on teaching ethics and morals. In Cambodia, little boys will often go to the temple to learn morals and values and then this is reaffirmed in the schools. Here, some of the Christian schools will do this. (personal interview, 2004)

A serious issue that faced Cambodian youth in Ontario was that they received little social recognition as a refugee group with special needs, and few non-Khmer expressed concern for their poor concepts of self and ethnic identity. During the mid-1990s, the conflicts facing older Cambodian youth were generally ignored, and the lack of meaningful intervention greatly contributed to the difficulties they had in finishing high school. The vice-principal of a high school in North York stated:

We have not done anything special for Cambodians. There are lots of traumatized youth here. But, the highest groups causing difficulties in the school are Vietnamese and Caribbeans; therefore, the programs are geared towards them. There is no data on the dropout rate by ethnicity. Part of the problem is defining 'dropout' – if they just disappear or go to another school. You have to make priority judgments based on the awareness of need. The access to programs and services is not equal. Those who get access are those who are most visible or acting out. (personal interview, 1994)

Few Cambodian youth in the mid-1990s were involved in scholastic and personal development counselling programs offered by Ontario boards of education, despite their almost 90 per cent dropout rate.[4] Second-generation Khmer youth today recognize that parental unfamiliarity with school expectations contributes to youth alienation and their educational difficulties. They also cited other factors that included Khmer parents' excessive involvement in social activities, parents dealing with overwhelming mental or physical health challenges, parents being too busy working two jobs just to cover household expenses, and conflicting family expectations. A Cambodian youth worker in Toronto commented on some of the family difficulties facing older youth:

I started working here about a year and a half ago and saw youth had problems with drugs, hanging out, and drinking – typical youth problems. I want to help them educate themselves, improve their lives, maybe move to a different location. Many say they don't like where they stay, the house/apartment is too crowded. Many [of their] Cambodian homes are welfare based, so when they turn twenty-one and don't move out, this causes problems with crowding, and with benefits reductions and expectations from welfare that they should help with the payment. The Cambodian expectation is also that the youth should help parents and help pay for a better living place by having a good job and contributing. But drinking and drugs, and a lack of education which means no good job to help sponsor themselves and their family, all cause problems.

Parents would want them to go but most of the youth cannot support themselves. The youth who live in this area do not see good examples to better themselves. You really can't blame the youth because this is what they have grown up with. Another problem is the youth whose Cambodian parents have drinking, drugs, or gambling problems which are destroying the family ...

Parents expect youth to think for themselves. Parents expect their kids to be better than them, but they don't tell or teach them how to have a better approach to life. Parents know that they themselves are not a good example for the children by drinking, gambling, low education. They know they are not a good role model, so they want the kids to do something different. But the kids grow up thinking that smoking, drinking is acceptable. Also, there is a cultural thing that the father will not tell the child that what the parent does is wrong. Parents will not admit their faults but still expect the youth to do better. (personal interview, 2004)

In trying to balance being Khmer with being Canadian, many youth sought new identities, new role models, and a sense of belonging outside their families and community. Their daily exposure to North American consumer culture, television, schools, and non-Khmer peers provided a variety of alternative ideas, values, and opportunities. Youth leaders note that the combined attraction of easy money, easy drugs, and lack of responsibility among school dropouts is a powerful lure for Cambodian youth. One young Khmer man commented on the consequences of these influences during his recent high school years:

The dropout rate was really high. There was a lot of skipping classes and everything like that. And I did get caught up in that. It was fun. I skipped school for a year, but then I realized I was not going to fuck around and blow it. I had spent a lot of time getting stoned, playing cards. When you find new friends, girls, too, you just want to hang around and you have too much fun. Mostly it was smoking marijuana. I also took some ecstasy when we would go to the raves, and shrooms, once or twice. I did the drugs for about five years, but then I just got bored. We also did a lot of alcohol ...

Struggling with the dropout was one of the youth problems, also the drugs, both male and female, and hanging out make a lot of fights with the parents. Especially the girls, they really had to fight to get their independence. Parents were really afraid of gang activity and teen pregnancy ... Lots of girls got pregnant and most kept the child. Many got married to the guy who got them pregnant but usually they got divorces within five years. After that, the girls tend to move back home to the parents. These women are the ones who tend to go out with non-Khmer guys, but I don't see them get married yet ...

Now I am twenty-three. Since I left high school, I have been looking for work, trying to find something that I like. I didn't have no skills, so I am just going through different kinds of jobs ... I wanted to go to university, but I cannot afford that time and money. We have to pay for the new house now. So I don't think I can ever go back to school. (personal interview, 2005)

Cambodian youth leaders feel that being unemployed, not finishing high school, chronic alcohol and drug use (marijuana, cocaine, steroids), and involvement in petty crime (breaking into cars, property theft, acquiring weapons) become the common characteristics in being involved with a gang. For Cambodian youth who are associated with gang-like groups, however, they state their participation is more concerned with issues of support and protection. A young Khmer man from the Jane-Finch area in Toronto recalled:

I started becoming aware of the youth issues in 1999. During that time there was a lot of police harassment towards the youth, till about the year 2002 or something like that ... They didn't know we were Cambodian, they just saw us as Asian, and they thought we were trafficking. I think there were Asian gangs going on at the time and there were Cambodians who were part of them ... There was also a lot of gang activity.

In school, there was Blacks against Asians. There were fights every day. They would catch each other walking by and they would catch one and drag him to the washroom and beat him up. Back and forth they would do that … The fights were probably over territorial control, maybe over the drugs, distribution. I also believe they were racist. The gangs were at school and parents were afraid of their kids' safety. The gangs had weapons and lots of fights, knives, and guns …

I didn't have so many fights. Down in my school there was a bunch of Cambodian guys so we kind of stick together, and if there's a problem with one guy, right, you know how high school is, you 'f'ing chink,' and stuff like that. Stuff might happen so we tend to stick together. (personal interview, 2005)

A young Khmer adult man who resettled in the same area during the mid-1990s noted a similar pattern:

I was twelve when I went to school here and I felt very lonely, but I didn't have people harming me, or making fun of me. But once when we got into groups [in high school], that's when the trouble was caused, groups against one another. It's a matter of understanding the turf, that's the problem. But also you get picked on, too, especially by the Black people; they are aggressive. Our people are more passive, you know, don't rock the boat, just live peacefully. Jane-Finch had a lot of violence, a lot of drugs and gangs. (personal interview, 2005)

The comments from a young Windsor Cambodian reflect a different racial element, but similar group dynamics:

When we first came to Windsor in 1980, there were maybe three or four families … I felt like a regular kid, hanging around with the other students all the time. It didn't hit me until high school that I started to see some of the other negatives of being a minority. There was racism, prejudice, bigotry, stuff like that. You live with it coming from the white brothers … In high school, yeah, some of those fights were racial. (Khmer Youth Workshop, 2005)

Youth gang involvements in Canada are correlated with racial differences in economic and social marginalization. Because they demonstrate considerable influence from American media gang imagery, especially the adopting of linguistic codes and dress styles, a clear recognition or identification of a youth association as a gang is often obscured (Wortley and Tanner 2006: 18–20). Although Khmer parents and youth leaders may refer to rebellious youth activities and their associations as 'gang-like,' the issues that typically define and characterize a gang are often absent. These include being associated with a specific name, clear organizational structures between leaders and followers, initiation rituals, common colours, control of territory, and involvement with crime (ibid.). Cambodian youth may have close socialization with one another that involves the use of alcohol and/or drugs, and provides an element of protection, but this does not necessarily imply organized criminal behaviour. Wortley and Tanner distinguish between 'criminal and social gangs,' noting that those who are frequent victims of crime and/or have low social status will seek out 'social gang' membership as a means of protection (2006: 24). Membership in this kind of youth 'social gang' is also strongly related to low levels of parental education; high levels of parental unemployment; residence in public housing projects; feelings of being stigmatized, isolated, and excluded from the outside world; and being denied access to employment or educational opportunities (ibid.: 33).

Ong notes that in the well-organized Cambodian gangs in California, including female-centred ones, gang membership became an effective social network for trading mutual obligations, for providing social structures that reinforced social and gender norms (especially patron-client systems and other forms of hierarchy and respect), and for developing strong and long-lasting social connections with each other (2003: 237–9). In Ontario, the friendship and patronage ties that arose through youth 'gang-like' affiliations have continued into adult relations as members mature and negotiate their own family and community patterns. A young Khmer adult from Toronto noted his ongoing association with former gang members:

> I still speak to them and they now have children, a big house near Keswick, near Newmarket. They had to do other things ... Many of those who dropped out, they got a job, and then they got children. (personal interview, 2005)

A youth leader from Windsor was surprised that individuals whom he once thought of as gang members now show up at youth-sponsored community events, bringing their own children along. These events are organized by a youth group started in 2005 called the Cambodiana Society of Windsor. Its leaders are older Khmer youth in their late twenties and younger Khmer, both male and female. Unlike the Khmer Athletics Association of Windsor (KAAW), an earlier sports-oriented group for young Khmer men, the Cambodiana Society targets youth from age eight and up. Their emphasis is on intergenerational activities and the reification of Khmer cultural identity through Buddhism.[5] Like youth leaders in Ottawa and Toronto, these Windsor youth leaders felt that the lack of Buddhist significance in the daily lives of Cambodian youth had contributed to their alienation from their parents and Khmer culture. A young Khmer woman explains why the second generation has such identity confusion:

> I think one of the biggest obstacles for Khmer youth out there is that they feel lost in their identity as Western and as Cambodian, that dual identity. You go to school and you speak English. And even in some schools you have to pray, even in public schools; that says Christianity is all over [the place], in Windsor, maybe not in Toronto. So when you go to school, you are faced with the Western culture, but when you come home, you have parents that speak to you in Khmer, which you don't even understand, but you have to try to understand. So I think the biggest obstacle there is for the two worlds to somehow meet in the middle, to find that even ground. (Khmer Youth Workshop, 2005)

Conflicting Youth Attitudes towards Buddhism

Buddhism is frequently seen as a fundamental aspect of Khmer identity and culture, but Cambodian youth express different attitudes regarding the importance of Buddhist activities in their lives:

> 1.5 generation man: Because of the younger generation, I think they're more Canadian than Cambodian. Most of them can't even speak Cambodian at home. So they're not very interested in the Cambodian holidays and the Cambodian culture. So when there's New Year's at the temple, they'll just think, 'It's just to go pray, stuff like that, and why don't I just stay home or go out with my friends instead.' I think that's the case. People of the younger generation, they're more Canadian than Cambodian.
> Young man: In some cases it's also religious affiliation 'cause Cambodian culture is so intertwined with Buddhism, like it's really moulded into one thing. Anytime there is a holiday there is an aspect of Buddhism involved, and those with affiliations with other religions don't really agree with that and they tend to stay away because of that Buddhism aspect of culture. (Khmer Youth Workshop, 2005)

Youth still accompany parents to temple events, but often unwillingly, as noted in the following comments:

> New first generation man: Do you guys find yourselves dragging your-selves out of bed to go the New Year's celebration, versus back home where everybody voluntarily goes there because they know there's some-thing there for them? Here, does your sister or brother want to stay home and watch TV on the Saturday instead of going out?
> Young man: Yeah, I've experienced that at home a few times to try to get my siblings to come along. I myself try to get involved with the event, and not just going there as an audience, but taking part in the cultural shows that they display for New Year's now. But my siblings, it takes a bit of prodding and pushing for them to come. So, they don't do it voluntarily, they're a bit hesitant to join in. (Khmer Youth Workshop, 2005)

Second-generation youth have stated that their resistance to commit to Buddhist beliefs, traditions, and temple leadership arose because they felt Khmer Buddhism was not relevant to their needs and identi-ties in Canada. Even youth who were seeking guidance and direction from Buddhist monks felt hesitant about going to the temple. This is in contrast to the situation in the United States, where bringing disturbed youth to a Buddhist monk often provides a process for healing that does not have the negative or stigmatizing connotations of visiting a psychiatrist (Sam 2003: 201). The recent increased presence of Buddhist monks and temples in Ontario could indicate that these benefits may be recognized here and acted upon in the future. It is more likely, how-ever, that youth will continue to be inhibited from temple participation due to the absence of a shared interpretive discourse between them-selves and what they regard as their parents' Khmer-Buddhist tradi-tion with its 'outmoded and irrelevant Cambodian family codes' (Ong 2003: 168).

In Ontario, many first-generation Cambodians continue to feel that Khmer Buddhist traditions will help retain Khmer family values in Canada, especially attitudes of respect and gratitude towards parents, moral discipline, the consequences of wrong or misguided actions, and ancestral veneration. These values remain central to their retention of Khmer identity. This correlation of Khmer Buddhist and ancestral prac-tices with the preservation of Khmer culture and tradition is evident in the comments of one middle-aged woman:

There are many things that I do to try and preserve culture while living in Canada. Some of these things are very simple to do, and are things that I do on a daily basis, such as speaking Cambodian, cooking traditional foods, and listening to Cambodian music. Other things take a bit more effort, such as going to the temple and performing religious ceremonies during special calendar days of the year. I try to go to the temple as many times as I can, but I mainly just go during the large celebrations, such as New Year's. I also try to keep up with all the important dates of the year, but there are a lot of them. But the important date I never miss is the celebration of remembering the dead. On this day, you pay your respect to your dead ancestors or relatives. You cook lots of food, and you invite the spirits to come and enjoy the feast. You also light incense and pray for the dead. You ask them to watch over you and to keep you safe. (personal interview, 2004)

The second generation shows little interest in participating in these kinds of Buddhist and ancestral events, or in finding the time necessary to become involved. A Khmer woman in her late twenties noted:

I feel that the youth involvement is not there. The older people don't take the time to show how to play the traditional Cambodian games, and on the weekend it's not so easy to do all the visiting so much. In Cambodia, the games used to be played on an empty field for the youth to get involved. Back home, they really had it organized. Here it's not going to happen so easily; people don't really have the time to become organizers, to come together ...

No Cambodian New Year is without that sticky rice cake, it's very important to have that *samkray* and *samjru*, that is, the sticky rice and banana inside and some mixed with the black pepper and salt. It's very unique; you can't find it anywhere, and they go together with every Cambodian New Year. But, it's time consuming. I work 9–5 and I'm tired when I wake up in the morning, so I only cook a small meal, maybe two pots, two dishes and that's all the time I have till I go to the temple; otherwise I'll be late. (Khmer Youth Workshop, 2005)

Yet, many youth do value the Buddhist temple, particularly its role in community cohesion and in preserving a sense of Khmer identity. The intergenerational activities organized by the Cambodiana Society of Windsor are specifically oriented towards increasing this cohesion, and they have made a concerted effort to involve older Cambodians in teaching the younger generation traditional Cambodian games and cuisine (see Sarorn Sim 2005 video). A young Khmer man commented:

> Being youth in Windsor, there's many Cambodian youth and I've noticed that most of them are losing their background. Most of them don't even know how to speak Cambodian, and the only words they know is the swear words. I've noticed that parents, new parents nowadays, they have to learn more English to speak to the kids, just because those kids are losing their background. I think that kids nowadays, they should be grateful for having a temple, and for having a youth group that we do have. What they do is that they really don't do anything, some of them are dropouts. The Cambodian youth nowadays, they're going in separate directions than what we usually want them to do. (Khmer Youth Workshop, 2005)

Two young Khmer men, who recently moved with their families from the Toronto area, noted that the Buddhist temple at Maple remains a significant cohesive community focus:

> First young man: I don't think we understood the importance of the temple, like what it does for the community and the surrounding area, especially for Cambodians like myself who live in pockets outside of Jane-Finch. We need the temple. It is the only string that we have to the rest of the community and that's what it serves as, as a cultural base for us to gather and to retain whatever traditions there are to respect.
> Second young man: For a place like Brampton, even though now we're starting to get a lot of Cambodian families in there, I think there will continue to be only one temple and there won't be any separation for Brampton. No matter how large the population gets in Brampton, we'll still continue to go to the temple in [Maple]. (Khmer Youth Workshop, 2005)

Much of the second generation's attitude towards traditional Khmer Buddhism has been influenced by what they perceive to be the North American emphasis on personal autonomy, self-responsibility, materialism, utilitarian competitiveness, and an egocentric rather than community-based religiosity. These influences provide alternative cultural relevance for Cambodian youth, particularly when traditional Cambodian values and practices are critiqued, as noted in the words of an Ontario Khmer pastor:

> One of the cultural facets of Buddhism is not to be assertive. Even if a per-

son is right, they will not speak. This is a huge challenge and it manifests in youth trying to find their identity in the face of peer pressure and the social, media messages, as well as the parental view who want the youth to stay with the Cambodian culture. But what is Khmer culture? Even the older generation is not sure beyond speaking the language, dress, food, and Buddhism. The problem is in finding a deep identity, on a spiritual basis. Christian education is the answer. (personal interview, 2002)

From certain Christian perspectives, conversion is the key to strengthening Cambodian youth to overcome cultural and religious confusion. To attract youth, many Christian churches overtly offer personal support, fun activities, and social connections. One Khmer youth commented on his religious conflict and the kinds of support he encountered with a Christian group in Newmarket:

Well, although I do believe in God, being Buddhist is still a connection with my culture. Just recently, I started going to church … I was raised with Buddhism, but believing in God offers support, lots of support from people around us. Because they are willing to do all they can to help you, and people find a lot of support actually. They give emotional support, and they are always listening to you. Before they say something, they must understand you, and all that.

Last year I went to the [Christian] Church in Newmarket. That's the first time I've been there. I felt that the kind of support they offered was what I needed in my life. I felt at home when I'm around them. They're always laughing. When something serious happened, they'd be serious. Yeah, it was something I was missing. There was a feeling of belonging, of finding my identity. And that's what I liked … the pastor made a good speech, a good talk, and I just felt a lot better. He explained what God can do for you. God can help you find a good job, make sure you keep good health, and if you want a beautiful wife that loves you, he can help you with that too … I believed him. I still believe that God can make wonderful things happen, but I don't go to church anymore, and the pastor said that to get things from God you must go to church. (personal interview, 2005)

For this youth, participation in diverse religious traditions contributed to identity confusion and caused additional pressures through his belief that even though God could help him achieve what he wants, God won't, because he is not able to commit and conform to the expectations of that particular church. Cambodian youth are being asked to make difficult choices between the Buddhism of their parents and a supportive church environment that, while offering a variety of benefits, places new types of demands on their attitudes, lifestyles, and behaviour. Conflicting religious values and beliefs can increase youth levels of insecurity and self-doubt, as noted by this Cambodian youth:

> Religion becomes an issue when you get older. When you begin to find out who you are. There is a lot of pressure on yourself to find out. Some of these questions are, 'Do I believe in Buddha or do I believe in the Lord Jesus Christ?' I believe in both of them. It's just that I was exposed to both of the teachings. I was part of the Christianity when I was younger, a lot younger, but I didn't take it seriously though. I used to go to a youth church where a lot of the time we played games, and they talk about God and everything about it. But I was just there for the games, so I wasn't aware that it was a church group. At home, I wasn't taught much of the Buddha's ways, of the Buddha's philosophy. It wasn't taught much. But my mother prayed to the Buddha all the time. I found out about Jesus Christ at another church when I was about twelve years old. I never had anyone to talk to about this, it was just kind of self-understanding, about what religion to go to. It's hard to explain. (personal interview, 2005)

Continuing Youth Struggles to Clarify Khmer Identity

The lack of representation or recognition in Canadian society of either Khmer Buddhism or Khmer culture has negatively impacted the efforts of Cambodian youth to clarify questions concerning ethnic, cultural, and religious identity. During one discussion at the 2005 Khmer Youth Workshop, several youth noted this confusion and the consequences:

> Young Windsor man: I think being Cambodian in Canada automatically puts us at a disadvantage because the Cambodian youth in Canada are not necessarily ignorant about their own culture, or it's not the fact that they don't want to learn about their own culture, it's the fact that they have no outlet. They have no resources or things available to them.
> Young Toronto woman: Yeah, you go to see at the library and there's maybe one or two books and it's on the[Cambodian] cooking.
> Young Brampton man: When I was in grade school, I never really felt like I was intimidated, or had anybody be racist towards me, because they

always called me Chinese, which I'm not [laughter]. I didn't take it personally, but as I got older I realized it was a stereotype that they all think we're Chinese, because there are so few of us.

1.5 generation Toronto woman: Yeah, exactly. I was in high school and all the people confused me as Filipino; they thought I looked like a Filipino or Chinese.

Young Toronto man: You tell them you're Cambodian and they say, 'What?' You say I'm Khmer, and they say, 'What?'

Young Toronto woman: Yeah, I have to tell them we're next door to Thailand.

Young Toronto man: Even restaurants that are run by Cambodians call themselves Thai/Viet.

1.5 generation Toronto woman: There's an automatic association that always happens, so my general conversation is, 'Oh, you're from Cambodia, so where's that again?' And I say, 'It's between Thailand and Vietnam, and we're a small country.' And they say, 'Oh you mean the *Killing Fields* one, is that the movie?' And then they always go on about the war, and say, 'So, are you people okay now?' This is an original stereotype that I get. It's always a general comment.

Young Toronto woman: In the 1990s you probably got a lot of that; 'Oh yeah, the *Killing Fields*,' but now the younger generation, if they're asked about Cambodia won't say the *Killing Fields* but will say, 'Oh Thailand, yeah that's near Indonesia, that's a really nice place.'

Young Toronto man: I think when they know where the Angkor Wat stands, that's what brings about [the recognition]. Like Angelina Jolie, she made the movie in Cambodia, now everyone is starting to be aware that Cambodia has these ancient monuments. Right now it's getting better.

1.5 generation Windsor man: Yeah, she also adopted a child. [People know that] Maddox is a little two-year-old kid that Angelina Jolie adopted while shooting the movie in Cambodia.

Young Toronto woman: *The Killing Fields, Tomb Raider, City of Ghosts, Two Brothers* have all featured Cambodia.

1.5 generation Windsor man: There is something about Cambodia that shows through in each of these movies ... We're proud of it. Like *Tomb Raider* showed the famous Angkor Wat, our national heritage. So more people know of it. People at work, they ask me about the trees and all that, and I can explain about them and the structure of the Angkor.

Young Brampton man: Yeah, it's mostly the only way that people of our generation will be able to distinguish what Cambodian is. It's basically these token images in pop culture, such as *Tomb Raider*. When they ask, 'Where's Cambodia?' you say, *'Oh Tomb Raider'* and they always get that token response ... But that's basically what it is, it's all just token images in the media and pop culture that distinguishes one from everybody else. But if you're going to talk to them about the real meaning of our culture, and even the *Killing Fields*, they wouldn't know. I wouldn't say all of them wouldn't, but most of them would not. (Khmer Youth Workshop, 2005)

Beiser et al. (2005: 23) suggest that youth who are secure in their ethnic identity as well as their Canadian identity are more likely to have high self-esteem, have a greater ability to initiate interethnic contact, and have greater academic achievement. The lack of social recognition for Cambodian refugees and their difficulties in resettlement have hindered the ability of second-generation youth to integrate parental expectations of retaining Khmer heritage with the demands of mainstream identification. It is especially difficult to identify oneself to others who have no recognition of one's distinct cultural background beyond token images. Cambodian youth have also felt the shame and embarrassment of growing up in poor refugee families, common among minority children (Rajiva 2005: 27). Living with the residual shame of family poverty or being perceived as different increases a negative or confused self-identity. One discussion at the 2005 Khmer Youth Workshop revealed how several second-generation youth come to terms with these feelings:

Young Brampton man: I'm really glad that we've actually talked about this stuff instead of holding it in. I know that a lot of Cambodian youth, they'd rather not talk about it because they feel, I would say, ashamed of their culture ... I think the whole Cambodian culture, the fact that they're immigrants and they live in Canada, I think they feel ashamed.

Young Toronto man: I have to agree with what [previous speaker] said that some Cambodian youth are ashamed of their culture, back then, when they came. Now I know my parents used all the resources that they can, that they had to find the cheapest things so that they can handle things, for example, shopping at Value Village. They'd buy my clothes there, or they'd buy the cheapest socks, or jean sales. I was really ashamed to go with them. I would hide in the car and peek out the windows to see if anyone was there to see me going into these places where they sold used clothes. It was the whole poverty and my parents struggling so hard, and having to go on welfare. That was one of the main things that I used to be ashamed of.

Young Toronto woman: My mother used to, you know when you got rice and you'd get it in that bag, my mother used to save the bags. She'd fold it, and after a while we'd go through a lot of bags, like ten or twenty stacked up. My friends would come over and see the bags. I'd ask her why she just doesn't throw them out 'cause she's going to get another bag.

Young Windsor man: [At] elementary school, I felt ostracized as soon as I got there. Our family couldn't afford the nicer clothes, and they made fun of us because we couldn't afford the shoes. Me and [my brother] wore the same clothes. So I'd wear a shirt one day and he'd wear it another day, and I'd hear about it. (Khmer Youth Workshop, 2005)

Each of these second-generation youth are now involved as youth leaders negotiating issues of racial differences, addressing the competing demands of their peers and parents, cultivating new types of cultural expectations within their families and communities, and seeking strategies to develop a sense of belonging as ethnic Khmer Canadians. There is, however, no consistency among Ontario Cambodian youth. Their emergent identities are quite varied, ranging from a longing to maintain restrictive traditional cultural practices, to an acceptance of cultural hybridity and/or loss, to the recognition that their Canadian-Khmer identity is an ongoing process, subject to change. One young Khmer man commented:

The whole problem with identity is that it always changes, it is never constant. Not just our identity here because we're something in between but we can even apply it to being Canadian. That's basically what's being highlighted here now, that they [the youth] see what life is like on this side then this changes when they go back [to Cambodia]. They then see life on this side and life on that side. Where are we? Where do we fit in? And the thing is, identity changes. It is not constant. (Khmer Youth Workshop, 2005)

The identity of first-generation Khmer remains tied to pleasant memories of being raised in Cambodia and to their suffering during the Khmer Rouge regime. One Khmer man notes that this distinguishes him from his children:

No matter how long I am in Canada, I still feel that I am a refugee because of what happened in Cambodia and living in the refugee camps. My children feel they are Canadian. I know other Cambodians who don't like to be called refugees but that's what I feel I am. (personal interview, 2004)

Resettlement in Canada has provided first-generation Khmer with opportunities to overcome differing regional, religious, and political identities in favour of an identity based on shared Khmer cultural values; to participate in homeland family support and country rehabilitation; and to cultivate future plans that rely on a peaceful and stable Cambodia. In contrast, the emerging identities among the second generation in Canada are part of a larger diversity of Khmer who were born and raised in different social and national contexts.

Growing numbers of second-generation Cambodian youth from across Ontario are concerned with overcoming limited family and community resources to achieve upward mobility through post-secondary education. A large number of these youth have come of age during a time when the majority of their parents have had a sustained period of full-time employment. Employment in relatively well-paid factory jobs or self-employment has coincided with the first-time purchase of homes and movement away from subsidized neighbourhoods. Simultaneously, there has been substantial growth in the number of Buddhist temples throughout Ontario, more stability in marriages, and more frequent visits to Cambodia. Increasingly, the second generation is concerned with the need to address prevalent issues in their communities. They are especially concerned with finding effective strategies to resolve youth difficulties of cultural alienation, identity confusion, high school dropout rates, and increasing gang activities. Younger Ontario Cambodians wish to develop a strong sense of identity that is based in Canadian social realities, such as finding their place within multiculturalism and correcting erroneous impressions that others may have of Cambodians. These concerns are expressed by two youth leaders:

New first generation Windsor man: [Our youth association groups] are pointing us in the right direction, showing us what we should be learning, what we should know, so we can pass it on to another generation, so our community can grow as Cambodian people. I've noticed that our [second] generation has gone down and our knowledge of our tradition and our background has decreased dramatically. Me being aware of this and following my tradition, I think I'm being a leader by still following it no matter what anyone says, sort of somehow educating those people who don't know anything about Buddhism or have heard false things about being Cambodian or being Asian. Some people still think we eat dogs. I always have to correct them, every single one of them who say that.

Young Toronto man: I work in an Italian restaurant and people say, 'Hey, what nationality are you?' I say, 'Cambodian' and they say 'but, it's the same thing as Chinese isn't it, like you guys don't speak the same language don't you?' 'No we don't, there's different countries and we all have different ways of life.' I'm like explaining 'cause that's been my experience of being Cambodian. Some of them they learn to respect me, my ways of living my life and my ways of following my traditions. In some way, I've educated them and this gives me the power that I am a leader. In a way, our community is growing and learning from our mistakes. (Khmer Youth Workshop, 2005)

These current youth attitudes contrast sharply with those of the first generation. The primary concerns of first-generation Cambodians were not about what others thought of them, but for their extensive loss of family members, changing social roles and traditions, adaptive difficulties, overcoming mistrust, the lack of community leaders, and low levels of social capital. The struggles of the first generation to rebuild community social structures that replicate familiar relations have provided the second generation with some of the support needed to achieve its particular goals. Family and community relations, networks of obligations, expectations, solidarity, and trustworthiness are more easily generated today. Cambodian youth not only have a strong ability to bond with one another, but also to create bridging opportunities with other Buddhist or Asian communities, and link their community needs to mainstream organizations.

Influence of Cambodian Entertainment Media in Constructing Ontario Youth Identities

The relative stabilization of Cambodia's political and economic situation within the last fifteen years has facilitated the rapid growth of a Cambodian-based entertainment and media industry. As CDs and videos are distributed and shared among diaspora Cambodians, trans-

national identities and connections are nurtured beyond family connections. Cambodians in Ontario constantly listen to classical and popular
Khmer music in their homes, especially through the hundreds of Cam-
bodian-produced videos and CDs (dances and songs) that are circu-
lated among friends, rented and bought at Cambodian-based variety
stores, or downloaded from the Internet. While traditional Khmer classical music and dance are associated with Buddhist ceremonies and life
cycle rituals, the non-religious popular forms have become the crucial
component of large community dances and informal parties with family and friends. Music and dance performances (either live or recorded)
are essential at New Year's celebrations, traditional Cambodian weddings, fundraising events, or as an enhanced feature during fashion
shows (see Sarorn Sim 2005 video).

Cambodian music plays a fundamental role in shaping the identity
of second-generation Khmer. They have been raised listening to their
parents' music and dance videos and cassettes, especially of popular Cambodian singers and songs from the 1950s and 1960s. Youth,
however, do not relate nostalgically to Khmer music and dance, but
seek new meanings through merging traditional, popular, and modern forms arising within transnational contexts. Global technologies
encourage youth to explore Cambodian music and dance, not only
to download recordings, but also for educational purposes, compen-
sating for the absence of community teachers. Youth gain historical
knowledge about different types of Khmer music and musical instruments, famous musicians and dancers; they learn the basic steps and
styles of traditional Khmer dance through video and online instruction; and in their online searches, come across other interests, such as
learning to read and write Khmer or connecting with other youth in
diaspora. For many Ontario youth, the Cambodia-based production
company Hung Meas (meaning 'golden phoenix') embodies the symbolic and institutional power of music and dance, and provides them
with strong historical and cultural links to Cambodia. Youth explain
that the golden phoenix is a symbol of the Khmer because, like Cambodia, it has a history of falling and rising again; it is about the destruction of war and being reborn to start over. Hung Meas' music combines
traditional classical with pop, jazz, and rap, creating new sounds that
Cambodian youth associate with a new beginning that connects and
unites them. For Ontario Cambodian youth, Hung Meas symbolizes
cultural fusion of traditional Khmer and Western cultures. One youth
noted that within this fusion, traditional musicians can provide a back-

ground for both breakdancers and Apsara dancers. During the 2005 Khmer Youth Workshop, several young Cambodian men discussed the importance of music:

First Windsor man: Music is tied to the identity. Music is what we claim a stake in. It's a big part of our culture. It's a medium that we use to communicate our language, and the message, whether it be social commentary or whatever. Music is another medium for language, and language is a huge part of culture. And the music itself is evolving to adapt to a new culture, to a new culture abroad, and to a new generation.

Brampton man: Well, someone said yesterday that in every single culture what's common is music. What they're trying to do is to unite Cambodians by music. I think that's what they're trying to do, and they're doing a good job, too. Like last night, we really had a great time (laughter) listening to all these songs.

Toronto man: If you look at all the movies that we said earlier, the ones made in Cambodia, what kind of songs do they play: traditional songs or modern? Like the *Tomb Raider*?

First Windsor man: They play traditional.

Second Windsor man: You know why? You should ask yourselves why they don't play the new music. Because they respect who we are, like our music, they want to play it, and show other people, to the whole world. They see the beauty of the old music. The new productions now, it's because of the new generation, because they are fading away, going to hiphop, rock and roll. If they can bring the traditional music back through this, they can bring the kids back, so they are more in tune with Cambodia.

Toronto man: I think that a lot of these movies play the traditional music because we immediately recognize it for what it is, being Cambodian. Whereas if you played new pop songs, something like that, you'd say, 'What's that? Is it our music?' The traditional music has its own beats, the instruments, how it's played, how it's produced, it's just really respectful. It makes it different ... I think that with the music in Cambodia that it just really connects different parts and different countries of the traditions together. Because even if you do listen to Cambodian music now, you are hearing the modern instruments, like the guitar, but you can still hear the traditional instruments, like the *sao*. No matter what you listen to, music just patches things up and merges things together, and gives us a better understanding. Music really educates us when it comes to the Cambodian traditions ... Yes, and through song and dance, too. Really, through music you can tell so many stories, and so many myths are told. It tells about life, about life for other people, and experiences.

Maple man: When you listen to Cambodian music and dance, I think you just feel yourself. You are not really thinking, you are just dancing, your body is just expressing itself, you are being the identity while you are dancing ... The party, the dance is something special you go to.

First Windsor man: During the dancing, I think we feel we are more Cambodian than Canadian. Pretty much everybody, if you go to a Cambodian party, you don't think you are a Canadian, you think that you are Cambodian. You belong to your group and you're there ... It's something you are proud of.

Popular Khmer folk dances such as the *Ram Vong* remain an important part of ethnic and cultural identity among youth. Dancing to Cambodian music binds the generations together, whether the dancing occurs at a private party or during a large community gathering. When asked, Cambodian youth envisioned that they would still be dancing when they are old, and they fully expect to share this activity with their own children and grandchildren. There was strong consensus that Khmer music, dance, and food would comprise cultural continuity for generations to come. Youth also recognized that through Khmer dancing, their increasing numbers of non-Khmer friends and spouses could easily participate in Cambodian traditions, as noted in comments by three young men during the 2005 Khmer Youth Workshop:

Brampton man: Even the non-Cambodians will dance. The reality is that there will be a lot of multiracial couples because we live in a very multiracial society. And you will definitely start to see other people getting involved in it. It's going to be a big thing.

Hamilton man: At first, nobody at the parties was non-Cambodian, but then afterwards, you notice that you start to have more nationalities than Cambodian.

Windsor man: We find that in Windsor as well ... I think it's because Cambodian kids are just so mixed with others from a lot of cultures that they understand where we come from, and I'm sure we understand where they come from. I, myself, go to Lao parties and Vietnamese parties and their activities. There are no borders anymore. It's like an Asian community. We all just understand that we're from the same part of the world kind of thing, it's not saying, 'You're Cambodian,' 'You're Vietnamese,' 'You're Chinese.' The borders are all open now. I think that's what everybody's coming to understand.

For Cambodian youth in Ontario, music and dance have become the prevalent transnational linkages for youth, connecting them with an ambiguous past and adding a sense of cultural certainty for the present and future. As one second-generation male from Brampton noted:

I think in both music and dance, I can see a hundred years from now, people will still be doing the same songs. (Khmer Youth Workshop, 2005)

7 Re-envisioning Khmer Identities within Transnational Networks

Developing Transnational Linkages

Faist (2000) suggests three kinds of transnational social spaces that reflect different degrees of integration and interaction within diasporic contexts: transnational kinship groups that focus on families and small-scale reciprocity; transnational circuits with a focus on cultural, economic, and ideological networks of exchange; and the transnational community as an agency wherein a diasporic collectivity and sense of solidarity are articulated. All three function to create social and symbolic ties (imagined and/or tangible) across geopolitical boundaries that increase peoples' connection to one another (ibid.: 196). The ability of first-generation Khmer in Ontario to develop transnational networks with Cambodia and other Khmer communities in resettlement has been limited to kinship and small-scale reciprocity. Cambodia's isolation during much of the 1980s, and the restricted and underdeveloped community-based cultural activities of Khmer in Ontario, has made it difficult for the first generation to create contacts and linkages beyond those of extended family and friends. However limited, these contacts played an important role in their resettlement. The fact that family and friends survived in Cambodia, or resettled in Australia, France, New Zealand, and the United States has helped first-generation refugees live with their own horrific pre-migration experiences and difficult adaptive and integrative circumstances. Over time, easier access to the homeland and others in resettlement has aided the first generation's transnational maintenance of traditional Buddhist identities, practices, institutions, and monastic/lay relations. The strong presence of Khmer-based music and dance produced in Cambodia has also been important. These foundations for global community contacts and circuits help retain traditional Cambodian ethnic and cultural identity in Ontario (McLellan 2004). Within resettlement, however, traditional identities and roles are simultaneously re-created and redefined, and thereby transformed. Generational dynamics, leadership development, changing attitudes towards Cambodia (especially in regard to financial support of extended-family or rehabilitation programs), and homeland visits, influence the ways Khmer identity is being re-envisioned.

Return visits to the homeland, also referred to as 'ethnic tourism,' provide frameworks that reinforce, reiterate, and solidify transnational social fields, particularly among those whose 'identities are multi-faceted and composed of complexly inter-woven strands of ethnicity, religion, and ancestry' (Coles and Timothy 2004: 7). Duval defines return visits as 'periodic, but temporary, sojourns made by members of diasporic communities to either their external homeland or another location in which strong social ties have been forged' (2004: 51). Visits to the homeland can function as an adaptive mechanism in resettlement, particularly to negotiate identities, reinvigorate social capital, and facilitate cultural continuity across multiple localities. Among Cambodians in diaspora there are numerous different attitudes regarding a return to Cambodia (Simon-Barouh 2005: 258). It is only since the early 1990s that Ontario Cambodians have been able to return to Cambodia.

Coles and Timothy identify six distinctive patterns of ethnic tourism 'associated with the spaces and places occupied and travelled through' by individuals, families, and groups in diaspora (2004: 13–16). Those that reflect Ontario Cambodian visits to the homeland include: secular pilgrimages to reaffirm and reinforce identity; a 'search for roots and routes' to maintain bonds of kinship or to discover the remains of family; and 'thanatourism' (visiting memorial sites that recall the Khmer Rouge genocide, areas of collective dislocation, and current conditions of village life) (ibid.). Return visits 'measure change and transformation' (Duval 2004: 57) for those in resettlement and in the homeland, and may result in troubling and disconcerting experiences that increase ambiguities and ambivalences (Nguyen and King 2004: 176). The motivations and experiences involved in visiting the homeland reflect differences in social hierarchy, religion, and age, particularly in the types and degrees of knowledge, that is, nostalgic as well as troubled memories from prior social and cultural contact, or information based on the recollections and attitudes of others. For first-generation Cambodians, return visits are understood as a significant obligation of family and religious piety. Visits to Cambodia, either alone or with family members, involve bringing large sums of money (upwards of $10,000) that may have taken years to save. These one-lump sums, and smaller more frequent remittances, significantly contribute to home village reconstruction and the welfare of extended family members. Formal business, political, institutional, or non-governmental organization affiliations are rare for Ontario-based Cambodians, especially when compared with Cambodians in Quebec (McLellan 2004). The informal remittance system relies on trusted friends to ensure personal deliveries of cash, rather than on banks or money-transfer businesses. Older Cambodians in Ontario also maintain diligent connections with Buddhist temples and monks in Cambodia in order to provide donations for rebuilding damaged structures and to ensure that monastics are supported.

Cambodians in diaspora still struggle with the disappearance of loved ones and the mass graves that deprived them of opportunities to perform necessary Buddhist rituals for death (Um 2006: 9; Overland 1999: 7). During the early years of resettlement, especially in locales where Khmer Buddhism was absent, Cambodian survivors of fractured families were unable to achieve closure, for both the dead and the living. Without closure, they remained in a liminal condition that inhibited them from easily rebuilding new lives or visions for the future (Um 2006: 19). Important ancestral and memorial rituals geared towards healing, appeasing angry spirits, honouring the dead, and accumulating spiritual merit depend upon the performance of ritual specialists and appropriate cultural ensembles (Men 2002). The lack of local temples or Buddhist monks in Ontario meant that many Cambodians were not able to effectively channel their powerful feelings of grief, loss, and reconciliation with the living and the dead. Their critical ontological concerns could only be alleviated through visits and remittances to Cambodian temples and monks. In lieu of local monks, personal and financial connections with reliable monks in Cambodia to perform overdue funeral and memorial ceremonies enabled them to achieve the necessary ancestral and cultural continuity. To some extent, memorial ceremonies have been held annually in private homes and in Ontario temples. When conducted in Cambodia, however, there is the possibility of a proper reburial for the deceased (if the remains are located), and surviving family members are able to participate collectively with several monks and ritual specialists. Similar to other Southeast Asians in diaspora (Nguyen and King 2004: 174), Cambodians feel that the home country provides the best maintenance of religious duties to ancestors and the strongest connection to relevant ancestral spirits.

Cambodians in Ontario began sending remittances to family members or friends who remained behind in Thai refugee camps, as soon as possible. Until the late 1980s and early 1990s, visits or sending letters and remittances to Cambodia was difficult. Following the 1993 elections, the movement of people, capital, and goods became easier, expanding rapidly once the repatriation of remaining refugees in Thailand began and the United Nations Transition Authority for Cambodia (UNTAC) partially stabilized Cambodia. Strong transnational ties through ongoing family remittances and donations to support infrastructural repairs in temples or home villages has continued, providing first-generation Cambodians in Ontario with new categories of social status and influence. Older Cambodians, although socially and economically marginalized in resettlement, gain increased merit-making and ethical standing when they financially support temples and monks in Cambodia. Despite limited education and economic means, participation in transnational cultural activities enables them to assume culturally appropriate positions of leadership in their local resettlement community and in homeland villages. These linkages with Cambodia enable them to become 'meaningfully engaged in the process of change, thereby validating their continued importance and relevance' (Um 2006: 13). In Ontario communities, when large sums of money are raised for emergency relief or special rehabilitation projects, it is one of these elders who carries the funds to Cambodia and who will be videotaped doing the necessary transactions. Upon the elder's return, the video is shown to either the fundraising committee or a wider audience to provide visual details on the local conditions and recipients, and to allay any feelings of mistrust.

Ontario Khmer invest in the well-being of surviving family members in Cambodia by purchasing land, equipment, animals, or small businesses there. Their investments ensure that they will have access to extensive social support upon their return to Cambodia, either for visits or retirement. These kinds of investments are particularly strategic for North American Cambodians who remain in low-wage, low-security employment sectors that are economically vulnerable (Um 2006: 13). Conversely, long-term remittances or investments may also have a negative impact on interpersonal relations if networks of obligation lead to economic hardship for Khmer in resettlement. Several Cambodian families in Ontario note that the money spent in Cambodia is at the expense of their children's education or the purchase of a home. As communications and visits to Cambodia steadily increase, there may be more requests for family financial aid or sponsorship opportunities. In the United States, Um notes several instances of family stress and destabilization that arise from severe debt or the demands to fulfil transnational obligations (ibid.: 17). The burden of sending remittances that involve distant relatives, either sole surviving relatives or new 'extended' families through transnational marriages, puts tremendous pressures on personal relationships and nuclear households. Within investment-based connections as well, the authority patterns characteristic of patron-client relationships can easily fuel irreconcilable expectations and/or resentment. Shifts in social relations at the village level particularly occur if collectively planned and decided projects, such as well digging, are undermined by overseas sponsors who override local participation and unilaterally determine the design and select the site for construction (ibid.: 18). First-generation Khmer in Ontario give little evidence that they have faced these negative aspects of their transnational connections. They state that land purchases and investment in small businesses in Cambodia demonstrate their social and economic success in Canada. Several who returned now maintain two residences, with constant travel between Canada and Cambodia. One Khmer man from Toronto noted this trend:

> I know people who have gone back to Cambodia to start a business. My friend's mother is going to do that, but I am not sure what kind of a business. I believe they want to retire there. Sell the house here and retire there. That's where their family and friends are. I would love to do that, too. A lot of people have done that. I am sure they are happy. They have a hundred grand in their bank, and that's in Canadian money, and when you convert that to Cambodian money, that allows them a lifetime of not having money problems there. And you have all your family and friends that you haven't seen for many decades. It's the country where you were raised ... But you know, back in 1994 or so, no one wanted to live in Cambodia. Now a lot of older people are talking about it. (personal interview, 2005)

Opportunities to return to Cambodia for political involvement or large-scale business interests remain limited for Ontario Cambodians, differing from those in Quebec and the United States. Quebec Cambodians are in great demand in Cambodia, highly valued for their professional expertise, trilingual ability (English, French, and Khmer), and pre-war status and connections (McLellan 2004). The United States also has a higher proportion of upper-class Cambodians, especially government officials, professionals, and army officers (Hein 1995: 135). Cambodia remains a 'stringently stratified society, where family names, educational achievement, former status, and even age continue to be reservoirs of traditional legitimacy' (Um 2006: 10). To assume important roles as investors, entrepreneurs, and critical intermediaries for firms seeking to do business in Cambodia, or to find positions in government and non-government arenas, overseas Khmer must possess business acumen and means, family and professional connections, as well as expertise and connections garnered in the West (ibid.: 11). Unlike many of the returning elites from Quebec, there are no Khmer doctors, engineers, bankers, or educators in Ontario. Few Ontario Khmer are trilingual or have the financial expertise and connections that would make their presence particularly useful in Cambodia's postwar reconstruction. With their working-class and farming backgrounds, most Ontario Khmer feel they do not have the ability to effectively connect with current political and financial agents in Cambodia. Community-based associations that provide affirmations and expressions of cultural and ethnic identity, local mobilization, and political activism, have more ability to develop strategic access to and structural links with Cambodia and other overseas Khmer communities (ibid.: 11). As noted earlier, the effectiveness of a community's leadership and advocacy depends on the availability of social and economic capital. Ontario Cambodians have not yet had the means and opportunities to conduct political or social service work in the homeland.

The current government in Cambodia remains fragile. Through the Internet and Cambodian satellite television, Ontario Cambodians are able to stay abreast of daily events. Social, political, and environmental disruptions continue to trigger the fears and memories of past horrors that are ever-present in people's minds (Kong 2003). While the burden of grief and worry for loved ones still in Cambodia remain a constant concern, visits and regular remittances to family, home villages, Buddhist temples or Christian missions provide first-generation Ontario Cambodians with meaningful frameworks to cope with and validate their life in Canada.

Second-Generation Visits to Cambodia

For the second generation, a visit to Cambodia and meeting extended family has a different significance. They are not reuniting with lost loved ones, nor are they overcoming pervasive fear, or confronting devastating memories. Instead, their visit becomes a crucial element in clarifying a bicultural identity as Canadian Cambodians. Cambodian youth in Ontario identify cultural confusion and a lack of belonging as one of the difficulties they face. As one second-generation Khmer male put it:

> It is very important to know you are Khmer and not deny it. It is important to question who you are, what Cambodia is. The biggest clash is between the two cultures, so it is necessary to find out who you are. Youth are still searching to find out what being Khmer is. (personal interview, 2005)

In Cambodia, Canadian-born and/or -raised youth are enveloped within extended family relationships that, hitherto, have only been understood through photographs or their parents' memories. Personal interactions demonstrate the shared biological and personality characteristics that they have with others, and help youth to recognize their parents' family values and traditions. Visits to Cambodia also entail meeting Cambodians from different countries of resettlement, enabling Canadian youth to realize that they are but one of many different expressions of being Khmer within a larger ethnic and cultural identification.

In February 2005, at the Northwood Community Centre in Toronto, the CCAO and Hong Fook sponsored the first Toronto community viewing of the documentary, *I am Khmer*. It was produced by Sarorn Sim, a second-generation Khmer from Windsor, and depicts his family's first return to Cambodia, over twenty years after their resettlement in Canada. The documentary captures the joy of the mother reuniting with her surviving family members, as well as the suffering when the father's brother is killed on the day the family arrives in the home village, murdered for U.S. $10 as he shopped for the celebratory feast. A visit to the Angkor Wat with extended family demonstrates how Sarorn slowly comes to terms with the complexity of Cambodia and his own identity as a second-generation Khmer Canadian. After viewing the documentary, several second-generation Khmer youth spoke about the changes they felt following their own visits to Cambodia:

> First young woman: I am heavily involved in the Cambodian community but have always felt Canadian first. My parents never taught me what it is to be Cambodian. You need to go back to Cambodia to find out. I went back three years ago, and it changed my life.

Second young woman: I grew up in Canada. I came here at about five months old. As a Canadian, I didn't know my own roots. I got lost, and then I went back to Cambodia to embrace my roots, my culture. I came back so fired up to help the community.

Third young woman: I am the same as my sister. It is only recently I have gotten in touch with my roots. I have always learned the language, but now after visiting Cambodia, I feel Cambodian. My brothers and sisters all feel the same.

What is notable in these comments is that their understanding of being Cambodian in Canada is not just tied to having a strong sense of cultural roots, but that these roots need to be discovered for oneself. This notion of quest and discovery was also evident in the responses two second-generation males gave to the question, 'How do you know you are Khmer?'

First young man: Like a lot of Khmer kids who grow up in Canada, I didn't know what it is to be Khmer. I heard stories from my mom, but I didn't know. Now, I am doing research, I'm searching. I'm trying to find out.

Second young man: My family, my heritage, our religion, the food we eat, the karaoke songs you sing, the dances, all these things tell you who you are. At one point you will realize it. (Khmer Youth Workshop, 2005)

During one discussion at the 2005 Khmer Youth Workshop, several young men described the effect that returning to Cambodia has had on their identity as Canadian Cambodians:

Second-generation Windsor man: You have to go back. This is where you come from, and that's your identity, and it's your homeland, and no matter how you try to deny it, it's where you're from. And no matter what happens, you'll always know that's where you're from. Those are where your roots are, where your ancestors and your parents. So there is no avoiding it ... everyone here is looking for that image of themselves, and who they are, and where they belong. It's important to find that. I think going to Cambodia helped me to find that.

Second-generation Hamilton man: A trip home is to find your identity, the identity of your parents. For me, it was a great way to find out who I am. Looking around the countryside, I saw what made up the characteristics of being Khmer and that's an important recognition for me. We're all evolving as Khmer. I realized that I would always be Khmer, even though no matter where I go, I am adapting to the culture. This just hits home. I looked at my sisters and I realized they have all the recognized character-istics of the Khmer. For me, personally, this is when I recognized myself as Khmer, and not a hybrid.

1.5-generation Toronto man: Sometimes when you [meet people in Cam-bodia] you don't know who they are, they look the same 'cause they're still Cambodian people. Even when they meet me, they don't know where I come from. But when they start to talk you see that they are different from the way others talk in Cambodia. You pick up that right away, and think, 'That's not Cambodian.' So you ask them, 'Where are you from? What do your people do there?' And they ask me the same thing. Lots of people return home from other countries. That's because they're con-nected. Regardless of what's happened to them, they're connected.

In visits to Cambodia, some youth become aware of the tremendous differences between Canadian and Cambodian society. They feel the absence of their previously taken-for-granted notions of security, access to health care, law, and civil order, and recognize that while Cambo-dia may be where their family and cultural roots lie, it remains a for-eign arena in which they do not belong. Following the viewing of the documentary *I Am Khmer* at the 2005 Khmer Youth Workshop, several second-generation youth observed that they felt similar elements of danger, violence, and alienation during their visit to Cambodia:

First young woman: I went back to Cambodia three or four years ago with my entire family ... We went to the cities like Phnom Penh, but we also went to the villages where my mom came from. During the first night there, we came across the guards, you know who come into your village, and they're telling you that if you don't give them money, they're going to have to kill somebody. And I think that's when I fully realized, 'Wow, this is not a vacation.' Our people said that they [those guards] come here every night and demand that you give them money. You just have to live with that. There is that reality in the country.

Second young woman: I remember when I was there I was riding on the motorcycle, and for whatever reason, the motorcycle went off course and we didn't go on the main streets, we were going on the rural roads, and when we finally got back with my family, everyone was panicking and crying at me. And I said, 'What's wrong?' And they said, 'It's just the way you look. You could have gotten killed. You are wearing expensive clothes. If you got robbed, we would have had to pay just to get you out.' And you think that in Canada, you're not worth that much, but to them, because you are a foreigner, actually because I'm fat, more than people there, because we look healthy and we have all these privileges, like glasses, and you know like a purse and a clean shirt, you are automatically identified as a foreigner, and as a target. And those realities don't hit us when we're walking the streets of our hometowns here [in Canada].

Young man: Well I think in Cambodia it's all about the darkness and beauty of the country, and also the darkness and beauty of life. And that's what I found so strong. Cambodia is all about pain and suffering, pain and reward, about triumph and tragedy ... That scene there [outside the Angkor Wat] shows the darkness and beauty of Cambodia. Here's this beautiful music, and they're playing that music in front of such a beautiful place, but if you look at the people that are playing it, I mean they have no limbs ... kids crying, there's suffering everywhere, and that's the whole thing about Cambodia, the darkness and beauty ... This is the image that I see what I see of my world, and that's what I have to accept. And I think everybody, everyone here, is looking for that image of themselves, and who they are, and where they belong. It is important to find that. I think going to Cambodia helped me to find that ... I hope it also gives people courage and persistence to keep moving, even within our small community, to keep pushing forward. Because if you look at our people and if you look at our country, they've gone through so much, yet with so little they've built so much. And that's something we can look at.

Second young woman: There really is an imbalance and injustice in Cambodia but at the same time, there is still hope to fix this. And I think that's what makes a lot of people to go back. You have to have the hope to fix it.

For some youth who have not had the opportunity to return to Cambodia, the process has become an idealized journey of self-discovery that would help resolve issues of confused identity, and finding meaning. Nguyen and King (2004: 180) found significant differences between those who travelled to the homeland and those who have not yet done so in terms of identity, happiness, and a sense of belonging. One second-generation Cambodian male in Toronto who has not visited Cambodia, commented on his identity confusion:

I have never been to Cambodia, but I would love to go. It would really make a difference in my sense of who I am. I have spoken with a few friends who have gone back to Cambodia and they all loved it. They enjoyed it. You know, growing up in a country where you are unable to see your relatives, when they go to Cambodia, they can see family. Cambodia is the country, not where I was born, but where I come from, where my roots are, and where they keep growing. I cannot explain it. It is a feeling of knowing that this is my country.

But I am a Canadian citizen too, so what does this mean? Things like religion, dual identity, would be different. If I had been raised in Cambodia, I would not have this dual feeling, like two identities or something. If I had been raised in Cambodia, I would have been exposed to everything – the teaching of the Buddhist philosophy, the ways, I wouldn't have to deal with Christianity. But once I'm in Canada, I'm here to stay and I'm going to be exposed to it. If I was raised in Cambodia, I would be all Cambodian. But in Canada, you are exposed to many things, different opportunities. In Canada, you can do basically anything you want because you have freedom. In Cambodia I would not have that freedom, I would be stuck with one religion, stuck with one way of life. But then again, I wouldn't have to go through all these identity crises. (personal interview, 2005)

During discussions at the 2005 Khmer Youth Workshop, several youth noted that through their experiences in Cambodia, not only did issues of identity confusion become clearer, but they also realized the extent of their parents' struggle during the early years of resettlement. Second-generation youth found that they became more appreciative of the things that they have in Canada, and no longer felt the shame of their parents' poverty:

Young woman: To go to the country and see what it's all about is an experience … and also this reflects a lot on our parents. Our parents gave us what they had when they came here. You look at them sometimes and you don't realize the history where they're coming from. Can you imagine what they've lived through and still be able to be strong today, to stand in front of all of us, and still pretend that nothing has happened.

Young man: But now I'm not [ashamed of my parents]. Now that I've gone to Cambodia I've seen what they used to do. I've seen how they used to live and I accept how we are now. It was the trip that made me accept, because before I was like it was up to me to do it. After seeing the things over there, and the things people would do for money, like begging.

Young woman: When you go to Cambodia you realize that bags are so valuable. Containers are so valuable. And you begin to understand your parents, why they do what they do when they came here.

Through visits to Cambodia, the second generation connect with their parents' past by staying in villages where their parents grew up, meeting relatives for the first time, and sharing in their memories. As stories unfold of survival, flight, and return, as bones of the dead are beheld, and as they attend memorial rituals, the second generation also begins to understand the parents' experiences under the Khmer Rouge. A second-generation young man from Brampton noted his sense of connection:

When I got back to Canada after visiting Cambodia I was pretty happy, even just being in the airport ... Cambodia is unexplainable. When I went there, I went to one of the places that they showed where people got killed. And when I went there, once you go in, you get this heart-clenching feeling. It hurt to go in there, and you see where they kept the people, where they were killed, the pictures they show how people were butchered, the weapons they used, it just really hits you really hard. And at the same time, you're like, 'Wow.' You get a feeling of like how they felt, you get such a feeling, that this really is home. (Khmer Youth Workshop, 2005)

Many second-generation youth who visited Cambodia spent time with extended family, participating in complex and elaborate memorial, ancestral, and healing rituals. One such ritual is the *hau bralin* (translated as calling or reconstituting the Khmer soul), an important ceremony performed by monks, *achaa*, or family members for people who return home to Cambodia and need to revive continuity with Khmer community and identity (Thompson 1996: 3).[1] Family in Cambodia assume that overseas youth have little understanding of the spiritual components of who they really are, so instruction and explanation are given in some detail (ibid.). Understanding the *hau bralin* enables Ontario Cambodian youth to better recognize the spiritual significance of modern ritual celebrations (the cutting of hair at birth and weddings, as well as invoking *hau bralin* for healing, funerals, and generalized blessings) and the power of these rituals for personal and community social cohesion. They begin to understand issues concerned with the survival of the Khmer soul as it is challenged by external and unsupportive contact in foreign lands of resettlement. Both the explanation and experience of the ritual become important means of communication and communion within a reaffirmed collective Khmer identity. The power of the 'performative' aspect of the *hau bralin* and other ritual activities is that in addition to being told or shown something, one is 'led to experience something' (Bell 1997: 160).

After a visit to Cambodia, for young men and women of the second-generation, the experiential reification of Khmer identity intensifies their religious and ethnic belonging. Their attitudes and lifestyles significantly shift as they construct different 'counter-memories' or 'new narratives' (Bottomley 1991: 304), and it becomes easier for them to live with cultural hybridity, to be fully Khmer while being Canadian. These deliberate re-ritualizations of social life are common among those who experience intense cultural changes and/or challenges (Cheal 1992: 366). Rituals that help define personal and social identities are, therefore, an important element in understanding a certain type of religiosity among the second generation. Buddhist-based rituals in Cambodia, with their embodied cultural symbols of ethnic and religious distinctiveness, help youth to clarify traditional patterns of relationships and the emotional commitments upon which they depend. This further strengthens their ability to find a presence and place in Canadian society when they return. The deepened sense of being Khmer that youth bring back to Canada frequently results in their undertaking committed involvements with community and temple activities. Having participated in unabridged and 'authentic' rituals in Cambodia, and with a better understanding of them, these youth are treated with more respect when they offer organizational assistance to the temple elders, or make requests of the monastics for more 'modern' teachings. With their new confidence, these youth actively address generational concerns and develop successful programs to teach younger children the basics of Cambodian Buddhism.

Discussions during the 2005 Khmer Youth Workshop demonstrated that second-generation youth become more aware of their educational and employment opportunities after a visit to Cambodia, further strengthening their appreciation of a Canadian-Khmer identity:

> First young woman: I admire the strength that my relatives in Cambodia have. My grandfather gets up even before the sun rises. And the kinds of energy that the kids have. I know they are unfortunate, but they have this hunger to learn. They were always asking me to teach them English. They would walk around, following me, asking me words. So when

coming back, you realize that your country just has so much, and you should take advantage of what you have. You look into your community here and you see that there's a lot of youth who don't finish high school, and they really take their free education for granted. You know, that's just the reality.

Second young woman: I think that is one of the great things about going back is that you can see the comparison, what you've done, and what they have, and what you have.

Young man: You don't realize what you have until you go back and see what they don't have.

New first-generation man: Same story with [name]; she was so spoiled until she goes back and sees her country. She came back a totally different person. She takes care, she's respectful, and she's learned cooking.

For many second-generation youth, the sense of belonging to, or identification with, Cambodia can be seen as more symbolic (Gans 1994) than actualized, since few seek a communal acceptance or social embeddedness grounded in living full-time in Cambodia. Reconnecting physically with Cambodia through short-term visits to relatives, parental home villages, and historical monuments (holocaust museums, palaces, Angkor Wat), however, provides a crucial step in helping the second generation to accept Cambodia as their ancestral homeland, and to acknowledge these roots as a crucial element of their identity. Homeland connections enable Cambodian youth to move beyond a bifurcated internal confusion. These youth now realize a multifaceted and expanded sense of identity that includes loyalties towards both Canada and Cambodia. Conversely, the cultural and ideological distancing encountered through a visit to Cambodia can also help the second-generation youth to clearly recognize that their life and future is within North América (Um 2006: 17). Numrich (1996: 104) also noted that for Sinhalese and Thai youth, the full extent of being 'North American' particularly became apparent when they visited their parents' Asian homeland or interacted with youth born and raised in Asia. In sharing their experiences of a visit to Cambodia with others, Ontario Cambodian youth described their feelings of social alienation, general disillusionment towards Cambodia's pervasive corruption and massive poverty, the poor sanitation, and their constant fear of violence.

Returning to Canada with a new sense of purpose, many of these youth have become active in advocating for programs to help their peers stay in school, to address drug and gang affiliation, and to access different kinds of leadership training. New youth associations developed in recent years are led by individuals who have gained a secure sense of Khmer identity by visiting Cambodia. They seek to help youth gain a greater involvement in traditional culture, and to establish closer interactions with the first generation. In June 2006, the Cambodiana Society of Windsor enabled youth and the older generation to participate, for the first time, in the city's annual multicultural festival. It has taken twenty-six years since their initial resettlement in 1980 for the community to share their Cambodian cuisine with non-Khmer and to showcase live performances of Khmer culture (music and dancing). The shared generational involvement in this festival enhanced community cohesion and demonstrated that they had finally broken through decades of representational isolation and social marginalization. As Bramadat notes, ethnocultural spectacles represent 'alternative economies of status' whereby ethnic minorities can express social prestige in ways that are understood by outsiders and enhance the recognition of their community characteristics and values (2001: 78). Through the planning and participation in these ethnocultural spectacles, particularly by making decisions regarding cultural displays and forms of entertainment, the second-generation youth clarify 'identity-generating links' between themselves and their parents, and between Canada and Cambodia (ibid.: 83). Second-generation leaders are especially aware of the opportunities that public festivals provide for ethnic minority communities to engage in the politics of identity recognition and representation.

A large segment of the current youth leadership is helping the second generation to overcome shame and develop pride in being Khmer. During the 2005 Khmer Youth Workshop, several youth noted that despite their enjoyment of Khmer music, dance, food, and community involvements, they have struggled to clarify what this pride embodies. Two 1.5 generation Khmer men commented:

First man: When I was growing up [in Hamilton], my struggle was, more or less, no respect. I was struggling with the fact that as a Cambodian, what do I have to show for pride? What can I say that we as Cambodians in Canada can take pride in? You flip on the TV and you see other ethnic cultures, but is there anything on Cambodians? So that itself, it hurts me because I have nothing available to relate back to. My friends have Caribana, and they say, 'Let's go.' Everyone knows what that is, right? so they have pride in there. That was my struggle.

Second man: Well, when I first came to Windsor, I found it really tough [for me] to handle. I was fourteen, and going to school I started ESL. So it was very hard. I was picked on, and I tried to hide where I was from, what I eat, and all that so I wouldn't get picked on. But I did anyway, they picked on me. Later on, I just discovered that this is me, I can't change it. I am Khmer, I am Cambodian. This is what I eat, this is what my mom, my dad, my parents or grandpa eats, so I had to tell them. I'm proud of it. So I urge everybody right now, you don't have to hide it. I go to work every day and I carry rice. People now say, 'I bet you've got rice in there.' That's what I eat, I love it. I cannot eat bread. I cannot change. So they start to respect you for who you are if you don't hide it. Just be yourself.

When asked, 'What are you most proud of as Khmer?' most youth noted the endurance of the Cambodian people in the face of great suffering, their ability to retain culture (especially food and music), and their strong family and homeland connections. The following quotes from the 2005 Khmer Youth Workshop highlight these facets of pride:

New first-generation young Toronto man: We have family, we have friendship, and we have unity. We can relate to each other, and we can have connections that we still talk about. We can still trust, still build relationships up within the community.

Second-generation Toronto man: I think because we Cambodians, we have been through so much, and we are still able to grow. That's what I take pride in. Like the golden phoenix, we fall down so many times and we get up.

1.5-generation Toronto woman: I feel that Khmer care for each other. There has been so much suffering in the past with the Khmer Rouge, or the civil war in the 1970s, the bombings – the Khmer have been through so much. Somehow, everybody still seems to care about each other. People send so much money back home to support those who are less fortunate. So you can see that even though we live far, we feel close. Even if some people can only send $10, $15, they send something.

Second-generation Hamilton man: What I feel about Khmer is that it doesn't matter where they are, they always come together. And that is something I'm really proud of. The connection is always there. If there's something going on in London, there is always Hamilton people, Kitchener people, Toronto – they're all there. And that is really great.

Second-generation Windsor man: I'm most proud of the people and the culture. On a smaller scale, I'm proud of the community that I live in. Mainly because we're so small and we've gone through so much. When all of us first came to Canada, we all came around the same time in the 1980s, and we really had to work hard. It took us so many years, for example, to just get a temple and be able to ritually pay respect to our elders. Yet throughout those twenty years, we never gave up. That says a lot about our people and the kind of people that we are as Cambodians. We should look to that and be proud of that.

Second-generation Toronto woman: What I'm proud of is what they teach you. They teach you to respect your elders, to respect your parents, that family is really basic. The education they're just starting to know, but they also value hard work. You work hard, you'll get somewhere.

Although youth easily cite characteristics that give them pride, they are still unsure of what defines being Khmer in Canada. Some youth argue that having the ability to communicate in the Khmer language is essential, while others feel that a qualified knowledge of Khmer cultural and religious traditions and familiarity with Cambodia is more important. The lack of clear guidelines remains a contentious issue that is not easily resolved and undermines a common sense of identity.

Conclusion

As a poor newcomer minority, Cambodian refugees in Ontario experienced a process of social exclusion from the wider social context. This impacted their intergroup relations; their access to settlement, health care, education, retraining opportunities, and labour market entry; and their establishment of religious institutions and cultural associations. Ong argues that during initial periods of resettlement, various administrative, economic, and social realms of support and welfare services (both governmental and non-governmental) act upon and influence the conduct of poor and at-risk newcomers (2003: 10). These supports and services seek to avert so-called personal failures and to achieve desirable qualities in their subjects' health, employability, wealth, and social integration. For Ontario Cambodians, resettlement services may have facilitated surface success in some areas, but they failed to address underlying issues of Cambodian mental health, the quality and conditions of employment (dangerous and poorly paid), the restrictions and obstacles of their illiteracy, their lack of community social capital and cohesion, and their extensive isolation.

In the mid-1990s, almost every Ontario Cambodian interviewed recognized common concerns in their own lives and in the lives of others in their communities (McLellan 1995). These included long-term difficulties in learning English (people cited their lack of concentration, memory, and capacity to absorb new information); numerous difficulties in obtaining employment; extended dependency on service providers (for escort, translation, or documentation needs); community divisiveness; general mistrust of leaders and others outside of close family and friends; extensive apathy within the community (associated with social withdrawal and isolation), especially among women; high youth dropout rates from school; increasing marriage breakdown (characterized by abandonment, divorce, violence, shifting gender roles); and enormous stress within families (associated with generational tensions, welfare, gambling, and alcohol consumption). Although these concerns reflected significant symptoms of post-traumatic stress, cultural bereavement, and social exclusion, most resettlement and government agencies in Ontario did not provide needed support. An American Khmer health professional notes that mental health support is still needed to deal with delayed reactions to the traumas suffered during the Khmer Rouge regime: 'We have a new group, people who have never talked about the past. They were doing fine with their lives, and then something happens, like a car accident, or somebody died in their family, then the trauma somehow gets triggered. So then those people now are starting to talk about their trauma. This car accident somehow makes them remember the trauma that happened during Pol Pot. To them, it's really fresh and new. So, you have different levels for different people' (Chea 2003: 245).

Little is known about the effect of the Cambodian genocide on the second generation in resettlement, particularly if there is a survival narrative that provides themes and metaphors around which identity is constructed and positioned or the ways parental trauma has been transmitted to their children (Kaufman 1998: 50; Boyarin and Boyarin 2003: 85; Kogan 1995: 150; Bek-Pedersen and Montgomery 2006). The issue is only beginning to be addressed in the United States, evidenced by the 2008 workshop held at California State University, Long Beach, one of the first events to target second-generation Cambodians (*Desert*

Sun, 31 March, 2008, B8). In Ontario, current concerns in Cambodian communities are with the loss of cultural and religious identity among youth; the lack of Khmer workers or volunteers in welfare services to act as advocates and interpreters; the shortage of community leaders to teach language and culture; generational tensions; and the high youth dropout rates from school. While young Cambodians speak English fluently, many have a limited ability to speak Khmer. Conversely, older Cambodians, especially those forty and over, continue to struggle with English proficiency or illiteracy. Cambodians who arrived in Canada as children were not able to turn to parents for school or career guidance and assistance, and feel the loss of role models for their life in Canada. First-generation adults fear that Cambodian youth who achieve mainstream success do so at the cost of their pride in, or adherence to, Cambodian values, traditions, and teachings. The worries that troubled American Khmer communities in the early 1990s (drugs, gangs, and an escalating increase in violence) have also become a problem in Ontario (Smith-Hefner 1993: 138).

Despite the challenges and difficulties, Cambodians and their communities have much to celebrate: steady employment with good wages, expanding business and home ownership, the greater proportion of youth in post-secondary education, rising community status and class positions, growing interest in leadership and community participation (especially from the second generation), the expansion of cultural programs through increased transnational networks, new ways of expressing Khmer identities, and a greater presence of traditional religious institutions. Buddhist temples are increasingly being utilized for local and homeland fundraising projects, providing opportunities for individual and collective involvement. The private and ceremonial context of Khmer material culture (home decoration, possessions, clothing, entertainment) has maintained generational continuity. The role of Cambodian food is particularly important as taste, smells, production, and consumption are associated with Cambodian homes, community celebrations, and the homeland. The same association of food with identity is shared among most immigrant and refugee groups (Petridou 2001: 100).

What Cambodian communities in Ontario continue to lack are visible signs of presence. Second-generation Cambodian youth, especially those that have affirmed their heritage, are slowly increasing the recognition and representation of Cambodians. Many of these youth have assumed positions of community leadership, become board members or directors of local Cambodian associations, created new liaison roles with various funding and social agencies (Maytree Foundation, Heritage Canada), and actively advocate on behalf of other Khmer youth. Their involvements and activities are evidence of increasing social capital within Cambodian communities. Age restrictions and lack of experience, however, somewhat limit their degree of community involvement, presenting difficulties in effective leadership functioning. Second-generation leaders must also overcome the community weaknesses of the past twenty-five years, especially the mistrust that people have towards those who run programs and attempt to provide community cohesion. In the United States, Um (2006: 17) observes that leaders from the younger generation now at the helm of many organizations frequently find themselves unable to negotiate the complex, multigenerational issues that beset the community. The second-generation leadership in Ontario also deals with the inherent resistence of older Khmer to younger, non-traditional leaders, and a tendency towards organizational instability. Part of their difficulty is the 'invisible system' (Mortland and Ledgerwood 1987) of patronage within Cambodian community associations, whereby leaders are given a 'patron' status with respect to the distribution and access of resources through services, promotion, representation, and fundraising. These traditional forms of community prestige and influence remain highly valued and continue to provide social status and respect; for example, at most community events when some form of financial contributions are involved, there will be public announcements of the names of donors who gave large sums of money. Younger Ontario Khmer leaders recognize the challenges and are working towards their solution by exploring other qualities of leadership, such as education, vision, and seeking external forms of representation.

Castles and Davidson (2000: 148) argue that in resettlement, immigrant politics and social activism move through three phases: from an initial focus on homeland issues, to more localized community and identity concerns, to clear demands for equal participation in the wider society. The last is particularly evident among children of immigrants who are highly sensitive to discrimination and the denial of equal rights or opportunities. They tend to mobilize in non-traditional ways (at the national level or within smaller community organizations) to achieve positive objectives. Inclusive citizenship arises when members of specific groups recognize themselves as social citizens and demand external recognition of their different cultural values and needs (ibid.). The second-generation Cambodian leaders in Ontario are rapidly moving towards this inclusive citizenship. Their shared aspiration is to raise the profile of Cambodians as a distinctive ethnic group in Canada, recognized and appreciated by others, and represented in pan-Asian affiliations, in mainstream organizations, and in local expressions of multiculturalism. They do not aspire to the Cambodian tradition of putting high value on personal prestige through patron/client relationships, but seek to raise their community's prestige through gaining access to valuable funding resources. Relying on their training as medical and social service professionals, younger Khmer members of the Cambodian Association of Ontario have written funding proposals for specific community programs that work towards improvements in mainstream service provision and access.

Second-generation youth work towards strengthening the bonds between the first and second generations that result in more frequent cultural and religious events and celebrations. In turn, this increased social cohesion enables the Cambodian communities in Ontario to initiate bridging capital (Putnam 2000) for interaction with other multicultural, multiracial, and multireligious groups. Through affiliation with pan-Asian associations, such as the Canadian Multicultural Council of Asians in Ontario, some Cambodian youth are developing linking capital (Voyer 2003). The ideals of some Cambodian youth leaders in Ontario are to increase relations between local communities, improve issues of representation, and expand transnational networks into more advocacy involvement. During the 2005 Khmer Youth Workshop, one second-generation community leader spoke about her expectations for other youth leaders:

> If identity changes, then the question isn't where are we, it is where do we want to be? ... Where do you want to be, how do you want to identify yourselves, socially, culturally? If identity evolves as you say it does, then you have the power to make the direction. If we want to be known as the culture that comes to Canada and doesn't go to school, and we're known as certain types of people negatively, then that's how we're defining ourselves, that's what we're doing. But if we're the type that says, 'Okay, you know what, we're making changes' then let's change it to a different type. What is this change going to be and who is going to do it? ... If you see a problem, if you are aware of the issues, then you need to fight for it. The

way that you can help here is by informing on companies here that we
believe are doing bad things in Cambodia. Our voices are here in Canada,
but we're also a strong voice for Cambodia as well.

As the younger generation increase levels of community social capital
and networks of interaction expand, new civic virtues of trust and tolerance will be included that further complicate issues of identity (Castles and Davidson 2000: 218). The second generation's aspiration for
effective and distinct community representation is countered through
the growing issue of hybrid and multiple identities in Ontario Cambodian communities. As 'identity entrepreneurs,' Cambodian youth
seek out different kinds of intellectual, aesthetic, and political coali-
tions, particularly with others of Asian descent under the pan-Asian
banner (Leonard 2000: 32). Increasingly, identities involve different
combinations of ethnic, cultural, racial, and religious diversity. Similar to other refugee youth, Cambodian youth invent, borrow, play, and
experiment with transnational cultural and identity forms that express
their ambivalence and hybridity of displacement, strategies of resistance, and syncretic acculturation (Diehl 1997: 147; Baily 1995: 86; Naficy
1993: 13; Frith 1987: 142). Past issues of community-based inclusion and
exclusion dealt primarily with Kampuchea Krom or mixed-heritage
Khmer. Now, they include children of racially and religiously mixed
marriages, new criteria for social status and class, and more flexible
definitions of who is Cambodian or who can claim Cambodian identity.
These issues affect the recognition and acceptance of leaders, local and
homeland community politics, and anyone to whom community activism is directed.

Despite more flexibility regarding concepts of 'recognition' or 'mis-
recognition' (Taylor 1994), many first-generation Ontario Cambodians
continue to identify Khmer Buddhism and language as the foundation
of their identity, similar to the experiences of Cambodians in other countries of resettlement (Ebihara et al. 1994; Smith-Hefner 1999; Overland
1999; Stevens 2001; Chan 2003). Buddhist beliefs and practices influence
daily life through adherence to traditional moral ideals, ancestral continuity, and holding ritual and ceremonial activities along Cambodian
times and seasons. The annual cycle of ceremonies commemorating
ancestral continuity, monastic and lay interdependency, New Year's,
and rituals associated with *hau bralin* remain significant for most Cambodian families and communities, structuring the enactment of cultural
tradition and framing the shared realities of being Khmer. Buddhism

remains correlated with Khmer culture, customs, arts, and behavioural expectations; it is identified as a symbolic embodiment of Khmer heritage and provides a trusted basis for social cohesion. Conversely, it is appropriate to question the extent to which Buddhism provides a link within or between Cambodian communities (Simon Barouh 2005: 259).

Ontario Cambodians recognize that they can retain only selected aspects of traditional Khmer culture and religion and that the Cambodian way of life will never exist in Canada. The awareness of this loss increases their tolerance for change in Canada, as well as their attempts to maintain strong connections and relationships with Cambodia, even though the Cambodia of today has dramatically changed from their memories of pre-war society. The retention of Khmer identity among Cambodians in resettlement, reflect Anderson's (1991: 6) concept of the 'imagined community' wherein people retain images of their communion with the homeland through shared feelings and understandings of the past. As Vasquez points out, the role of religion in these 'imagined' processes can have positive consequences: 'Religious institutions shape the morphology of migration by providing transnational networks which generate, concentrate, and distribute social capital among individuals and localities … Religion helps immigrants imagine their homeland in diaspora and inscribe their memories and worldviews into the physical landscape and built environment. In addition, religion regenerates and re-centers selves challenged by the migration process, producing new habituses, introducing new forms of collective and individual identity, and new understandings of citizenship, locality, and community' (2005: 238).

Many Cambodians in Ontario feel that local Khmer Buddhist temples provide the most tangible elements of a shared Cambodian memory, and are the most stable community-based associations. Spiritual continuity, ceremonial centres, and rituals function as 'a magnet attracting persons, authority and other resources' (Wellmeier 1998: 186). The associated qualities of authority, power, and credibility within Cambodian temples provide a focus for personal and collective involvement, and funnel scarce economic and social capital into cohesive and strengthening activities. Buddhist rituals, such as the New Year celebration or praying for the dead, represent an idealized symbolic unity that helps to integrate past, present, and future times within scattered spatial allegiances. During religious ceremonies people can re-create and share their closest memories of the Cambodian homeland. The ritual objects, monastic chanting, smells of incense, decorations, traditional styles of clothing, sounds of music, kinds of food offered, and the types of communal participation all evoke Khmer values, practices, and behaviours. For Ontario Cambodians who remain identified with Buddhism, the Buddhist temple provides a positive and culturally appropriate basis to organize community events and forge new identities. Traditional religious activities within the temple, especially Buddhist ceremonies and bereavement rituals, particularly address and meet ongoing health, mental health, social, and cultural needs of older Khmer. For those Cambodians who have little or no involvement with Buddhist temples or ceremonies, the combined issues of religion, Khmer culture, and physical or mental health are often categorized into distinct specializations.

On an idealized level, most Khmer continue to recognize the Buddhist temple as the embodiment of traditional Cambodian culture wherein ethnic identity is reaffirmed and expressed. The monastic presence in Ontario especially represents a continuity with Cambodia, since this is the preferred country for textual and ritual specialists. The rituals invoking merit making, ancestral honouring, and remembrance particularly strengthen connections between the living and the dead, deeply linking Canada and Cambodia. As government funding for resettlement-based associations decreased, Buddhist temples have become an institutional base for community leadership, giving high social status to older men and businesspeople. For many ethnoreligious groups in diaspora, experiences of marginalization, social isolation, and racism led to religious solidarity being used as a key form of resistance (Castles and Davidson 2000: 137). Buddhism provided many first-generation Cambodians with self-esteem, traditional moral values, ethnic pride, and a sense of belonging that transcended space, time, and national borders. The shared beliefs and practices of Buddhism, however, are not necessarily a unifying element. Kampuchea Krom Buddhism is affiliated with a distinct agenda to maintain and inculcate a specific internal identity that is different from Cambodian-based Khmer. Similar to other politicized members of ethnoreligious groups in exile, Kampuchea Krom seek governing power, access to resources, and redress for centuries of domination and exploitation in Vietnam. Kampuchea Krom have high linking capital that enables them to affiliate with regional and international bodies such as the United Nations and enlisting non-governmental organizations, the media, and other academics to further their cause (Wellmeier 1998: 190–1).

In Ontario, most Khmer from Cambodia do not equate Buddhism and the temple as part of a larger political agenda but as a representation of peace, and a space of social familiarity in which they can meet, talk, discuss and solve problems. There is the expectation that Buddhist temples in Ontario will offer educational activities to youth on weekends or after school, teach traditional language, dance, music, arts and crafts, and expand programs and events for older Khmer. Many older Khmer feel that the preservation of Khmer culture and traditions is fundamental to enhancing the community's sense of well-being, pride, and identity. Because the new residential neighbourhoods that many Cambodian families have moved into are mainly accessible by car, it is unclear to what extent the Buddhist temple can be used by Khmer youth or the elderly. Even without regular programs, the presence of a Buddhist temple and monks is still meaningful. When necessary, Buddhist monks can provide traditional rituals and ceremonies that help some Cambodians resolve post-traumatic, transitional, and adaptive stresses. Monastic intervention is especially important for somatic ailments that may have a spiritual basis. Monks are entrusted to perform services that are categorized in Western terms as individual, family, and marital counselling. People will listen to the authority of a monk and respect his advice, which is generally based on Buddhist and Cambodian moral principles. Since religious memory is subject to constantly recurring construction, monastics represent a lineage of belief, affirming and manifesting 'authorized memory' that legitimates, unifies, and controls its mobilization (Hervieu-Leger 2000: 124–5; Connerton 1989). The rituals and religious practices of Khmer monastics operate as a form of social exchange, reminding the community of its identity and maintaining continuities between the generations (Lee 1992: 1). The few bilingual monks or leaders of the Buddhist temples or associations are especially beneficial as brokers, advocates, and liaisons between their Cambodian members and the larger service agencies and Canadian social systems, especially in providing information about Buddhism and its contributions to Asian cultures and values.

Cambodian youth in Ontario still require supportive counselling in defining their academic goals and life options. Ongoing family conflicts, generation gaps, school dropout rates, and substance abuse reflect their high levels of stress and fragile emotional well-being. Many second-generation Cambodians have expressed an interest in learning Buddhist meditation to increase their positive attributes, coping skills, and self-help resources, but opportunities to do so at Khmer temples have been scarce. The valiant attempts by underfunded and over-worked youth leaders in Ontario Cambodian communities to develop youth programs through sports, recreation, and community activities have had a significant positive influence. As Cambodian youth participate in mentorship programs, conferences, and workshops, they develop leadership skills that, in turn, benefit others. Through these supportive group settings, participatory and democratic leadership skills are taught, enabling youth to explore issues of family, trauma, and multicultural identity issues in an atmosphere of trust. The symbolic construction of identity among some second-generation Cambodians has enabled them to retain continuity with traditional forms of Khmer Buddhism, with material objects and activities in their home, with new expressions of Cambodian culture, and with ideal or imagined connections with Cambodia. Differences between Kampuchea Krom monastics and more traditional ones from Cambodia, however, can cause confusion among the youth; for example, when one youth asked a Kampuchea Krom monk in Ontario about the significance of the *hau bralin* ritual, he was told 'Kampuchea Krom do not believe in this ritual; it is an outdated belief.'

Some Ontario Cambodian youth have cultivated multiple linguistic, religious, and cultural competencies that enable them to negotiate different cultural and material lifestyles. In one American example, Douglas and Mam note the inclusion of Wiccan as a new mode of healing and cultural enhancement (2005: 64–9). Other youth, however, are more conflicted and feel enormous stress in balancing traditional Khmer expectations, values, and behaviours with those that they perceive to be mainstream or Christian. For youth who have attended Buddhist and Christians events, the significance of particular observances, beliefs, and rituals may be unclear, and their difficulty to choose one or the other can increase their feeling of exclusion from both. Christianity offers a wide range of denominational options for Cambodian youth (Baptist, Catholic, Christian Reformed, Evangelical, Mormon, and Seventh-day Adventists), but unless they have received ministerial training, few understand doctrinal distinctions. Initially, the weekly congregational format, often with additional mid-week study sessions, provided an ongoing connection for youth to explore new forms of Christian fellowship, prayer, and singing. When pressures to increase their levels of commitment through conformity, witnessing, and active proselytization of friends and family arise, many youth are not comfortable. Some Cambodian youth stated that the new obligations or expectations on them increased their sense of identity confusion, especially when they were asked to make a clear choice for inclusive belonging to the particular group.

The active participation of Christian women in playing music, singing hymns (individually or in small choirs), leading Sunday school, and giving inspirational talks is in direct contrast to the Khmer women's role in Buddhism, even though male pastors and elders continue to embody Christian religious leadership. New religious allegiances that overtly conflict with Buddhist practices or Khmer cultural events and activities further increase generational tensions (Douglas 2005: 136). Many Cambodian youth try to accommodate the differences between Buddhism and Christianity by recognizing their ethical/moral commonalities, and by saying they believe in both God/Jesus and Buddha. Minimizing religious boundaries has been somewhat successful for the first generation, especially when adherence to Christianity was an obligation to those who had provided sponsorship or resettlement assistance, and Buddhist and ancestral practices were retained. Second-generation youth, however, do so at the cost of a committed involvement and secure identity.

The process of migration, resettlement, and return to the homeland changes religious, ethnic, and civic identities, particularly affecting the organizational structures and practices that frame religious traditions. The move towards organizational congregationalism, for example, entails a legal incorporation necessary to qualify for Canadian tax-exempt status, but alters formal decision-making structures and introduces new forms of membership, new types of support for religious specialists, and different criteria for leadership and authority positions (Ebaugh and Chafetz 2000; Yang and Ebaugh 2001). The result for most Asian Buddhist groups is a complex interplay between traditional continuities and modernist transformations that depict a mix of hybrid combinations of homeland and localized North American loyalties. Components of modernism and traditionalism shift and are expressed according to context and situation (Stepick 2005: 15). A specific community's or temple's position on this continuum is influenced by several factors. Educational and generational differences impact the degree to which specific religious practices and beliefs are retained as representations of homeland-based ethnocultural identity. New kinds of transnational networks and linkages are developed to inform and influence particularized Buddhist identities in diaspora and, in some cases, levels of social capital within the community. Shifts in traditionalism also reflect the willingness (or necessity) of a religious institution to transform from an ethnic to a multiethnic organization (Mullins 1987), or to assume congregational forms (Ebaugh and Chafetz 2000; Cadge 2008). Being raised within competing value systems and changing expectations of cultural behaviours and relationships provide second-generation youth with multiple religious, ethnic, and social alternatives of identity. Douglas and Mam cite the example of a young Khmer man who became a Wiccan priest, attempting to combine Cambodian traditional practices with magical systems and techniques (2005: 64–6).

Overall, Cambodian refugees who resettled in Ontario twenty-five years ago have found a future in Canada and a sense of belonging through citizenship. Their social and economic prospects, compared with Cambodia, have been beneficial, providing numerous opportunities for themselves and extended family in Cambodia. Despite long-term employment, learning English, investing in houses and businesses, and establishing new social networks, most first-generation Cambodians retain an identity as Khmer in Canada that is always related to Cambodia, past and present. The second-generation Cambodians in Canada clearly identify themselves as Canadian and recognize Canada as home, yet they continue to struggle with what a Canadian identity means to them, and how much of it involves identifying with Cambodia and Khmer culture. Many youth have cultivated flexible identities that vary according to context (home, local community, educational, leisure, work, multicultural, multiracial, or travel settings). The fluidity and highly personal nature of their identity determines the extent to which different facets of being Khmer are acknowledged or expressed, and in what kinds of situations. There are many ways to be Khmer.

Ontario youth who maintain an active involvement in Khmer cultural and religious traditions are more comfortable with a hybrid identity as Cambodian Canadians and tend to be more closely associated with the community as leaders or as advocates. Their close identification does not prevent them from questioning what they perceive to be shortcomings in religious or associational services, practices, or leadership. Youth leaders today are becoming a bridge between the generations, a catalyst in searching out different ways of acknowledging community difficulties and in expanding ways of self-identifying and being recognized as Khmer. Their ability to develop a secure sense of ethnic, religious, and cultural continuity in Canada is enhanced through a closer awareness of and identification with Cambodia, as well as through Canadian educational and career achievements. The strength and resiliency of Ontario Cambodians continue with those born and/or raised in Canada, their Khmer spirit evident in the words of two youth leaders, both second generation:

Young Windsor man: People always understand Cambodian people as always related to suffering. But what we need to is try to break that image. Because if someone mentions Cambodia, for those who are educated, for those who know, the first thing that comes to mind is suffering. What we are trying to do and what they are trying to do in the country is to shed that image, to try to teach how to look at Cambodians more, of what is. I see Cambodians here with kids who are educated and who are trying to start something. But people still see Cambodians as a tragedy, as a suffering. And that will never go away, but hopefully, as time goes by, maybe we can teach the whole spectrum of life; that Cambodian people in Ontario do have a bright light at the end of the tunnel.

Young Hamilton man: I am most proud of the fact that I am Khmer and there's no one single thing that weighs more than the other. From my parents, to my home country, to what we eat, to everything [in my culture], those are the things that I'm proud of. That's what distinguishes me from another person. I can walk up to another person and I can say, 'I am Khmer because of these things.' That's what is becoming deeper and deeper for me every time I explore these issues. I think that the youth of tomorrow will struggle with these issues also, and we recognize today that there is no one single thing that makes us different ... They know deep in their hearts that they are Khmer. And those are the challenges that we will face tomorrow, that these things we know as identity will change according to the youth. Yet, they'll still be Khmer. (personal interviews, 2005)

In response to the recent economic downturn, a second-generation Windsor man described his community's reaction:

It's a scary situation out there, and sadly, there's little hope of a recovery anytime soon. In the Windsor community alone, I can count over thirty Khmer families with parents that do not have jobs. But, in traditional Khmer fashion, Khmers aren't picky when it comes to how they earn their money. Most Khmer parents resort to the farm or greenhouses in the winter for their income ... basically taking jobs that the normal Canadian would brush off, even if they were desperate. Nope, not Khmers, they'll do anything. An in the end, they'll prosper by saving every penny. I have hope that they'll be fine; because in all honesty, they've been through much worse. (personal interview, 2008)

Following the example of their parents, these second-generation Khmer increasingly symbolize themselves with Hung Meas, the spirit of the golden phoenix, rising from the flames to begin anew and shine in different ways.

Notes

1 A Brief History of Cambodians

1 Since the end of the nineteenth century, Buddhist modernism has exercised a significant presence in all Asian Buddhist countries. Harris (2005: ix) describes the following characteristics of Buddhist modernism in the Theravada tradition: a preference for modes of thought and behaviour specifically authorized by the 'scriptural tradition' as expressed in the Pali canon (Tripitaka) and its commentaries; a marked tendency towards laicization and the employment of modern proselytizing techniques (pamphlet production, technological distribution); presenting itself as a movement of purification, reform, return to the 'original truth' of the Buddha's vision; and affiliating these modern Buddhist ideals with the development of various national liberation struggles. In Cambodia, the Thommayut (Dhammayut) and the Mahanikay disagreed over the interpretation of some elements of monastic discipline (vinaya), particularly the wearing and composition of the monastic robe; they had differences in their liturgical deliveries, pronunciations, and in ceremonial celebrations; and they enjoyed different levels of aristocratic support, although the Mahanikay retained strong influence in rural areas (Harris 2005: 107–8, 110–12). Hansen details further arenas of difference, as well as the subsequent internal strife of the Mahanikay as they became influenced by the reformist ideas being introduced and the French colonialist response (2007: 97–9).

2 Cambodian Resettlement in Canada

1 Ontario community leaders tend to approximate the number of people based on known families, and on the numbers of Cambodians who attend

community festivities. At a Toronto New Year's evening dance in 1990, over 800 people attended, mostly older youth and young adults. When community leaders account for the older generation, and the mothers and young children who did not come, they suggest the total community in the Toronto area alone would approximate 4,800. The 1991 census lists the total Cambodian population in Ontario as 4,575. The 1994 assessments given by Cambodian leaders in various Ontario cities were as follows:

- Hamilton has approximately 250 Cambodian families, indicating over 1,000 people. Many of these families have come from Edmonton, Saskatchewan, Alberta, and British Columbia.
- Ottawa has approximately 250 families, indicating over 1,000 people.
- over 500 Cambodian families are in the London area, with estimates of more than 2,000 people. The numbers had significantly increased in 1989 due to secondary migration from Edmonton, Alberta. In nearby St Thomas, over thirty-seven families (approximately 200 people) were initially resettled, but most have since moved away to London and other Ontario cities.
- Toronto has more than 5,000 Cambodian people, when the regions of Brampton, Newmarket, Vaughan, and Maple are taken into account. In addition, there are several hundred Kampuchea Krom and numerous Khmer who claimed Vietnamese identity. Many families in Toronto were initially resettled in Kingston, but since 1986, over twenty-five families have come to Toronto for school or employment, with fewer than ten families remaining in Kingston.
- In the Windsor area there are approximately 135 families, indicating over 550 people, including seventeen families in nearby Leamington.

2 Until early 2000, the majority of Cambodians in Ottawa lived in three main subsidized housing areas: fifty to sixty families lived in West End Bayshore; sixty to eighty families lived in Rochester Heights near the Cambodian Buddhist Cartwell Temple; and forty to fifty families lived in Chinatown, near Wood Street. During the early 1990s, certain apartment blocks in Ottawa were identified by Cambodians as being comprised of 'Khmer Rouge,' a derogatory labelling discussed in chapter 3. In Windsor, two main residential areas for Cambodians developed. The 'east side' in downtown Windsor had very few families relying on assisted housing, whereas over half the families lived in assisted housing in the 'west side.' Many of the 'west side' families have remained on welfare due to unemployment, ill health, handicaps, or single-parent needs. In the London area, over 136 Cambodian families were initially concentrated in low-cost rental

apartments in the northeast end of the city, especially along Cheyenne Avenue and Huron Street, close to the Cuddy Food Products plant where many of them worked.

In the greater area of Metropolitan Toronto, Cambodians were initially concentrated in one specific newcomer area of the former city of North York. Referred to as the Jane-Finch area, it includes several subsidized apartments, apartment buildings, and townhouses. Cambodian community leaders in Toronto have separated this large area into smaller units, based on the housing authority names: Jane-Finch (largest concentration), Shoreham Village (second largest), then Woolner, Driftwood, and Grand Ravine. Sino-Cambodians (those with Chinese ancestry or identity) tend to congregate in Regent Park, a government subsidized housing district in downtown Toronto. Regent Park is recognized for its large concentration of Chinese from Vietnam, Cambodia, and Laos. There are about thirty families from Cambodia living here.

3 In November 1989, a London landlord of two Cheyenne Avenue apartments made several racial slurs about Cambodians to the local press, describing them as 'little pigs living in the jungle who regarded cockroaches as pets.' Although this landlord was fined and convicted for consistently not complying with city-ordered building repairs dating back to 1987, his defence was to blame the deteriorating structure on Cambodian renters.

4 At one Chalkfarm apartment building near Jane and Wilson Blvd., thirty Cambodian families left during the early 1990s. Cambodians at the Woolner Building, at Jane and St Clair, experienced similar harassment and left as well, with over twenty-five families moving to other areas such as Jane and Finch, Regent Park, and Newmarket. The loss of these families from the Woolner Building adversely affected the only existing Khmer Heritage Language Program in Toronto, which had been housed in the building's George Sam Centre. Several of the families who moved to Newmarket and Brampton, however, cited employment and the opportunity to buy houses as their primary motivation. These Cambodians tended to be young adults, recently married and/or with very young children.

5 In a 1993 workshop on sexual assault given to a Cambodian ESL class for women, the Cambodian Community Association requested a guest speaker from the Jane-Finch neighbourhood women's assault centre to help Cambodian women understand their rights. The guest speaker was a young Black woman student from the University of Toronto. Her talk was about sexual harassment in the office environment, a situation totally alien to most Cambodian women, especially those enrolled in the ESL class. To illustrate sexual harassment, she spoke of men referring to women's large

breasts (unusual in Asian women). When she handed out a picture of many men from all racial backgrounds in different occupations and asked, 'Who is likely to be an assaulter? ' all the Cambodians in the class picked the Black man. Her point had been that all men are potential abusers, but for many Cambodians living in the Jane-Finch area, sexual harassment and assault was identified with Black men.

6 In the late 1980s, government funding for Khmer settlement workers decreased, as did most ISAP support. The Canadian Cambodian Association of Ontario, located in Toronto, was the only remaining organization to employ settlement counsellors for Cambodians until that funding completely ended in 2001. Both Khmer and non-Khmer settlement workers throughout Ontario increasingly requested the province to support programs for various Cambodian communities. From the late 1980s, throughout the 1990s, funding was sought from the Ministry of Citizenship and Culture, Ministry of Health, Ontario Women's Directorate, and the Ministry of Community and Social Services. Yet, as one consultant from Field Services, Ministry of Citizenship noted in the early 1990s, 'there is no provincial mandate for mental health or for specific community problems.' Ontario funding sources were geared towards such mainstream general programs as welfare or re-education, not for unique difficulties. The type of settlement services available and their accessibility for Cambodians adversely affected adaptation and integration.

After ten to fifteen years of living in Canada, the need for settlement services among Cambodians still had not diminished (McLellan 1995). By the mid-1990s, Cambodians in Ontario who still required support and assistance had few services available to them. In 2003, only two Ottawa Community Health Centres, the Toronto-based Jane-Finch Family and Community Centre, and Hong Fook Mental Health Association continued to assist Cambodians through funded programs. Overall, the resettlement services available to Cambodian refugees in Ontario were not easily accessed; they were not provided for an adequate length of time; they were not specialized to acknowledge or meet the unique needs of Cambodians, especially as survivors of genocide; most services were not oriented towards long-term integration; and few were provided by qualified individuals.

7 The CCAO received ISAP funding for Cambodian refugees until the late 1990s. Mr Serei Kang, executive director in 1992, identified three goals of the CCAO: to create a network for Cambodian immigrants; to maintain Cambodian culture and traditions; and to educate Cambodians regarding their rights and obligations so they can become good Canadian citizens.

The association provided a variety of educational activities (language instruction, workshops, information-sharing sessions) for Cambodians. In 1993, approximately $200,000 was funded by Employment and Immigration Canada to provide salaries and benefits for three settlement counsellors, a part-time LINC (Language Instruction for Newcomers in Canada) teacher, a part-time LINC coordinator, and two part-time LINC child-care workers. LINC, however, could only be offered to those Cambodians who had not yet become Canadian citizens. The salary of the association's full-time executive director was paid by an OSIP grant from the provincial Ministry of Citizenship and Culture. Although the Cambodian Association of Ontario received federal resettlement service funding for over fourteen years, until the early 1990s, it provided only limited programs, which were accessed by a small proportion of the total community (McLellan 1995). Given the levels of distrust among Cambodian refugees, and the dynamics of patronage, the CCAO's early history was mired in political disputes, controversial leaders, unqualified service workers, and ineffectual programs. Although government personnel from the specific funding departments attended the CCAO annual general meetings, these meetings were conducted in Khmer, and translators may have been unwilling to elucidate contentious or damaging issues. For several years, therefore, government workers remained unaware of the difficulties in service provision, in the absence of community participation, and the lack of annual elections. In the mid-1990s, a program coordinator position, primarily concerned with community development, was funded through Canada Heritage (formerly Multiculturalism and Citizenship Canada). The first program coordinator was a non-Khmer woman with extensive experience in working with Cambodians (in London and Toronto) as well as with Laotians. Several innovative programs were developed, including leadership training and Khmer community outreach workers. Large portions of the community that were previously marginalized by the association were connected with services.

To keep the CCAO functioning, additional funding was provided by the Municipality of Metropolitan Toronto for office expenses. Canada Heritage and the Ontario Women's Directorate also contributed to occasional educational programs offered in the LINC classes, to deal with topics such as sexual assault, wife abuse, and racial problems. The non-Khmer coordinator worked with the nearby Jane-Finch Family and Community Centre to develop its first programs for Cambodian women and youth.

8 One young man featured in the documentary stated: 'When I first came, I was depressed. Everything was new to me. I wanted to continue my

studies but lacked money. I was not prepared for the Canadian job market. I felt frustrated, hopeless, and lonely. Then, with help from Immigration Canada, I attended school and got a job at a factory. I didn't like my first job, but I worked hard to earn a living and save for my education. I believe my future in Canada will improve because there is freedom and opportunity. I learned to solve problems by reading, newspapers, and watching TV. I also sought advice from those around me ... At first, I tried to solve them [problems] by myself. I discussed some difficult ones with friends. They found me a job as a hotel servant. With my ability to speak several languages, I became a reception clerk within a month. My salary was increased. Since then, I knew I could pursue my dreams. I managed to take an evening course, and I then started to study full-time. I will graduate very soon.'

A thirty-eight-year-old woman also emphasized success: 'I was born in Phnom Penh. I was a government official until I fled to Thailand (Kao Dao heard). From there, I applied to come to Canada ... When I arrived in Toronto, I had several problems. My past job experience was not applicable here. I needed to earn enough money to bring my kid from the refugee camp in Thailand. I didn't have the bare necessities of life. I attended English as a second language classes and worked at night. Later, I took a job-training course. I talked with my friends, relatives and teachers in an effort to find solutions to my troubles. I learned to relax through leisure activities. I never let my problems dominate me.'

The documentary ended with various scenes of Toronto, a Khmer Buddhist celebration, Cambodian community park picnic, and a political event sponsored by the CCAO to honour the visit of H.E. Son Sam, Prime Minister of the Coalition Government of Kampuchea (featuring musicians playing traditional music and the performance of an Apsara dancer) while the Hong Fook Khmer worker spoke the following words: 'We must have good health to build our future. To maintain good health we need to reduce stress and keep active. We need to relax and reduce job pressure. Talking to family and friends reduces stress. We should spend a few hours a week relaxing. Exercising promotes physical and mental health. Problems left unresolved can worsen. If we can't solve a problem by ourselves we should seek help from family, friends, or MDs. Also the Cambodian Association and Hong Fook provide friendly, confidential, and attentive services. Therefore, we shouldn't hide our problems.'

This Khmer worker developed several life skills programs for Khmer women, and her continuing presence at the Hong Fook provides a crucial connection to the Cambodian community. In 2004, Hong Fook and the

Cambodian Advisory Committee produced a CD called *Life Beyond the Rain* dramatizing the kinds of mental health concerns that young Khmer women are facing, and encouraging them to seek help.

9 The London Cross-Cultural Learner Centre provided substantial assistance and support to Cambodian refugees throughout the 1980s and early 1990s. ISAP services were introduced in 1980, enabling the hiring of a full-time Khmer service worker and the development of a variety of Khmer educational programs. With funding from the Refugee Settlement Branch of Employment and Immigration Canada, the Cross Cultural Learner Centre implemented a needs assessment survey in 1988. Serious problems were identified in the sample group taken from one-third of the London Cambodian population. More than 90 per cent of those surveyed said they had the following difficulties: lack of Cambodian support group (95.85%); problems with the English Language (95.83%); problems in understanding Canadian society (95.65%); problems in dealing with the Canadian government (91.30%); and lack of help with getting a job (90.47%).

Furthermore, of those adults with school-aged children, almost 80 per cent stated they experienced difficulties relating to their children's education and school. These results indicated that existing government services designed to enhance adaptive and integrative capacities were not working for the Cambodians. As a result of this survey, the London Cross Cultural Learner Centre developed different types of Cambodian community development programs. The Cambodian Women's Integration Project and the Cambodian Leadership Training Program were funded by alternative provincial and federal government grants from Multiculturalism and Citizenship Canada. The Ministry of Culture and Citizenship employed more part-time Khmer workers to assist the full-time Khmer worker. ISAP funding, however, was not extended, forcing the Cambodians into a choice between employment or studying English.

10 Community Health Centres (CHC) in Ottawa recognized that access of opportunity is the premise upon which integrative processes are realized for newcomers. If refugees lack the cultural capital, ability, or knowledge to access opportunity (such as services, programs, training, employment, or education), addressing this lack must be a fundamental focus for any settlement service. The short-term provision of settlement services by CHCs were therefore linked to long-term programs that enabled newcomer groups to access and participate in mainstream resources. The CHCs incorporated a dynamic approach to implementing programs and services, taking into account that the durations needed for resettlement and the processes of integration differ enormously among individuals and within specific groups.

11 During most of the 1990s, the Somerset West Community Health Centre in Ottawa (formerly Dalhousie Community Health Centre) employed two Khmer workers, one as a part-time community health worker and one full-time in social services. Half the members of the community (more than 100 families) in Ottawa were listed as active clients in 1994. Initially, programs were concerned with issues of family dynamics, gender, and intergenerational conflict. Later, they were also geared towards developing the community's capacity for equitable representation, self-sufficiency, and mainstream integration through skills training. The Khmer social service worker at Somerset West CHC described how she facilitated opportunities to provide services for Cambodians: 'As a Cambodian outreach worker, my emphasis is on providing accessible, culturally, and spiritually sensitive services, such as to the Seniors' Cambodian Women's Group, which meets in the Cambodian Buddhist temple. I have also worked with the Women's Sewing Group and would like to develop a parents/youth program. Also, the mental health problems are increasing in the Cambodian community. I play a bridging role to get clients to mainstream services, for example, to meet psychiatric social workers from the hospital. Through SWCHC, we arranged a meeting with all the Cambodian workers in Ottawa, including leaders from the Cambodian Association, to discuss difficulties in providing services. We looked at roles and referrals and how to develop a coordinated plan to include the community and develop more self-help initiatives. Another Cambodian worker is still working one day here at SWCHC in the Health Section, and spends the rest of the week with the Carleton Board of Education as a liaison' (personal interview, 1994).

12 A Hamilton-based former Khmer service worker commented: 'Cambodians needed escorting service, not just phone service which is what the government usually provides. The Chinese and Vietnamese groups are more organized and articulate and they set the pace. Among the Cambodians, most people over forty cannot learn English. Escorting service is needed for at least the next ten years. There was an ethnic counsellor conflict at settlement services over the escorting service and the fact that most Cambodians are seen outside of the office. For example, one social worker wanted a Cambodian family to pick up the welfare cheque, but the family couldn't find the place and couldn't read the map to figure it out. Other ethnic groups can be told this. Cambodians must be taken ... Because many feel so discouraged from Pol Pot and feel so tired, they still feel fear from the "nightmare" and have no courageous sense to improve here, to know the city better, to help themselves with a problem' (personal interview, 1994).

A non-Khmer service worker in Toronto had similar observations: 'The LINC class is open to all "newcomers" because the LINC teacher feels that this will force the Khmer to speak English ... Also, the LINC teacher feels that issues such as violence, of sexual assault, or other themes brought up in the workshop are common to all "newcomers" and thus can be talked about in a generalized fashion. But, my feeling is that the particular historical context of Khmer experiences is not fully appreciated, nor is their particular cultural interpretation or response to the issues presented. This is a problem occurring within all service agencies. The Khmer community is small, and they are being addressed as just one more "newcomer" community. Unfortunately, the communities who will get the interpreters or the specialized programs will be those with large population numbers, those who actively advocate for specialized services, or those who act out in a way that draws attention to youth violence or abuse' (personal interview, 1995).

13 A Cambodian in St Thomas commented: 'The [non-Khmer] elder responsible for the Cambodian group was the only church member who really realized what had happened to us, our different backgrounds, our experiences under Pol Pot, and why we have such difficulty to trust. He has had numerous discussions about this with us and has read several survival books to gain more information. He has shared this understanding with the Christian pastor here but feels that regular people don't want to know about the past of the Cambodians ... I think this is why the Christian church feels so cold to me [people being polite but unfriendly] and why I don't like to go even though I am a devout Christian' (personal interview, 1993).

One private sponsor affiliated with the Christian Reformed Church recalled: 'Neither sponsors nor administrators in the Reformed Church were aware of the extreme psychological devastation among Khmer people. The Reformed Church never offered special programs for Khmer people in Canada. Executives like myself, who had been in the camps and talked with people, didn't follow through with their knowledge. When churches began to sponsor and resettle people, this process was accomplished through a "national" organization under the master agreement. The Christian Reformed Church was a national organization with a master agreement that enabled local churches (Christian Reformed or other ones) to sponsor resettlement. Outreach was the responsibility of local churches. The Christian Reformed Church failed to develop a "responsive outreach." Long-range goals for Cambodian refugees were not accomplished. In the manual on long-range goals under Refugee Sponsorship and Resettlement

it states, "5B: Work with the deacons, and deaconal conferences to encourage sponsorship and resettlement; and develop a responsive outreach and
ministry to locally resettled refugees realizing their needs as well as their
potential." The Christian Reformed Church, as the 'national' organization, did not initiate an overview of Cambodian resettlement or provide
specific areas to address in specific programs. Difficulties were met ad hoc.
Reaction and response arose as the needs were noted' (personal interview,
1994).

Another private sponsor noted that in general: 'People sponsored boat
people out of a sense of guilt, that something needed to be done, something compassionate. But, they didn't really realize what was going on
or what was needed. This was why no program was established. The
response to sponsorship was enough to fill this sense of guilt. No more
was needed to be done' (personal interview, 1993).

14 During the early 1980s, most Khmer service workers in Ontario were men.
Although men felt uncomfortable with interpreting the needs of women,
men were thought to be more assertive in telling clients what to do and
being listened to. A former female Khmer settlement worker in Toronto
stated: 'A man by his sheer presence is respected. If a woman speaks up
she is looked as aggressive, but if she doesn't she is walked over' (personal
interview 1994).

15 A Khmer woman from London thought that cultural misunderstandings
particularly affected women: 'Medical personnel here are not aware. The
traditional practice of coin-rubbing is misinterpreted. The "roasting" of
new mothers and herbal wine consumption is also not understood. Wine is
thought to help strengthen the uterus and flush out old blood, but nurses
only warn against the dangers of alcohol and won't allow. Here there are
no facilities to lie on the fire after a baby is born, "roasting," where lots
of heat is needed. The tradition is hot drinks, herbs, and ginger. But here,
doctors give ice packs and cold drinks. Steaming is not allowed in the hospital. Also, traditionally, women are not to move for at least one week or
allow the child to be taken out. Cambodian women are upset when forced
to move. Because women can't practise traditional medicine, many feel
that they are not as healthy as their parents and grandparents' (personal
interview, 1994).

Toah (touh) is a Khmer term that refers to the somatic symptoms women
get when they fail to follow cultural food restrictions or when they suffer
from depression and extensive grief (Eisenbruch and Handelman 1989;
Sargent, Marcucci, and Elliston 1983). Symptoms include loss of appetite,
sleeplessness, weakness, crying spells, and loss of energy. When these

symptoms are diagnosed for Cambodians according to Western systems of health and treatment, the result is ineffective treatment and non-compliance. As Eisenbruch and Handelman (1989: 244) note, the result of misdiagnosis and culturally inappropriate treatment is often intractable illness behaviour (repeat visits to no avail) at a great cost to both the patients and the health care systems. One Khmer service worker felt that the overall failure to provide culturally sensitive and preventive health care meant that diagnosis often came too late, to the point where symptoms were incurable. She also pointed out that the opposite occurred as well, with Khmer misunderstanding the system (going to the hospital for a cold), overusing the system (claiming to always be sick), or misusing the system (getting prescriptions that are then sent to Cambodia or to get extended health disability benefits).

16 In the Toronto Cambodian community, services to Cambodians were provided exclusively through the Cambodian Association, and paid positions were particularly seen to be based on patronage rather than merit. One former federal government worker familiar with the Cambodian community from 1980 to 1986, commented: 'Federal government money equals power, and power equals the ability to dispense favours. This is the Cambodian way, to give positions and services to members of their family first. Attempts have been made by the board of directors to start hiring family members to share the wealth. But, none of these hired were capable of providing settlement services and even knowing about them. Annual general meetings were very bitter and angry. Some meetings had to have a police presence. You could see a lot of troubled faces. The most contentious issues were always about leadership, who would be the president of the association ... Cambodians have so little inkling of how to provide settlement services, or what to provide, that it is better that these services be in a non-Khmer association. Part of the problem is that highly traumatized individuals are being expected to help other traumatized people. The workers needed are inverse to the community, the fewer the workers, the greater the need' (personal interview, 1994).

17 Many Cambodian men have not been able to advance beyond introductory levels of English, despite repeated ESL classes. This has restricted them from accessing government retraining programs or pursuing high school and post-secondary education. Cambodian women faced several difficulties in learning English, particularly arising from their high Khmer illiteracy rates. In general, Cambodians' struggles to learn English is exacerbated by structural differences between Khmer and Western languages (script, verb tenses, phonemes); cultural differences between Cambodian and

Canadian styles of teaching; low educational levels among the majority of older Cambodian adults, indicating a lack of experience with or comfort within a formalized classroom structure; almost ten years of interrupted education (during the Khmer Rouge regime and in refugee camps) among younger Cambodian adults; and extensive impaired memory or learning capacity among Cambodians in general, symptomatic of post-traumatic stress disorder (Eisenbruch 1991; Payne 1990).

18 In 1995, the Cambodian community worker in St Thomas noted that 50 per cent of public school Cambodian children were still in ESL classes and 100 per cent of Cambodian youth in the high school still required ESL training, but did not receive it. An elementary school principal in Toronto commented: 'Cambodian children born in Canada are still using ESL services. They do poorly in needs assessment. Their English fluency is challenged because parents don't speak English ... The Cambodian children who arrive in early elementary still need six or seven years ESL to have the confidence and skills needed to cope. Therefore, those who arrived in Grade 7 or up never got the support needed to help. Cambodian kids don't have a snowball's chance in high school unless parents can be educated in the value of education and the system, for example, through culture-specific parent/teachers associations. We need to take the school out to the community, for example, to rent halls in the apartment buildings and have the school staff go out' (personal interview, 1994). In the smaller communities such as Ottawa or St Thomas, ESL instruction was funded until the late 1990s. In Toronto, however, ESL instruction for Cambodians declined by the early 1990s.

3 Community Distinctions and Divisions

1 Common economic activities in a rural village consisted of the cultivation of rice, fruit, and vegetables, and involvement in fishing and crafts, such as producing cloth and pottery. Some rural Khmer who had migrated to the larger cities before 1975 had begun to work in factories, and some had established small trade businesses. Upper-class ethnic Khmer from Phnom Penh and Battambang, the largest urban cities in Cambodia, were frequently engaged in government, military, professional, and educational work. Business ventures, financial opportunities, and entrepreneurial roles tended to be developed and filled by Vietnamese and Chinese minorities in the cities and towns.

2 The St Thomas Cambodian community was unique in that all of the families except one shared a similar background. During the early 1990s most

of the St Thomas community consisted of extended families and friends, originally from the farming areas of Battambang, Kompong Thom, and Siem Reap. Because many of the adults were less than fifteen years old when the Khmer Rouge shut down all the schools in 1975, they all shared a low educational background (only one or two adult males had some secondary schooling), although several of the men learned carpentry skills and other trades in the Thai camps. Most of the women had no education at all. The one family, where the husband had been a military government official, had a difficult time being accepted by the rest of the community because of differences in their speech and lifestyle.

3 Upper-class Khmer who worked in government, military, professional, and educational arenas represent less than 10 per cent of Cambodians who resettled in Ontario. None have found occupations even remotely similar to what they held in Cambodia, and they continue to find it difficult to work in what they perceive as low-status jobs of unskilled labour.

4 In early 1980, a unique program called Project 4000 was started for Indochinese refugees in Ottawa. It provided an occupational assessment to establish the refugees' skills (according to Canadian standards), and then direct them into retraining and apprenticeship programs. Few Cambodians were advised about the program or received placement in training for a skilled job. In other Ontario communities, local boards of education set up refresher courses for Indochinese refugees ready to enter the local workforce. Courses were taught in English, and included typing, keypunching, commercial sewing, auto mechanics, and dry cleaning. Most Cambodians were unfamiliar with the areas covered in these courses, and the courses were provided at a level inappropriate for their language and educational capacity.

5 Having a steady income is a priority for most Cambodians. Since their initial resettlement, individuals and households have contributed to the welfare of surviving family members in Cambodia. Remittance arrangements, while informal (personally delivered through trusted friends), provide relatives in Cambodia with basic food, medicine, education, household goods, farming equipment, and capital for small home-based businesses.

To make extra money, many Cambodian men, women, and youth engaged in informal, seasonal work, such as night worm picking. In London, Windsor, and Hamilton, a large number of Khmer women worked in local mushroom farms, while elderly and pregnant women assisted by babysitting. Women were also informally engaged in sewing, cooking, and cleaning. Several Cambodian women worked two jobs. One job would consist of factory work, often industrial sewing, while the other would involve home piecework sewing or flower arranging. When the women were laid off, or forced to leave due to ill health, the second job provided some economic continuity. A few of these women have turned their part-time jobs into full-time home-based businesses. Some operate small stores, or have a booth in a local market. Piecework home sewing, however, meant that women worked in isolation, often in unsafe or unhealthy conditions, and lacked contract security or grievance procedures (Ong 2003: 233). Some Cambodian men make extra money playing popular music for Cambodian parties, and those with classical music skills are in constant demand for weddings and religious celebrations. Now that Cambodians can return to Cambodia, visits entail thousands of dollars for family members, as well as gifts and donations to help rebuild religious and cultural institutions and village infrastructures (roads, bridges, wells, schools) in Cambodia.

6 Cambodians were well aware of the cycle of poverty that arose from the lack of English language skills and made valid suggestions to overcome the problem. A Cambodian man in Ottawa had this suggestion, which unfortunately, was not implemented: 'About training, some people want to be a carpenter or baker but we don't know English, it is very difficult to learn. We want to have class training starting from basic level to intermediate and advanced level. The basic level is the general level. But the intermediate level should be specialized. It should teach terminology for a specific job, for example, terminology for baker, technician, or mechanics, so that people know the specific language for that job training' (personal interview, 1994).

7 Cambodians in Ottawa/Hull had an unemployment rate of 25.0 per cent, and in Kingston 27.3 per cent (Statistics Canada 1991: Special Tabulations). Data for Hamilton show that Cambodians had over twice the unemployment rate of non-Cambodians. In the Kitchener area, the Cambodian unemployment rate of 22.2 per cent far exceeded the 9.0 per cent overall unemployment for the region. The common pattern for Cambodians in Ontario during the 1990s recession was high unemployment and low labour force participation (ibid.). Informal surveys conducted by the Cambodian Association and the South East Asian Services Centre in Toronto in the mid-1990s, supported by information from numerous interviews with Cambodians throughout Ontario at this time, indicated that unemployment figures for Cambodians were underrepresented. In Kingston, 90 per cent of adult Khmer had been laid off from their factory jobs. The only employment they were able to access was occasional office cleaning,

pumping gas, or short-term jobs that required no skills. In St Thomas, almost twenty-two families lost their employment at the United Technology Factory when in closed in 1990.

8 A Khmer service worker commented: 'Women's position has changed so radically here that men can't adjust and family separation results. The single mother situation teaches children dependency and abuse of the system and no ethics for hard work and no example for good role models. Mothers on welfare are not respected but looked at as lazy, not capable' (personal interview, 1994).

9 In the Toronto area , the majority of employed Khmer work in manufacturing jobs in North York, Brampton, and Newmarket. At the Rimply Company in Newmarket, for example, Cambodians comprise almost half of the 1,000 workers in the factory. In Hamilton, factories such as York Barbell, StressCrete, and Cramarose Tarpaulin employ significant numbers of Cambodians. In Ottawa, although most employed Khmer do unskilled labour in manufacturing, office cleaning, or landscaping, there is a growing number who do electronic assembly work at Apsopulse, and a small group of Khmer Evangelicals who do similar work at the New Bridge Networks Corporation. In London, Khmer men and women work at Cuddy Food Production, cutting chicken, while other men work in construction jobs or at the Siemens Auto Parts Factory. In St Thomas, six families (husbands, wives, and children) work at the Preston Factory making car parts, and several people commute to the Siemens factory in London. In Windsor, men tend to work on the assembly lines in car factories. Khmer men and women also work in related manufacturing firms such as InterCrom, which makes car seats, belts, and wheel covers. Beginning in 2008, however, economic conditions have resulted in a severe loss of manufacturing jobs in Ontario, particularly affecting those associated with the auto industry.

10 Many of their chronic health problems are understood to be lingering effects of experiences under the Khmer Rouge. The Khmer medical doctor in Toronto commented: 'The physical complaint of many Cambodians is mostly joint and neck pain. Sometimes they feel chilled. The motivation is slow, as is their thinking. Mistrust to everyone is rampant in the community. One patient told of the hard labour that he endured. He worked from dusk to dawn carrying soil to build a dam. He had crushing pain to his neck and chest during this time, and the damage is permanent. During anatomical examination (X-ray) the damage is not apparent, but the man feels the pain and crushing sensation. This becomes especially apparent when he has flashbacks and relives the trauma. During these times his

body ceases to function. It is a miracle that the Cambodians here can cope and work with this kind of experience' (personal interview, 1994).

11 Apart from the low pay and lack of opportunity within unskilled labour positions, Cambodian workers may face additional health problems from the factories. Payne (1990) suggests that Cambodians who endured malnutrition and the harsh, severe work under the Khmer Rouge and then work continuously in heavy labour jobs may experience long-term physical deterioration, especially as they age. Cambodians' frustration with their poor English ability was exacerbated by their mostly unsuccessful experiences in trying to get employers to understand their physical disabilities, in filling out the forms needed to access workers' compensation benefits, and in obtaining effective treatment. One Cambodian woman commented on the damage done to the bodies of the men and women who work at a food-processing factory: 'We work in the constant cold. Heavy gloves are required, and scissors, and always standing. Therefore there is a lot of hand operations and dislocated shoulders, joint seizures, numbness in hand, assembly line work to keep up with production. Cambodians are shy to complain to Workers' Compensation, which doesn't accept their complaints. Company personnel will do short-term solution, for example, temporary light work, but puts them back eventually on the line. The company gives subtle message that lots of others want jobs' (personal interview, 1994).

12 In 2005, Cambodian businesses in Ontario included service industries (signs, portraits, printing, video production, marble supply); grocery stores, a large supermarket, and several food supply companies (e.g., ocean seafood); upholstery, furniture, and appliance stores; wedding specialists and beauty salons; florists; car repair shops; jewelry stores; travel agents; remittance networks; bakeries, delis, and restaurants; life insurance, real estate, and investment companies; and fast food outlets (Coffee Time, Baker's Dozen, Dairy Queen, Subs).

4 Re-creating Cambodian Buddhist Temples and the Significance of Tradition

1 The Pagode Khmer du Canada in Montreal is the oldest (founded in late 1970s), largest, and best-supported Khmer Buddhist institution in Canada, maintaining several monks and numerous *duan chee* (nuns who follow ten precepts). Renovated from three rowhouses, it incorporates traditional Khmer architectural style, several Buddhist shrines and meditation areas, and is surrounded by a large courtyard and garden.

2 Until 2004, it was a small two-storey single house in a residential neighbourhood, with no indication from the outside that it was a Buddhist
temple. The ground floor comprised a kitchen and large shrine room;
bedrooms on the second floor for the monks; and in the basement, an area
for tables and chairs, a cleared space for sitting on the floor, and a public bathroom. In 2004, the temple relocated to a building in a semi-rural
location near Ottawa. The larger space now allows for a library, rooms for
cultural activities (language and dance instruction), youth programs, and
accommodates more parking.

3 The Wat began in a small one-bedroom apartment in a building that
housed several Khmer families, and later moved to a slightly larger two-
bedroom townhouse (stacked rowhousing) in the same area. No markers
were provided on the outside to identify its religious or cultural significance, but inside, the living and dining room area was converted to a
Buddhist shrine and meditation area, with walls covered in pictures of the
Angkor Wat and other scenes reminiscent of Cambodia.

4 The entire ground floor comprises two separate shrine areas, a large
office, and a small meeting room; the upper floor has four bedrooms and
a bathroom; and the lower floor provides a large kitchen and communal
eating area, separate bathrooms for men and women, and a large activity
room with walkout to the backyard. The Maple temple houses the abbot,
who arrived from Cambodia in 1996; any recently arrived Khmer Buddhist
monks who come to Canada on visitor visas (due to Canadian government
restrictions on sponsorship); monks who become temporarily ordained;
and *duan chee* who live there temporarily to provide cooking, cleaning, and
temple maintenance service for the monks.

5 In 2005, the Windsor community rented a large hall and kitchen for the
entire day to hold New Year's/*Bun Chaul Chhnam* ceremonies in the morning, a communal lunch, and a community dance in the evening. Tickets
for the evening food (prepared by the community) and drinks were sold
to cover costs. Local Khmer and visitors from Hamilton, London, and
Michigan attended. Since Toronto and Ottawa hold similar events, the
communities arrange their Buddhist celebrations on different weekends to
accommodate out-of-town friends and family, as well as to share the few
available monks.

Most New Year's celebrations in Ontario are reduced to one or two days,
usually held on a weekend in April or early May, as close to the full moon
as possible. The temple in Hamilton does not rent a large hall, but holds
morning religious ceremonies for New Year's on three days (Friday to Sunday) to avoid large crowds on any one day. Communal meals follow each

religious service, but the temple does not include performances by the Hamilton Cambodian Folk Dancing group.

6 About thirty older Khmer (those over fifty-five) and two monks sat in chairs, semi-circle around a Buddha and two vases of water. The rest of the participants lined up, each with a flower (previously handed out from a large bucket), then went to the shrine and wet the flower from a vase on the right. They stroked the Buddha's face, arm, and chest with the flower and then put the flower in the vase on the left for more moisture. They either repeated stroking the Buddha or went directly to the monks, and after bowing, touched the monk's hands with the moistened flower as he gave blessings. They bowed again, and then went to the elder sitting next to the monk. Along the line, people went to each Khmer elder, often bowing before they touched the elders on the hand with the flower, and the elders would smile and say blessings in return.

7 The large beautifully constructed 'flower money-trees' are prominently displayed with paper money (usually $5, $10, $20, and $50 bills) folded into flower blossoms. Each money-tree demonstrates the creativity, commitment to the temple, and generosity of particular community groups, businesses, families, or individuals. At large fundraising events with numerous money-trees, a representative for each money-tree carries it in a mini-parade for blessing by the monks, and donor groups and individuals are publically identified. At the end of the 2004 *Chol Preah Vassa* retreat in Hamilton, about 500 participants raised over $32,000 to pay off the temple mortgage, with another $20,000 donated from Cambodian businesspeople in Toronto. A similar fundraising event at the Maple temple in July 2002 enabled the Maple temple to pay off its mortgage (about $25,000) and build an extension onto the back of the house. The extension now serves as an additional communal space for people to cook and eat together, and for the monks to hold private ceremonies away from the more public shrine area.

8 Some of the Cambodian games include *Toet Sei* (a male-only team game with a badmintonlike birdie that is kicked); *Chol Chhoung/Bah Choong* (a rolled scarf that acts as a ball is tossed back and forth between two teams divided by gender); *Rout Pong Moan* (running with an egg); *Leaq Konsaeng* (men and women form a circle and crouch down, facing inward, and a person with the rolled scarf ball drops the scarf/ball beside/behind one of the people in the circle and then runs away to avoid being hit by the person who discovers the ball); *Lot Antheaq* (skipping rope, usually youth, teenagers, and older women); *Bah Angkuing* ('throwing the angkuing seed,' in which members of two teams, gender specific, separated by about

fifteen feet, take turns rolling/bowling angkuing (large seeds from a tree) to hit a target in front of the other team; and *Teanh Proat* (a rope tug of war between men and women). During the Ottawa games, musicians played traditional music and gradually, many women came to join the group and sing, continuing long after the games had ended.

9 The customary minimum fee for one monk to perform a home blessing (accompanied by at least one *achaa*) is $250, with additional gifts of food or goods (such as pots and pans) for the temple. Each monk and *achaa* who recite chants and blessings for a wedding receive approximately $60 to $80. Several times a month, Khmer monks are asked to recite prayers for the dead (*bangskaul*) at the temple, in funeral halls, or in people's homes.

10 During one visit to the Maple temple in 2004, people gave the following comments:

Woman, age 50: Monks in Canada share the same roles and responsibilities as those monks in Cambodia. They are a source of spiritual teaching. They help to make sense of the complexities of the world. They are a very important part of spiritual celebrations.

Woman, age 71: Monks are the source of spiritual enlightenment. The monks in Canada do not have to face hardships like those in Cambodia. They have a nice place to live, they are driven to places, and they do not have to beg for food.

Man, age 60: Monks in Canada are a source of spiritual leadership ... They do not really do much more than perform blessings, and they represent a source of goodness and purity.

Woman, age 68: Monks are symbols of the Buddhist religion. They perform blessings and prayers for people and certain events, and they teach people prayer at the temple. They teach anyone who is willing to learn, no matter what your age.

Man, age 62: Monks teach people prayers, and they perform blessings during critical moments of a person's life, such as a wedding, a home blessing, or blessing a person if they have run into a lot of bad luck.

Woman, age 50: Most monks enjoy living in Canada. They feel that they have better living conditions in Canada. They do not have to bang door to door for food and they have the luxuries of televisions, cars, and telephones.

11 During the first part of a Cambodian wedding, usually held in the morning at the bride's home or at the temple, the monks and *achaa* perform a blessing ceremony. Before Khmer monks were available in Ontario, monks were invited from the United States or Montreal, and their transportation

costs and accommodation added considerable expense to the wedding costs, which always includes a large donation to the temple. Depending on the number of guests, a hall may be rented to accommodate everyone, or to avoid being conspicuous to neighbours. During the blessing ceremony, traditional wedding music is played by Khmer musicians. When there is community concentration, some weddings feature a neighbourhood procession where the groom's family and friends, accompanied by the musicians playing music, bring many dishes of food to the bride's house for a second ceremony. The monks and the *achaa* give additional blessings and prayers to invite ancestral and guardian spirits, while parents exchange ceremonial offerings. The *achaa* ritually cuts a lock of the bride and groom's hair, which some Khmer in Canada have explained is symbolic of the Buddhist ritual when heads are *shaved* for ordination, signifying the cutting away of the past. The monks are then offered food, and after they have eaten and returned to the temple, an afternoon feast follows for the guests. In the evening, the bridal party, families, and friends go to a restaurant for another meal and to be entertained by Khmer folk dancing or the performance of traditional Khmer music. Near the end of the evening, the *achaa* solemnly ties a white cotton string around the wrists of the bride and groom who are now officially 'married' in the eyes of the community. Some guests may also tie strings on the bride and groom to signify their new identities as a married couple.

12 The Maple temple holds weekly language classes for Khmer children, and when teachers are available, provides classical dance training. At the Hamilton temple, funding from the Hamilton Wentworth Board of Education in 2004 enabled the abbot, the Venerable Truong Thach Dhammo, to hold a three-month Khmer language course for more than sixty students in Grades 6 to 12. They met every day for two hours in two groups, a beginners program and an intermediate level. One day per week was spent learning traditional cooking. The Cambodian Canadian Youth Society of Ottawa (CCYSO) is part of the Ottawa Buddhist temple. One of the founding members of CCYSO had taken temporary ordination at the Montreal temple for several months, and another's father was the *achaa* (lay leader) at the Ottawa temple. Their motto 'honouring our past as we enter our future,' manifests itself in activities both traditional and innovative. Traditional activities have included helping to organize the Cambodian New Year's (*Chaul Chnam Khmer*) celebrations in Ottawa, promoting classes in Cambodian classical dance, and hosting parties/picnics. Innovative projects include field trips to skate on the Rideau Canal, visiting Fulton's Pancake House and Sugar Bush, arranging two school scholarships (worth $500 each), and creating an Internet Cambodian Youth Magazine that

reports on current news in Cambodia, leadership profiles, entertainment, sports, culture, Cambodian history, interviews, business, science/education, health issues, general commentary, research, and analysis.

13 Harris (2005: 74) identifies different novice ordination rituals, including ordination to fulfil a vow (*puos tingun*); following the death of a close relative (*puos phloeung*); and one-day sessions (*puos muoy samkamn tamri*) to be purified for particular ceremonial obligations. Preceding the Hamilton ordination ceremony, the youth made several offerings to ancestral and other spirits, and their parents provided a special feast for relatives and friends, with monks providing blessings and prayers. The young men all wore a sarong (*hole*) with a white lace scarf (*krama*) around one shoulder, and the young women wore white robes from neck to ankle (arms covered), with a white upper robe across their shoulder. Unlike the young men, the young women did not have their heads and eyebrows shaved. The ordination candidates participated in a symbolic re-enactment of Siddhartha's renunciation, whereby they led a procession through the streets surrounding the temple, followed by family and friends carrying ritual offerings (monk's robes, food, *dana* bowls) and playing musical instruments. The ordination ceremony began with the boys in one vertical line in front of the shrine and the girls farther back in a horizontal line. Each youth faced his mother, who sat in front of him. The youths bowed to their mothers first with *sampeah* and then began to recite the ordination prayers specific to undoing any bad feelings they might have had for their mothers, to clear away family problems, and to become aware of the mistakes they have made concerning their attitudes or behaviours to parents. Most of the youth, and many of the mothers cried during this ritual of forgiveness, especially when the youth repeated the words of the *achaa* as he recited what they may have to apologize for (saying mean things to their parents, treating them disrespectfully, wanting to win arguments, and so forth).

The Caucasian monks then explained in English that the meaning of the longer Pali recitation is three-fold: to pay respect to parents and to show gratitude for all that they have done for the children (looking after them, cleaning their bodies, worrying about them, loving them); to recognize their good fortune in having met the Buddha's teachings and this tradition in their life; and to be aware that whatever unwholesomeness they have done in the past towards their parents, they must ask forgiveness for any harm done and, through the forgiveness, to progress to letting go of past hurts and harm. Afterwards, parents took a white string, dipped it in water, and tied it round both wrists of the youth. Family and friends came up to the youth and gave blessings and symbolic gifts (such as watches) to help them keep their vows and be aware of their responsibilities. During this time, the youth were photographed and the monks took turns to provide a continual commentary on current events (locally and in Cambodia), and made humorous comments about the novices.

14 For more than 100 years, Kampuchea Krom temples in Vietnam have actively inculcated strong Khmer cultural and national identities and firm resistance against the imposition of Vietnamese political authority. When Khmer villages were forced to adopt Vietnamese names, Kampuchea Krom villagers continued to identify each other by their local Khmer temple name. Khmer Theravada Buddhist beliefs, institutions, monastic practices, and such annual ceremonies as New Year's or Wesak remained distinct from the Vietnamese Mahayana Buddhist traditions. Strategies to resist ongoing Vietnamese educational attempts to assimilate the youth included developing Khmer Buddhist educational activities for all the children, organizing inter-village temple-based sports teams, and supporting higher education outside of Vietnam, especially for monks.

15 Ontario-based Kampuchea Krom Buddhist associations include the Khmer Kampuchea Krom Buddhist Temple in Hamilton, Khmer Association of Kitchener, Cambodian Association of St Catharines, Khmer Buddhist Temple in Windsor, and Khmer Buddhist Temple in London.

16 In the early years of Cambodian resettlement in Ontario, Kampuchea Krom men were active organizers of the Cambodian temple in Toronto and maintained strong relations with Khmer community leaders. Once the Buddhist temple appeared stable, however, some Kampuchea Krom noted that the attitudes of the temple's board and leaders seemed to change towards them, causing them to withdraw from active involvement to avoid conflicts or divisions. Some continued to work on temple committees until they became involved in establishing a second Buddhist temple in Hamilton, then more recent ones in London and Windsor.

17 The Caucasian monk also provided a congregational Sunday-style religious service for the English-speaking students during his residence. This is the only Ontario Khmer example of a 'parallel congregation' (Numrich 1996).

18 On selected days, Monday to Friday, the monks would walk to specific Khmer homes where a pre-arranged gathering of family and friends offered food and other *dana* (gifts) to the monks. Non-Khmer neighbours on the 'route' became familiar with the sight of the monks in their robes with their alms bowls and sometimes would participate in offering food.

19 During visits to the Maple Temple in 2003, several members gave their opinion when asked about the relationship, 'to be Khmer is to be Buddhist':

Woman, age 71: You do not have to be Buddhist to be Khmer, and you should not feel you have to. You are given a choice, and Buddha would not want you to do something you do not truly want to do.

Man, age 60: Many Cambodians are Buddhist, but being Buddhist is not the only factor that makes you Cambodian or Khmer. How you live your everyday life, what you read, eat, wear, act, is also a big part of being Khmer.

Woman, age 50: No, Buddhism allows you to believe in other religions. You are still Khmer if you are not a Buddhist.

Man, age 62: Well, in Cambodia being Buddhist is a big part of being Khmer, but in Canada, that is not necessarily the case.

Woman, age 68: Yes, many Cambodian families have sakkarak (shrines) in their homes where they place Buddhist symbols like Buddha, pendants, or necklaces. They honour meba (ancestoral spirits) on the special days, such as an anniversary of the person's death, to pray and offer food to the relatives. Being Buddhist is part of Cambodian culture, connecting children to their parents and grandparents. Cambodian people are usually very friendly and peaceful people; this can be related to the fact that we are Buddhist.

These same individuals were also asked about the relationship of Khmer ethnic identity and culture and those who convert to Christianity:

Woman, age 71: It really depends on them. Some people want to blend in completely, they try to change everything. Our people [who we see at the temple] who convert to Christianity still maintain a part of their culture, the way they decorate [their homes], the foods they eat, and the way of thinking does not change. Becoming Christian does not mean that you have to lose your culture.

Man, age 50: When a Khmer converts to Christianity they can lose their ethnic identity because they try very hard to fit in or be as normal as possible, and this involves changing some of their customs. But then, there are some Khmer who are not Christian who still get caught up in fitting in and want material things. It depends on who you are, the way how you view the culture, do you want to be a part of it.

Man, age 62: Everyone who comes to Canada changes a bit or loses a bit of their ethnic identity because the lifestyle is so different here. But I do notice that people who are Christian change a lot more than other people.

Woman, age 64: Religion plays a big part of who you are but no matter what you believe in, just as long as it promotes forgiveness, respect for all things, and to overall be a good person. Buddhism allows you to believe in other things, it is very open. But no matter what you believe in, you cannot completely change your ethnic identity because you cannot change the way you look or your ancestral past. You should bring who you are, your ethnic identity, into your future. Never forget where you are from.

6 Challenges and Concerns of Ontario Cambodian Youth

1 KYAOH arranged a youth forum in 1997 that featured talks, short plays, and a keynote speaker from Phnom Penh to help counter the contentious generational issues between youth and their parents. The Hamilton youth wrote, directed, and acted in two short plays: the first featured rebellious attitudes and actions of the youth and the resultant parental tirades of anger and physical force; the second depicted alternative ways to behave, emphasizing increased listening and speaking, as well as peer mediation.

2 The Khmer Youth Association of Windsor was founded in 1996. Since they were geared towards male members over sixteen, it was later renamed Khmer Athletic Association of Windsor (KAAW). One founding member spoke of his necessity to connect with other Khmer and the kinds of struggles the youth in Windsor faced:

> Cambodians who settled outside Toronto were scattered ... When you get a lot of people scattered like that and not in one particular group you can't fall back on traditional values, that's respect for your elders. And another bad thing about being spread out like that, it's hard to find yourself, it's hard to find an identity for yourself, because at the same time you're promoting it, at the same time you're trying to integrate into the North American way of life. So, what drives us is that hunger of being recognized, and of being who we are ...
>
> Our group was basically built on friendship ... Our need was not to, when we first evolved and developed, it was not for a youth group purpose, it was basically trying to learn ourselves, while learning from others. It was the first time a lot of Cambodians our age, especially from Windsor where there's not a lot to choose from, actually bonded together. We tried to understand each other and the passion just flared up. And then, we want to fight, whether it is fighting in public office, or fighting for our rights and freedom, or

just for our ethnic culture, and that's what developed us. We find sports is a major way, just like music. Music is very big cultural beginning for a lot of ethnic backgrounds, and sports is no exception to that rule. Sport bonds us together, and since we grow older, and our bodies, we just can't take it anymore, back hurting, kids coming. That's when we find a need.

Only about five years ago that we actually clicked into the mind that 'Hey, we need to form a youth group.' Because there are kids that's grown up and if we don't form a youth group, all we're going to do is play basketball, that's all these kids are going to know is how to play basketball. So that's what we tried to do, to form a youth group so they can have a basis to fall back on. Not just basketball, but a basis to fall back on, of their identity, of their self-respect, respect for others, and respect for just the parents. To fall back on to the Cambodian tradition, to think with each other, to respect yourself, to just try to gain a momentum that is oriented towards the future, something concrete. That's what we're trying to do with our life. (Khmer Youth Workshop, 2005)

3 The Cambodian Canadian Youth Society of Ottawa (CCYSO), founded in 2002, began with a strong commitment to address the difficulties facing Cambodian youth. Their website listed an ambitious agenda to strengthen Cambodian families, overcome youth alienation towards Buddhism, provide scholarship opportunities for youth, preserve, and foster Khmer ethnic heritage, and promote equitable social, economic, and educational access for Cambodians. In practice, the CCYSO leaders were able to organize Buddhist celebrations, sports, and recreational activities for about two years before other commitments intervened.

4 At one high school in North York attended by a large number of Cambodian youth, extensive individual tutoring and support was available for at-risk teens through a special program, Cities in Schools. In 1993–94, only three Cambodian girls participated, with two subsequently leaving due to feelings of exclusion. A similar program called Change Your Future (funded and coordinated jointly by the Ministries of Citizenship and Education), specially geared to racial minority students at risk of dropping out of school, had no Cambodian youth at all (McLellan 1995).

5 During the 2005 Khmer Youth Workshop, three male leaders of this group commented on why they felt it necessary to strengthen ties with the older generation:

The reason for us starting our youth group is that we found a need to bridge the gap between the young and the old. We found that ever since the older generation created their [Buddhist] association, we felt that we were left out. We felt that the youth in the community didn't have a place at all. And that's the reason why we formed. So our mission is to reduce the gap between the young and the old and try to bring us all together as a community, for us to work together, and to learn off each other. We do activities where we can bring the young and the old together.

We try to build up that because the kids that are growing up right now, they don't know what's the meaning of going to the temple. So we try to show them. How we do it is to try and get the elders to show the kids. And we are the ones that open the door for them. We also want to work on a dance troupe and all that which is our culture. We don't have any dance teachers in Windsor, we are still searching for one right now, because of the population of the Cambodians, it is very hard to find. We are working really hard to try and get one. And that's one of our main goals.

I think in Windsor we feel a little disadvantaged because of the elders that are here. Most of them are not educated like the elders are in Toronto, you have more in Toronto and they probably come from a background where they are more educated. Whereas in Windsor, because there are not that many people, you find it hard to find the right leader to lead us. That's also a reason why we formed the youth group, hopefully we are those leaders. We hope to have something good.

7 Re-envisioning Khmer Identities within Transnational Networks

1 Thompson (1996: 15) notes that three particular circumstances (homecoming, shock, and illness) occasion performance of the *hau bralin* as a specific ritual to bring the individual out of danger and back to his or her full forces or proper place within the community. The attempt to retrieve, to preserve, and to reintegrate the *bralin* of an individual is similar to the Lao ritual of *sou khuan/soukhouan*, a process that involves tying protective strings around the wrists of those people for whom a given ceremony is performed and ultimately ties individuals tightly into their community and re-establishes personal and social equilibrium following disruption (Rajah 1990: 309; Van Esterik 2003: 66–70, 126).

References

Abbott, Max. 1989. *Refugee Resettlement and Well-Being*. Auckland: Mental Health Foundation of New Zealand.

Adelman, Howard. 1988. Refugees as Over-Achievers: The Case of the Indo-Chinese. Paper presented at Mosaic 88: Conference on the Contributions of Immigrants and Refugees, Toronto, 22 Nov.

– 1983. *Canada and the Indochinese Refugees*. Regina: Wigle Educational Association.

Adelman, Howard, Charles Le Blanc, and Jean-Philippe Therien. 1980. Canadian Policy on Indochinese Refugees. In Elliot Tepper (ed.), *Southeast Asian Exodus: From Tradition to Resettlement*, 135–50. Ottawa: Canadian Asian Studies Association.

Akcapar, Sebnem K. 2006. Conversion as a Migration Strategy in a Transit Country: Iranian Shiites Becoming Christians in Turkey. *International Migration Review* 40(4): 817–53.

Anderson, Benedict. 1991. *Imagined Communities: Reflections on the Origin and Spread of Nationalism*. London: Verson.

Andras, Robert. 1980. A Historical Sketch of Canadian Immigration and Refugee Policy. In Howard Adelman (ed.), *The Indochinese Refugee Movement*, 3–9. Toronto: Operation Lifeline.

Baily, John. 1995. The Role of Music in Three British Muslim Communities. *Diaspora* 4(1): 77–87.

Bankston, Carl, and Min Zhou. 1995. Religious Participation, Ethnic Identification, and the Adaptation of Vietnamese Adolescents in an Immigrant Community. *Sociological Quarterly* 36(3): 523–34.

Beiser, Morton. 1990. Migration: Opportunity or Mental Health Risk? *Triangle* 29(2/3): 83–90.

Beiser, Morton, and F. Hou. 2001. Language Acquisition, Unemployment and Depressive Disorder among Southeast Asian Refugees: A 10-Year Study. *Social Science and Medicine* 53(10): 1321–34.

Beiser, Morton, Linda Ogilvie, Joanna Anneke Rummens, Robert Armstrong, and Jacqueline Oxman-Martinez, eds. 2005. The New Canadian Children and Youth Study: Research to Fill a Gap in Canada's Children's Agenda. *Canadian Issues* (Spring): 21–4.

Beiser, Morton, Jay Turner, and Soma Ganesan. 1989. Catastrophic Stress and Factors Affecting Its Consequences among Southeast Asian Refugees. *Social Science and Medicine* 28(3): 183–95.

Bek-Pedersen, Katherine, and Edith Montgomery. 2006. Narratives of the Past and Present: Young Refugees' Construction of a Family Identity in Exile. *Journal of Refugee Studies* 19(1): 94–112.

Bell, Catherine. 1997. *Ritual: Perspectives and Dimensions.* New York: Oxford University Press.

Berry, John W, Jean S. Phinney, David L. Sam, and Paul Vedder, eds. 2006. *Immigrant Youth in Cultural Transition: Acculturation, Identity and Adaptation across National Contexts.* Mahwah: Erlbaum.

Bezanson, Kate. 2006. Gender and the Limits of Social Capital. *Canadian Review of Sociology and Anthropology/RCSA* 43(4): 427–43.

Bit, Seanglim. 1991. *The Warrior Heritage: A Psychological Perspective of Cambodian Trauma.* El Cerrito, CA: Seanglim Bit Publishers.

Boehnlein, James K. 1987. Clinical Relevance of Grief and Mourning among Cambodian Refugees. *Social Science and Medicine* 25 (7): 765–72.

Bottomley, Gillian. 1991. Culture, Ethnicity, and the Politics/Poetics of Representation. *Diaspora* 1(3): 303–20.

Boua, Chantou. 1991. Genocide of a Religious Group: Pol Pot and Cambodia's Buddhist Monks. In Timothy Bushnell, Vladimir Shlapentokh, Christopher Vanderpool, and Jeyarantnam Sundram (eds.), *State Organized Terror: The Case of Violent Internal Repression,* 227–40. Boulder: Westview.

Boyarin, Daniel, and Jonathan Boyarin. 2003. Diaspora: Generation and the Ground of Jewish Identity. In Jana Evans Braziell and Anita Mannur (eds.), *Theorizing Diaspora: A Reader,* 85–118. London: Blackwell.

Bramadat, Paul A. 2001. Shows, Selves, and Solidarity: Ethnic Identity and Cultural Spectacles in Canada. *Canadian Ethnic Studies* 33(3): 78–99.

Cadge, Wendy. 2008. De Facto Congregationalism and the Religious Organizations of Post-1965 Immigrants to the United States: A Revised Approach. *Journal of the American Academy of Religion* 76(2): 344–74.

Canda, Edward, and Thitiya Phaobtong. 1992. Buddhism as a Support System for Southeast Asian Refugees. *Social Work* 37(1): 61–7.

Cantanzaro, Antonino, and Robert John Moser. 1982. Health Status of Refugees from Vietnam, Laos and Cambodia. *Journal of the American Medical Association* 247(9): 1303–8.

Carole, Linda Flies. 1991. Cambodian Adolescent Survivors of Genocide: A Community-Based Group Intervention. In Ferne E. Atkinson (ed.), *Treatment of Torture: Readings and References*, 233–41. Ottawa: Ferne E. Atkinson.

Castles, Stephen, and Alastair Davidson. 2000. *Citizenship and Migration: Globalization and the Politics of Belonging*. New York: Palgrave.

Chan, Sucheng, ed. 2003. *Not Just Victims: Conversations with Cambodian Community Leaders in the United States*. Chicago: University of Illinois Press.

Chan, Raymond, Mony Mok, and Samantha Yin. 1999. *Trauma and Its Impact on Mental Health: A Study of Resettled Cambodians in Metro Toronto*. Report submitted to Hong Fook Mental Health Association and Cambodian Association of Ontario, Toronto.

Chandler, David P. 2000. *A History of Cambodia*, 3rd ed. Boulder: Westview.

– 1991. *The Land and People of Cambodia*. New York: Harper Collins.

– 1983. Revisiting the Past in Democratic Kampuchea: When Was the Birthday of the Party? *Pacific Affairs* 56(2): 288–300.

Chea, Dharamuni Phala Svy. 2003. A Holistic Approach to Mental Health. In Sucheng Chan (ed.),*Not Just Victims: Conversations with Cambodian Community Leaders in the United States*, 241–58. Chicago: University of Illinois Press.

Cheal, David. 1992. Ritual: Communication in Action. *Sociological Analysis* 53(4): 363–74.

Cheran, R. 2006. Multiple Homes and Parallel Civil Societies: Refugee Diasporas and Transnationalism. *Refuge* 23(2): 3–7.

Chhim, Him S. 2003. Long Beach, California, the Capital of Cambodian America. In Sucheng Chan (ed.), *Not Just Victims: Conversations with Cambodian Community Leaders in the United States*, 45–64. Chicago: University of Illinois Press

Clarke, Greg, William H. Sack, and Brian Goff. 1993. Three Forms of Stress in Cambodian Adolescent Refugees. *Journal of Abnormal Child Psychology* 21(1): 65–77.

Cohen, R. 1997. *Global Diasporas: An Introduction*. London: UCL Press.

Coleman, Cynthia M. 1987. Cambodians in the United States. In D. A. Ablin and M. Hood (eds.), *The Cambodian Agony*, 354–74. Armonk: M. E. Sharpe.

Coleman, J. S. 1990. *Foundations of Social Theory*. Cambridge, MA: Harvard University Press.

– 1988. Social Capital in the Creation of Human Capital. *American Journal of Sociology* 94: 95–120.

Coles, Tim, and Dallen J. Timothy. 2004. 'My Field Is the World': Conceptualizing Diasporas, Travel and Tourism. In Tim Coles and Dallen J. Timothy (eds.), *Tourism, Diasporas and Space*, 1–29. London: Routledge.

Connerton, Paul. 1989. *How Societies Remember*. Cambridge: Cambridge University Press.

Dang, Bach-Tuyet. 1983. Physical Health Problems of South East Asians. In *Health Consultation South East Asian Community*, 3–7. Toronto: Department of Public Health.

DePaul, Kim, ed. 1997. *Children of Cambodia's Killing Fields: Memoirs by Survivors*. New Haven: Yale University Press.

Diehl, Keila. 1997. When Tibetan Refugees Rock, Paradigms Roll: Echoes from Dharamsala's Musical Soundscape. In Frank J. Korman (ed.), *Constructing Tibetan Culture: Contemporary Perspectives*, 122–55. Quebec: World Heritage Press.

Dirks, Gerald. 1979/80. Contemporary Canadian Responses to the World's Refugee Phenomenon. *Multiculturalism* 3(4): 3–23.

– 1977. *Canada's Refugee Policy: Indifference or Opportunism?* Montreal: McGill-Queen's University Press.

Dorais, Louis-Jacques. 1991. Refugee Adaptation and Community Structure: The Indochinese in Quebec City, Canada. *International Migration Review* 25(3): 551–73.

Douglas, Thomas J. 2005. Changing Religious Practices among Cambodian Immigrants in Long Beach and Seattle. In Karen Leonard, A. Stepick, M. A. Vasquez, and J. Holdaway (eds.), *Immigrant Faiths: Transforming Religious Life in America*, 123–45. Walnut Creek: AltaMira Press.

– 2003. 'The Cross and the Lotus: Changing Religious Practices among Cambodian Immigrants in Seattle. In Jane Iwamura and Paul Spickard (eds.), *Revealing the Sacred in Asian and Pacific America*, 159–75. New York: Routledge.

Douglas, Thomas J. , and Sophon Mam. 2005. Ritual and Magic: Two Diverse Approaches to Inner Healing in the Cambodian American Community. In Linda L. Barnes and Susan S. Sered (eds.), *Religion and Healing in America*, 59–69. New York: Oxford University Press.

Duval, David. 2004. Conceptualizing Return Visits: A Transnational Perspective. In Tim Coles and Dallen J. Timothy (eds.), *Tourism, Diasporas and Space*, 50–61. London: Routledge.

Ebaugh, Helen Rose, and Janet Saltzman Chafetz, eds. 2002. *Religion across Borders: Transnational Immigrant Networks*, Walnut Creek: Altamira Press.

– 2000. *Religion and the New Immigrants: Continuities and Adaptations in Immigrant Congregations*. Walnut Creek: AltaMira Press.

Ebihara, May. 1985. Khmer. In David Haines (ed.), *Refugees in the United States*, 127–45. Westport: Greenwood.
- 1974. Khmer Village Women in Cambodia: A Happy Balance. In C. Matthiasson (ed.), *Many Sisters: Women in Cross-Cultural Perspective*, 305–47. New York: Free Press.
- 1966. Interrelations between Buddhism and Social Systems in Cambodian Peasant Cultures. In Manning Nash et al. (eds.), *Anthropological Studies in Theravada Buddhism*, 175–96. New Haven: Yale University Southeast Asia Studies.

Ebihara, May, Carol Mortland, and Judy Ledgerwood, eds. 1994. *Cambodian Culture since 1975: Homeland and Exile*. Ithaca: Cornell University Press

Eck, Diana L. 2001. *A New Religious America: How a 'Chrirtian Country' Has Now Become the World's Most Religiously Diverse Nation*. New York: Harper.

Eisenbruch, Maurice. 1992. Towards a Culturally Sensitive DSM: Cultural Bereavement in Cambodian Refugees and the Traditional Healer as Taxonomist. *Journal of Nervous and Mental Disease* 181(1): 8–10.
- 1991. From Post-Traumatic Stress Disorder to Cultural Bereavement: Diagnosis of Southeast Asian Refugees. *Social Science and Medicine* 33(6): 673–80.

Eisenbruch, Maurice, and Lauren Handelman. 1989. Development of an Explanatory Model of Illness Schedule for Cambodian Refugee Patients. *Journal of Refugee Studies* 2(2): 243–55.

Employment and Immigration Canada. 1980, 1981, 1982, 1983. *Annual Report to Parliament on Immigration Levels*. Ottawa: Author.
- 1980–92. *Immigration Statistics*. Ottawa: Author.

Faist, Thomas. 2000. Transnationalization in International Migration: Implications for the Study of Citizenship and Culture. *Ethnic and Racial Studies* 23(2): 189–222.

Frith, Simon. 1987. Towards an Aesthetic of Popular Music. In Richard D. Leppart and Susan McClary (eds.), *Music and Society: The Politics of Composition, Performance and Reception*, 133–49. Cambridge: Cambridge University Press.

Gans, Herbert J. 1994. Symbolic Ethnicity and Symbolic Religiosity: Towards a Comparison of Ethnic and Religious Acculturation. *Ethnic and Racial Studies* 17(4): 577–93.

Garry, Robert. 1980. Cambodia. In Elliot Tepper (ed.), *Southeast Asian Exodus: From Tradition to Resettlement*, 33–54. Ottawa: Canadian Asian Studies Association.

Giddens, Anthony. 1990. *The Consequences of Modernity*. Cambridge: Polity Press.

Gosling, David. 1984. Discussion Notes: Buddhism for Peace. *Southeast Asian Journal of Social Science* 12(1): 59–70.

Guest, Kenneth J. 2003. *God in Chinatown: Religion and Survival in New York's Evolving Immigrant Community*. New York: New York University Press.

Haines, David. 1985. *Refugees in the United States*. Westport: Greenwood Press.

Haller, Deiter. 2004. Economy, Spirituality and Gender in the Sindhi Network. In Waltraud Kokot, Kachig Toloyan, and Carolin Alfonso (eds.), *Diaspora, Identity and Religion: New Directions in Theory and Research*, 189–203. London: Routledge.

Hansen, Anne. 2007. *How to Behave: Buddhism and Modernity in Colonial Cambodia, 1860–1930*. Honolulu: University of Hawai'i Press.

– 2004. Khmer Identity and Theravada Buddhism. In John Marston and Elizabeth Guthrie (eds.), *History, Buddhism and New Religious Movements in Cambodia*, 40–62. Honolulu: University of Hawai'i Press.

Harris, Ian. 2005. *Cambodian Buddhism: History and Practice*. Honolulu: University of Hawai'i Press.

– 1998. Buddhism in Extremis: The Case of Cambodia. In Charles Keyes, Laurel Kendall, and Helen Hardacre (eds.), *Buddhism and Politics in Twentieth Century Asia*, 43–73. Honolulu: University of Hawai'i Press.

Hefner, Robert W. 1993. *Conversion to Christianity: Historical and Anthropological Perspectives on a Great Transformation*. Berkeley: University of California Press.

Hein, Jeremy. 1995. *From Vietnam, Laos, and Cambodia: A Refugee Experience in the United States*. New York: Twayne.

Hervieu-Leger, Daniele. 2000. *Religion as a Chain of Memory*. Piscataway: Rutgers University Press.

Himm, Sokreaksa. 2003. *The Tears of My Soul*. Grand Rapids: Monarch Books.

Hitchcox, Linda. 1990. *Vietnamese Refugees in Southeast Asian Camps*, New York: St Martin's Press.

Hopkins, Mary Carol. 1996. *Braving a New World: Cambodian (Khmer) Refugees in an American City*. Westport: Bergin and Garvey.

Kalab, Milada. 1994. Cambodian Buddhist Monasteries in Paris: Continuing Tradition and Changing Patterns. In May Ebihara, Judy Ledgerwood, and Carol Mortland (eds.), *Cambodian Culture since 1975: Homeland and Exile*, 57–71. Ithaca: Cornell University Press.

—. 1976. Monastic Education, Social Mobility, and Village Structure in Cambodia. In David J. Banks (ed.), *Changing Identities in Modern Southeast Asia*, 155–69. The Hague: Mouton.

Kaufman, Debra Renee. 1998. Gender and Jewish Identity among Twenty-Somethings in the United States. In Madeleine Cousineau (ed.), *Religion in a Changing World: Comparative Studies in Sociology*, 49–56. Westport: Praeger.

Keyes, Charles. 1994. Communist Revolution and the Buddhist Past in Cambodia. In Charles Keyes, Laurel Kendall, and Helen Hardacre (eds.), *Asian Visions of Authority: Religion and the Modern States of East and Southeast Asia*, 43–73. Honolulu: University of Hawai'i Press.

Kiernan, Ben. 1983. Wild Chickens, Farm Chickens and Cormorants: Kamupuchea's Eastern Zone under Pol Pot. In David P. Chandler and Ben Kiernan (eds.), *Revolution and Its Aftermath in Kampuchea: Eight Essays*, 136–211. Monograph Series No. 25. New Haven: Yale University Southeast Asia Studies.

Kiljunen, Kimmo. 1983. The Tragedy of Kampuchea. *Disasters* 7(2): 129–41.

Kinzie, David J. , William Sack, Richard Angell, et al. 1989. A Three-Year Follow-up of Cambodian Young People Traumatized as Children. *Journal of the American Academy of Child Psychiatry* 28(4): 501–4.

– 1986. The Psychiatric Effects of Massive Trauma on Cambodian Children. *Journal of the American Academy of Child Psychiatry* 25(3): 370–6.

Kinzie, J. D. 1988. The Psychiatric Effects of Massive Trauma on Cambodian Refugees. In John Wilson, Zev Harel, and Boaz Kahana (eds.), *Human Adaptation to Extreme Stress*, 305–17. New York: Plenum.

Kogan, Ilany. 1995. *The Cry of Mute Children: A Psychoanalytic Perspective of the Second Generation of the Holocaust*. New York: Free Association Books.

Kong, Chhean. 2003. On Buddhism and Psychotherapy. In Sucheng Chan (ed.), *Not Just Victims: Conversations with Cambodian Community Leaders in the United States*, 65–91. Chicago: University of Illinois Press.

Kral, V. A. , L. H. Pazder, and B. T. Wigdor. 1967. Long-Term Effects of a Prolonged Stress Experience. *Canadian Psychiatric Association Journal* 12(2): 175–81.

Krulfeld, Ruth M. 1994. Changing Concepts of Gender Roles and Identities in Refugee Communities. In Linda A. Camino and Ruth Krulfeld (eds.), *Reconstructing Lives, Recapturing Meaning: Refugee Identity, Gender and Culture Change*, 71–4. Toronto: Gordon and Breach.

Kubat, Daniel, ed. 1979. *The Politics of Migration Policies: The First World in the 1970s*. New York: Centre for Migration Studies.

Kwon, Ho-Youn, and Shin Kim, eds. 1993. *The Emerging Generation of Korean-Americans*. Seoul: Kyung Hee University Press.

Langer, Lawrence. 1991. *Holocaust Testimonies: The Ruins of Memory*. New Haven: Yale University Press.

Lanphier, Michael. 1981. Canada's Response to Refugees. *International Migration Review* 15(1/2): 32–49.

Ledgerwood, Judy. 1990. Portrait of a Conflict: Exploring Changing Khmer-American Social and Political Relationships. *Journal of Refugee Studies* 3(2): 135–54.

Lee, Richard R. 1992. Religious Practice as Social Exchange: An Explanation of the Empirical Findings. *Sociological Analysis* 53(1): 1–35.

Leonard, Karen. 2000. State, Culture, and Religion: Political Action and Representation among South Asians in North America. *Diaspora* 9(1): 21–38.

Leonard, Karen I. , Alex Stepick, Manuel A. Vasquez, and Jennifer Holdaway, eds. 2005. *Immigrant Faiths: Transforming Religious Life in America*. Walnut Creek: AltaMira Press.

Levitt, Peggy. 2001. *The Transnational Villagers*. Berkeley: University of California Press.

Lowe, Lisa. 1991. *Critical Terrains: French and British Orientalisms*. Ithaca: Cornell University Press.

Mabbett, Ian, and David Chandler. 1995. *The Khmers*. Cambridge: Blackwell.

Maira, Sunaina Marr. 2002. *Desis in the House: Indian American Youth Culture in New York City*. Philadelphia: Temple University Press.

Majumdar, R. C. 1980. *Kambuja-Desa or, An Ancient Hindu Colony in Cambodia*. Philadelphia: Institute for the Study of Human Issues.

Makio, Morikawa. 1997. When 'Orientals' Are Not Socially Weak: A Conflict between the Chinese and Canadians in Markham, Ontario. In Chieko Kitagawa Otsuru (ed.), *Diversified Migration Patterns of North America: Their Challenges and Opportunities*, 217–32. Osaka: Japan Center for Area Studies.

Marcucci, John. 1994. Sharing the Pain. In May Ebihara, Judy Ledgerwood, and Carol Mortland (eds.), *Cambodian Culture since 1975: Homeland and Exile*, 129–40. Ithaca: Cornell University Press.

Marston, John, and Elizabeth Guthrie. 2004. *History, Buddhism, and New Religious Movements in Cambodia*. Honolulu: University of Hawai'i Press.

Martin, David. 1990. *Tongues of Fire: The Explosion of Protestantism in Latin America*. Oxford: Blackwell.

McCrasson, Paul. 1980. Current Refugee Policy. In Howard Adelman (ed.), *The Indochinese Refugee Movement*. Toronto: Operation Lifeline.

McLellan, Janet. 2004. Cambodian Refugees in Ontario: Religious Identities, Social Cohesion and Transnational Linkages. *Canadian Ethnic Studies* 36(2): 101–18.

– 1999. *Many Petals of the Lotus: Five Asian Buddhist Communities in Toronto*. Toronto: University of Toronto Press.

– 1995. *Cambodian Refugees in Ontario: An Evaluation of Resettlement and Adaptation*. Toronto: York Lanes Press.

McLellan, Janet, and Marybeth White. 2005. Social Capital and Identity Politics among Asian Buddhists in Toronto. *Journal of International Migration and Integration* 6(2): 235–53.

Mehmet, Ozay, M. Tahiroglu, and Eric A. L. Li. 2002. Social Capital Formation in Large-Scale Development Projects. *Canadian Journal of Development Studies* 23(2): 335–57.

Men, Chean Rithy. 2002. The Changing Religious Beliefs and Ritual Practices among Cambodians in Diaspora. *Journal of Refugee Studies* 15(2): 222–33.

Miyazaki, Hirokazu. 2000. Faith and Its Fulfilment: Agency, Exchange, and the Fijian Aesthetics of Completion. *American Ethnologist* 27(1): 33–51.

Mollica, Richard F. , C. Poole, L. Son, C. Murray, and S. Tor. 1997. Effects of War Trauma on Cambodian Refugee Adolescents' Functional Health and Mental Health Status. *Journal of the American Academy of Child Adolescent Psychiatry* 36(8): 1098–1106.

Mollica, Richard F. , Grace Wyshak, and James Lavelle. 1987. The Psychosocial Impact of War Trauma and Torture on Southeast Asian Refugees. *American Journal of Psychiatry* 144(12): 1567–72.

Mortland, Carol. 1994. Khmer Buddhists in the United States: Ultimate Questions. In May Ebihara, Judy Ledgerwood, and Carol Mortland (eds.), *Cambodian Culture since 1975: Homeland and Exile*, 72–90. Ithaca: Cornell University Press.

Mortland, Carol, and Judy Ledgerwood. 1987. Refugee Resource Acquisition: The Invisible Communication System. In Y. Y. Kim and W. B. Gudykunst (eds.), *Cross-Cultural Adaptation: Current Approaches*, 286–306. Newbury Park: Sage.

Mysliwiec, Eva. 1988. *Punishing the Poor: The International Isolation of Kampuchea*. Oxford: Oxfam Publishing.

Mullins, Mark. 1987. The Life Cycle of Ethnic Churches in Sociological Perspective. *Japanese Journal of Religious Studies* 14(4): 321–34.

Naficy, Hamid. 1993. *The Making of Exile Cultures: Iranian Television in Los Angeles*. Minneapolis: University of Minnesota Press.

Nagata, Judith. 1989. Conversion as a Social Process: Christianity and Islam in South East Asia and North America. Paper presented at the 13th annual meeting of the American Society for the Study of Religion, Philadelphia, 28–30 April.

Neuwirth, Gertrud. 1987. Socioeconomic Adjustment of Southeast Asian Refugees in Canada. In John Rogge (ed.), *Refugees: A Third World Dilemma*, 324–43. Totowa: Rowman and Littlefield.

Ngor, Haing. 1987. *A Cambodian Odyssey*. Chicago: Warner Communications.

Nguyen, San Duy. 1983. Mental Health Services for Southeast Asian Refugees. In *Health Consultation, South East Asian Community*, 9–22. Toronto: Department of Public Health.

Nguyen, Thu-Huong, and Brian King. 2004. The Culture of Tourism in the Diaspora: The Case of the Vietnamese Community in Australia. In Tim

Coles and Dallen J. Timothy (eds.), *Tourism, Diasporas and Space*, 172–87. London: Routledge.

Numrich, David Paul. 1996. *Old Wisdom in the New World: The Americanization in Two Immigrant Theravada Buddhist Temples*. Knoxville: University of Tennessee Press.

Ong, Aihwa. 2003. *Buddha Is Hiding*. Berkeley: University of California Press.

– 1995. Southeast Asian Refugees and Investors in Our Midst. *Positions* 3(3): 806–13.

– 1993. On the Edge of Empires: Flexible Citizenship among Chinese in Diaspora. *Positions* 1(3): 745–78.

Overland, Gwynyth. 1999. The Role of Funeral Rites in Healing the Wounds of War among Cambodian Holocaust Survivors. Paper presented at the 20th Nordic Sociological Congress, Bergen, 17–19 June.

Payne, Donald. 1990. The Psychiatric Sequelae of Torture: Diagnosis and Treatment. Paper presented at the XVIth International Congress on Law and Mental Health, Toronto, June 20–4.

Petridou, Elia. 2001. The Taste of Home. In Daniel Miller (ed.), *Home Possessions: Material Culture behind Closed Doors*, 87–103. Oxford: Berg Press.

Poethig, Kathryn. 2001. Visa Trouble: Cambodian American Christians and Their Defense of Multiple Citizenhip. In D. N. Hopkins, L. A. Lorentzen, E. Mendieta, and D. Batston (eds.), Religions/Globalizations: Theories and Cases, 187–202. Durham, Duke University Press.

Portes, Alejandro, and Ruben Rumbaut. 2001. *Legacies: The Story of the Immigrant Second Generation*. Berkeley: University of California Press.

Portes, Alejandro, and Min Zhou. 1993. The New Second Generation: Segmented Assimilation and Its Variants. *Annals of the American Academy of Political and Social Science* 530 (Nov.): 74–96.

Putnam, Robert. 2000. *Bowling Alone: The Collapse and Revival of American Community*. New York: Simon and Schuster.

Rajah, Ananda. 1990. Orientalism, Commensurability, and the Construction of Identity: A Comment on the Notion of Lao Identity. *Sojourn* 5(1): 308–32.

Rajiva, Mythili. 2005. Bridging the Generation Gap: Exploring the Differences between Immigrant Parents and Their Canadian-Born Children. *Canadian Issues* (Spring): 25–28.

Reid, Janice C. , and Timothy Strong. 1988. Rehabilitation of Refugee Victims of Torture and Trauma: Principles and Service Provision in New South Wales. *Medical Journal of Australia* 148(7): 340–6.

Reynell, Josephine. 1989. *Political Pawns: Refugees on the Thai-Kampuchean Border*. Oxford: Refugee Studies Programme.

Richmond, Anthony. 1994 *Global Apartheid: Refugees, Racism and the New World Order.* Oxford: Refugee Studies Programme.

– 1988. *Immigration and Ethnic Conflict.* London: Macmillan.

Ross, Andrew, ed. 1988. *Universal Abandon? The Politics of Postmodernism.* Minneapolis: University of Minneapolis Press.

Routledge, Paul. 1985. *The Role of Religion in Ethnic Self-Identity: A Vietnamese Community.* Lanhan: University Press of America.

Rosseau, C. , A. Drapeau, and R. Platt. 2004. Family Environment and Emotional and Behavioural Symptoms in Adolescent Cambodian Refugees: Influences of Time, Gender, and Acculturation. *Medicine, Conflict and Survival* 20(2): 151–65.

Rumbaut, Ruben. 1996. The Crucible Within: Ethnic Identity, Self-Esteem, and Segmented Assimilation among Children of Immigrants. In Alejandro Portes (ed.), *The New Second Generation,* 119–70. New York: Russell Sage Foundation.

– 1991. Migration, Adaptation, and Mental Health: The Experience of Southeast Asian Refugees in the United States. In Howard Adelman (ed.), *Refugee Policy: Canada and the United States,* 381–424. Toronto: York Lanes Press.

Sam, Sam-Ang. 1994. Khmer Traditional Music Today. In May Ebihara, Judy Ledgerwood, and Carol Mortland (eds.), *Cambodian Culture since 1975: Homeland and Exile,* 39–47. Ithaca: Cornell University Press.

– 2003. The Cambodian Network Council. In Sucheng Chan (ed.), *Not Just Victims: Conversations with Cambodian Community Leaders in the United States,* 186–204. Chicago: University of Illinois Press.

Sandos, James. 2004. *Converting California: Indians and Franciscans in the Missions.* New Haven: Yale University Press.

Sargent, Carolyn, John Marcucci, and Ellen Elliston. 1983. Tiger Bones, Fire and Wine: Maternity Care in a Kampuchean Refugee Community. *Medical Anthropology* 35 (Fall): 67–79.

Satzewich, Vic, and Nikolaos Liodakis. 2007. *'Race' and Ethnicity in Canada: A Critical Introduction.* Toronto: Oxford University Press.

Schieffelin, Edward. 1981. Evangelical Rhetoric and the Transformation of Traditional Culture in Papua New Guinea. *Comparative Studies in Society and History* 23(1): 150–6.

Shawcross, William. 1979. *Sideshow: Nixon, Kissinger, and the Destruction of Cambodia.* New York: Simon and Schuster.

Sim, Sarorn. 2005. *Memories: Celebrations of Remembrance.* A documentary film by Windsor-based 4 Front Communications Inc. Available for viewing at www.sarornsim.com.

Simmons, Alan, and Dwaine Plaza. 2006. The Caribbean Community in Canada: Transnational Connections and Transformations. In Vic Satzewich and Lloyd Wong (eds.), *Transnational Identities and Practices in Canada*, 130–49. Vancouver: UBC Press.

Simon-Barouh, Ida. 2005. Ethnicity and Diaspora: The Case of the Cambodians. In Andre Levy and Alex Weingrod (eds,), *Homelands and Diasporas, Holy Lands and Other Places*, 247–69. Stanford: Stanford University Press.

Smith, Frank. 1994. Cultural Comsumption: Cambodian Peasant Refugees and Television in the 'First World. ' In May Ebihara, Judy Ledgerwood, and Carol Mortland (eds.), *Cambodian Culture since 1975: Homeland and Exile*, 141–60. Ithaca: Cornell University Press.

Smith-Hefner, Nancy. 1999. *Khmer American: Identity and Moral Education in a Diasporic Community.* Berkeley: University of California Press.

– 1998. Rebuilding the Temple: Buddhism and Identity among Khmer Americans. In Carol Mortland (ed.), *Selected Papers on Refugee and Immigrant Issues*, vol. 6, 51–72. Arlington: American Anthropological Association.

– 1994. Ethnicity and the Force of Faith: Christian Conversion among Khmer Refugees. *Anthropological Quarterly* 67(1): 24–37.

– 1993. Khmer Education, Gender, and Conflict. *Anthropology and Education Quarterly* 24(2): 135–8.

Statistics Canada. 1981 and 1986. *Census. Canadian Khmer-Mother-Tongue. Cambodian Populations by Metropolitan Areas.* Cat. No. 93–156. Ottawa: Author.

– 1991. *Census. Canadian Khmer-Mother-Tongue. Cambodian Populations by Metropolitan Areas.* Cat. No. 93–313. Ottawa: Author.

– 1991. *Census. Special Tabulations of Ontario Khmer-Mother-Tongue Cambodian Populations.* (Compiled for Janet McLellan. 1995. *Cambodian Refugees in Ontario: An Evaluation of Resettlement and Adapatation.* Toronto: York Lanes Press.) Ottawa: Author.

Stepick, Alex. 2005. God Is Apparently Not Dead: The Obvious, the Emergent, and the Still Unknown in Immigration and Religion. In Karen I. Leonard, Alex Stepick, Manuel A. Vasquez, and Jennifer Holdaway (eds.), *Immigrant Faiths: Transforming Religious Life in America*, 11–38. Walnut Creek: AltaMira Press.

Stevens, Christina A. 2001. Perspective on the Meanings of Symptoms among Cambodian Refugees. *Journal of Sociology* 37(1): 81–98.

– 1995. The Illusion of Social Inclusion: Cambodian Youth in South Australia. *Diaspora* 4(1): 59–76.

Stubbs, Richard. 1980. Why Can't They Stay in Southeast Asia? The Problems of Vietnam's Neighbours. In ElliotTepper (ed.), *Southeast Asian Exodus: From Tradition to Resettlement*, 115–24. Ottawa: Canadian Asian Studies Association.

Suh, Sharon. 2004. *Being Buddhist in a Christian World: Gender and Community in a Korean American Temple*. Seattle: University of Washington Press.

Tambiah, Stanley J. 2000. Transnational Movements, Diaspora, and Multiple Modernities. *Daedalus* 129(1): 163–94.

Tauch, Sokhom. 2003. Cambodians in Portland, Oregon. In Sucheng Chan (ed.), *Not Just Victims: Conversations with Cambodian Community Leaders in the United States*, 205–25. Chicago: University of Illinois Press.

Tapp, Nicholas. 1989. The Impact of Missionary Christianity upon Marginalized Ethnic Minorities: The Case of the Hmong. *Journal of Southeast Asian Studies* 20(1): 70–95.

Taylor, Charles. 1994. The Politics of Recognition. In Amy Gutmann (ed.), *Multiculturalism: Examining the Politics of Recognition*, 25–73. Princeton: Princeton University Press.

Tenhula, John. 1991. *Voices from Southeast Asia: The Refugee Experience in the United States*. New York: Holmes and Meier.

Terr, Lenore. 1989. Family Anxiety after Traumatic Events. *Journal of Clinical Psychiatry* 50(11): 15–19.

Thach, Bunroeun. 2003. The Khmer Krom. In Sucheng Chan (ed.), *Not Just Victims: Conversations with Cambodian Community Leaders in the United States*, 259–74. Chicago: University of Illinois Press.

Thompson, Ashley. 1996. *The Calling of the Souls: A Study of the Khmer Ritual Hau Bralin*. Clayton: Monash Asia Institute.

Thomson, Suteera. 1980. Refugees in Thailand: Relief, Development, and Integration. In Elliot Tepper (ed.), *Southeast Asian Exodus: From Tradition to Resettlement*, 125–32. Ottawa: Canadian Asian Studies Association.

Um, Khatharya. 2006. Diasporic Nationalism, Citizenship, and Post-War Reconstruction. *Refuge* 23(2): 8–19.

United Nations High Commissioner of Refugees (UNHCR). 2000. *The State of the World's Refugees, 2000: Fifty Years of Humanitarian Action*. New York: Oxford University Press.

Van Esterik, Penny. 2003. *Taking Refuge: Lao Buddhists in North America*. Monographs in Southeast Asian Studies. Tempe: Arizona State University Press.

Van Hear, Nicholas. 2006. Refugees in Diaspora: From Durable Solutions to Transnational Relations. *Refuge* 23(1): 9–15.

– 1998. *New Diasporas: The Mass Exodus, Dispersal and Regrouping of Migrant Communities*. London: University College London Press.

Vasquez, Manuel A. 2005. Historicizing and Materializaing the Study of Religion: The Contribution of Migration Studies. In Karen I. Leonard, Alex Stepick, Manuel A. Vasquez, and Jennifer Holdaway (eds.), *Immigrant Faiths: Transforming Religious Life in America*, 219–42. Walnut Creek: AltaMira Press.

Vertovec, Steven. 1999. Conceiving and Researching Transnationalism. *Ethnic and Racial Studies* 22(2): 447–62.

Vickery, Michael. 1984. *Cambodia, 1975–1982*. Boston: Southend Press.

– 1983. Democratic Kampuchea: Themes and Variations. In David P. Chandler and Ben Kiernan (eds.), *Revolution and Its Aftermath in Kampuchea: Eight Essays*, 99–135. Monograph Series No. 25. New Haven: Yale University Southeast Asia Studies.

Voyer, Jean-Pierre. 2003. Diversity without Divisiveness: A Role for Social Capital? *Canadian Diversity* 2(1): 31–2.

Warner, Stephen, and Judith Wittner, eds. 1998. *Gatherings in Diaspora: Religious Communities and the New Immigration*. Philadelphia: Temple University Press.

Welaratna, Usha. 1993. *Beyond the Killing Fields: Voices of Nine Cambodian Survivors in America*. Stanford: Stanford University Press.

Wellmeier, Nancy J. 1998. *Ritual, Identity, and the Mayan Diaspora*. New York: Garland.

Whitmore, John. 1985. Chinese from Southeast Asia. In David Haines (ed.), *Refugees in the United States*, 59–75. Westport: Greenwood.

Wicker, Hans-Rudolf, and Hans-Karl Schoch. 1988. Refugees and Mental Health: Southeast Asian Refugees in Switzerland. In Diana Miserez (ed.), *Refugees – The Trauma of Exile*, 153–79. Dordrecht: Martinus Nijhoff.

Winland, Daphne. 1992. The Role of Religious Affiliation in Refugee Resettlement: The Case of the Hmong. *Canadian Ethnic Studies* 24(1): 96–119.

Woolcock, M. 2001. The Place of Social Capital in Understanding Social and Economic Outcomes. *ISUMA: Canadian Journal of Policy Research* 2(10): 11–17.

– 1998. Social Capital and Economic Development: Toward a Theoretical Synthesis and Policy Framework. *Theory and Society* 27(2): 151–208.

Woolcock, M. , and D. Narayan. 2000. Social Capital: Implications for Development Theory, Research and Policy. *World Bank Research Observer* 15(2): 220–38.

Wortley, Scot, and Julian Tanner. 2006. Immigration, Social Disadvantage and Urban Youth Gangs: Results of a Toronto-Area Survey. In Marc Vachon et al. (eds.), Our Diverse Cities: Challenges and Opportunites. *Canadian Journal of Urban Research* (special edition), 18–38. Winnipeg: Institute of Urban Studies.

Wuthnow, Robert. 2002. Religious Involvement and Status-Bridging Social Capital. *Journal for the Scientific Study of Religion* 41(1): 669–84.

Yang, Fenggang, and Helen Rose Ebaugh. 2001. Transformations in New Immigrant Religions and Their Global Implications. *American Sociological Review* 66(2): 269–88.

Zhou, M. , and C. Bankston. 1994. Social Capital and the Adaptation of the Second Generation: The Case of Vietnamese Youth in New Orleans. *International Migration Review* 28(4): 821–45.

– 1998. *Growing Up American: How Vietnamese Children Adapt to Life in the United States*. New York: Russell Sage Foundation.

Zhou, M. , C. Bankston, and R. Y. Kim. 2002. Rebuilding Spiritual Lives in the New Land: Religious Practices among Southeast Asian Refugees in the United States. In P. Gap Min and J. Ha Kim (eds.), *Religions in Asian America*, 37–70. Walnut Creek: AltaMira Press.

Index